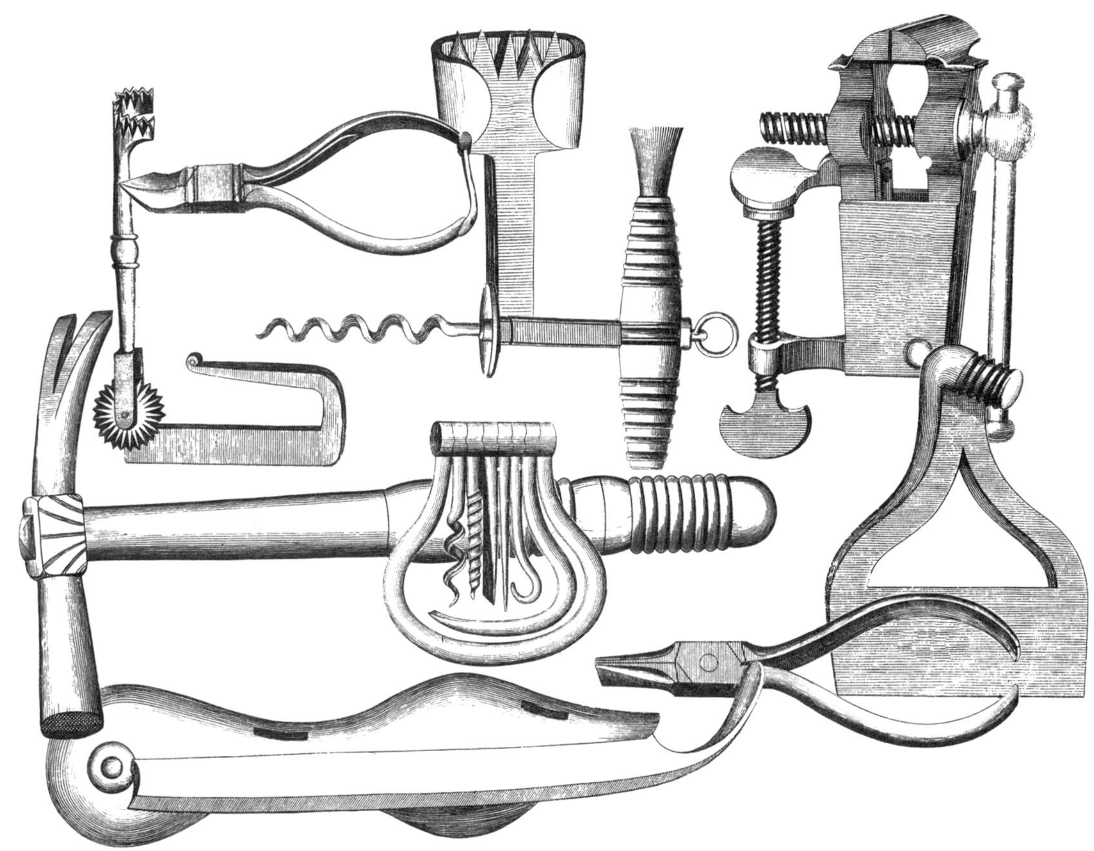

A Pattern Book of Tools and Household Goods

Introduction by Jane Rees and Elton W. Hall

Published by the Early American Industries Association in cooperation with the Peabody Essex Museum, 2006

This is a reprint of the Pattern Book, catalog number 672.2/S19/v.9, in the Phillips Library of the Peabody Essex Museum, reproduction courtesy of the Peabody Essex Museum.

Reproduction of the W. & C. Wynn List of Prices 1810 courtesy of Jane Rees

ISBN 0-943196-04-3

This book was made possible by the Mark Rees Publication Fund of the Early American Industries Association and the kind permission of the Peabody Essex Museum, Salem, Massachusetts, the owner of the original pattern book.

All photographs by Jane Rees unless otherwise noted.

Published by the Early American Industries Association, Inc.
167 Bakerville Road, South Dartmouth, Massachusetts

Printed in the United States of America by The Stinehour Press
Lunenburg, Vermont

This book is dedicated to

Mark Rees (1939–2001)

whose vision it was to reprint this pattern book and whose enthusiasm and knowledge have inspired and benefited tool collectors and researchers the world over.

Foreword

The publication of primary source material has always been among the most important functions of an historical association. In the course of his research into the history of English tool manufacture and the distribution of English tools far and wide, including America, Mark Rees became aware of the importance of the books of engravings illustrating the manufactures of Birmingham and Sheffield. The Peabody Essex Museum in Salem, Massachusetts, has in its Phillips Library one of the most extensive collections of these now very rare pattern books. During the course of his service as a board member of the Early American Industries Association, Mark proposed that the Association publish a reprint of one of the books, believing that it would be of great usefulness not only to tool historians and collectors on both sides of the Atlantic, but also those interested in many facets of material culture, historic preservation and the history of trade. He also believed that the publication should reflect the size and clarity of the original.

Regrettably, Mark died before the project could be carried out. Fortunately, his wife Jane shared his enthusiasm for the undertaking. Her determination to see this project through to completion has been the most important element in bringing it to pass. In addition to her scholarly contributions, she has been a major force in the establishment of the Mark Rees Publication Fund, a revolving fund to support the ongoing publication program of the Early American Industries Association, of which the present volume will be the first undertaking.

Many others have helped with this publication. William T. La Moy, formerly Librarian and Director of Publications at the Peabody Essex Museum, now Curator of Rare Books at Syracuse University, and Jay Gaynor, Director of Historic Trades at the Colonial Williamsburg Foundation, were supportive of the project from the outset and helped advance it in a variety of ways. Other members of the Peabody Essex Museum staff have also been involved. Jeffrey Dykes captured the images of the plates and price list digitally. William Phippen, Deputy Director; Lynda Hartigan, Chief Curator; and Peter Doran, Assistant Controller; all assisted with the numerous details. Colonial Williamsburg provided an illustration, and its Historic Trades bookbinders made the marbled paper reproduced on the covers. This book is worthy fruit of their collective labors.

Elton W. Hall
Executive Director

View of Birmingham from Wrightson's 1830 directory.

A Pattern Book of Tools and Household Goods

Jane Rees

From the Colonial Period until after the Civil War, the principal source of tools and other hardware used in America was England, and more specifically the manufacturing cities of Birmingham and SheYeld.

The industrial and consumer revolutions of the eighteenth century resulted in the production of vastly increased quantities of goods and an ever increasing demand for them. English manufacturers sought to fulfil existing markets and develop new ones. Consequently they began to look at ways of advertising themselves and their wares not only in the domestic market but also in the overseas markets, particularly the North American colonies.

Marketing

One of the traditional means of identifying a business was by a hanging sign outside the premises. This had the advantage of being comprehensible to those unable to read but only attracted customers who happened to pass by. Hanging signs also had an inherent safety problem and in 1672 a proclamation was issued in London prohibiting them. Advertisements in newspapers were used from the sixteenth century, as were broadsheets, listing the services and wares offered by a business. Trade cards, depicting the goods made, were another useful tool.

By the mid-eighteenth century the trades directory, which was eventually to become a universal means of advertising, was firmly established in London, soon to be followed in other major manufacturing centers. The forerunner of the trades directory, a list of merchants in and around the City of London, was published in 1677. This was intended for commercial use and included only wholesale businesses, but it was to become the pattern for future directories.[1] From 1734, London directories were published annually.

The first Birmingham directory was published in 1763 by James Sketchley, although the earliest extant directory for Birmingham is Sketchley's third edition, published in 1767. It was Sketchley's intention that his directory would provide a means for traders and merchants to make contact with each other and with their suppliers. In the preface to the 1767 directory, he presents this possible situation "Let us suppose a merchant in Birmingham, Walsall or Wolverhampton, who wants to purchase a parcel of Buckels (*sic*) and Spurs and is not particularly acquainted with any maker," then reference could be made to Sketchley's classified list of manufacturers to find what was wanted.[2]

From that date on, directories for Birmingham were published on a regular basis, often with descriptions and engravings of the city and also, in the case of the early nineteenth-century directories, illustrated with trade cards from a wide range of firms. A look at some of these directories confirms the importance of the overseas market, with two specialist American merchants listed in Wrightson's Triennial Directory of 1821, William Chance & Son and Joseph Goddard & Co., and other specialist merchants listed for various European countries.

The issuing of pattern books and catalogues was another effective method of advertising. They could be widely distributed at a lower cost than samples and enabled manufacturers to show an extensive range of products and designs.

Pattern books

A pattern book is a bound set of "engraved plates," printed from copper plates, illustrating the goods produced and/or sold by a manufacturer. The pages are often numbered and indexed and each item illustrated is assigned a consecutive stock number. The majority of the surviving pattern books of the late eighteenth and early nineteenth centuries are of a very similar design. Although pattern books, catalogues, and prices lists had been issued for some commodities since the sixteenth century, books, scientific instruments, and printing type being among the earliest, the proliferation of manufactured goods greatly increased the number and range of such books.

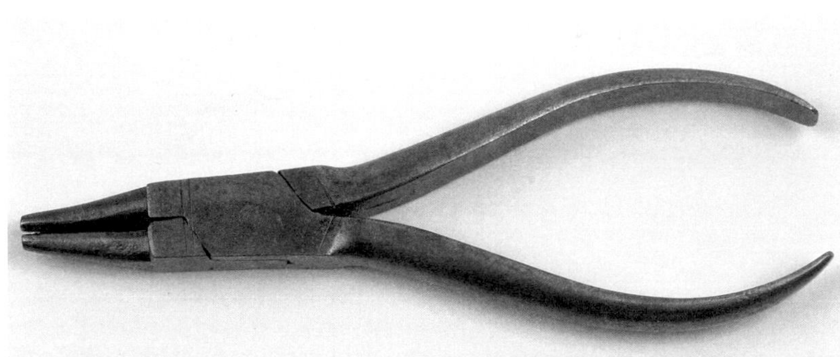

A pair of round nosed plyers, marked W & C. WYNN, *as shown on Plates 34 and 35 of this pattern book. These plyers are 6 in. long.*

Copper plates are made by incising the surface of a smooth, flat piece of copper with a variety of engraving tools with deeper lines for the outlines and lighter lines for shading to give a three-dimensional effect. The plates are then spread with an oil-based ink over the entire surface which is lightly wiped off leaving the engraved lines filled with ink. Damp paper is placed on the plates and the whole passed through a pair of rollers, thus transferring the ink to the paper.

The same plates continued to be used, though often altered and added to, for many years. Indeed some catalogues dating to the early twentieth century still contain some of the engravings found in those dating from the early nineteenth century. Copper is a relatively soft material, and it is possible to correct mistakes, remove items completely or make alterations by smoothing the previously engraved lines with a burnisher and then re-engraving. Other items were also added in the spaces between the previous images.

One notable feature of a whole range of Birmingham pattern books and catalogues dating from the late eighteenth century to the mid-nineteenth century, although issued by different firms, is the similarity between the articles depicted – indeed many are identical. Judging by the number of engravers listed in the trade directories for the early nineteenth century – there are sixty-two in the Birmingham directory published by Wrightson in 1830 – there were many different engravers involved in this work. One possibility is that there was considerable plagiarism between the engravers; another could be that there was a standard pattern book to which engravers could refer.

The illustrations were likely to have been drawn from actual examples of the tools. The perspective employed at times appears strange to our eyes, but it served to illustrate various features of tools that more conventional drawings would not. Once the viewer deciphers this system, the engravings prove to be extremely accurate renditions of surviving examples of the products. The majority of the products were rendered life-size.

Exactly how the pattern books were used has to be a matter of conjecture as no records or descriptions of their use have survived, but it is apparent that they were intended for the wholesale rather than the retail market. Very few carry the name of the firm that issued them – the user of the books certainly did not intend his customer to find out his sources – and the prices of all but the largest goods are quoted as "per dozen."

Products were offered and illustrated in a wide range of designs, materials, qualities, and sizes. In the pattern book reproduced here, the wide selection of some items, such as corkscrews (Plates 51 to 53) or pencil holders (Plate 49½), was intended to give buyers choices based upon varying forms, finishes, or decoration. There was something to suit almost any taste. Other design variations were grounded in function: square- versus round-nose pliers (Plates 34 and 35), hammer types intended for specific trade uses (Plate 70), a wide range of drill bits (Plates 27 and 28). Form and decoration variations, or "patterns" as they often were called, occasionally were designated by a place name: "Kent Hammers" (Plate 70), and "London Pattern Hammers." Other tools were named based upon their specific functions (such as carrot and turnip scopes and cheese and butter tasters) or the trades whose practitioners were their principal users: Carpenters, Glaziers, Shoemakers, Upholsterers, Saddlers. Several tools are defined as "Gentlemens" or "Ladies" – smaller, lightweight tools intended for casual use.

Given the full-scale drawings, sometimes the alternative sizes available are shown by a note such as "A Size Larger" or, very occasionally "A Size Smaller." Some items, such as the steak tongs shown on Plate 22, could be had one, two, three, or four sizes larger. Other items could be obtained in sizes stated in inches. Plate 65 shows compasses that could be had from five to twelve inches and callipers from six to twenty-four inches.

Before the 1830s, the prices of goods were not included in the pattern books but were supplied in separate price lists, although in many of the early pattern books, including that reprinted here, the prices have been marked in ink, presumably by the user.

In many instances, the wholesalers who used these pattern books were expected to pay for them but when a new book was issued, the out-of-date book could be returned and a new one issued in its place. It is of note that there are considerably more pattern books extant in the United States than there are in Britain and although this might be a reflection of their

A pair of rule joint compasses, with steel points, marked W & C WYNN, *as shown in Plate 65 of this pattern book.* (Colonial Williamsburg Foundation)

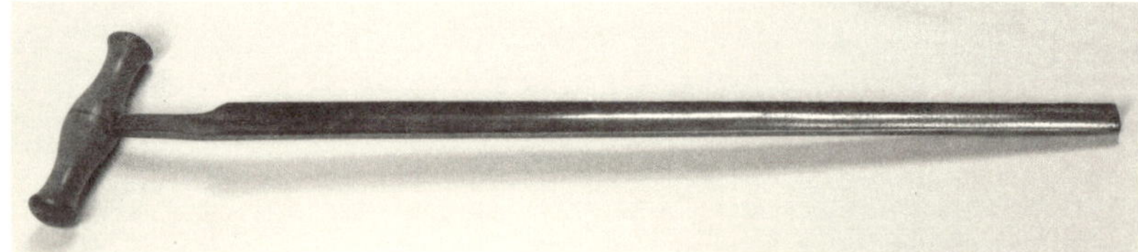

A butter or flour tryer (tester), 24 in. overall, with a wooden handle. Marked W & C WYNN CAST STEEL, *this style of tryer is shown in Plate 33½ in this pattern book with, right, a detail of the mark. In the price list, these are called butter testers.*

use in the export market, another explanation may be that the difficulty and expense of returning the books was such as to make it more economical to purchase a new book without returning the old one.

The return and pirating of pattern books was a source of much litigation. In 1850, R. Timmins and Sons (another Birmingham manufacturer) accused one of their clerks of obtaining a pattern book by false pretences. Their statement to the court gives a good insight into the reasons why the owners were so concerned to keep control of their books. It says that "Although the value of the book was not great, the loss to the firm was past calculation because if these books got into the hands of small makers, they copied from the patterns and put their spurious goods into the market, greatly to the detriment of the high class and respectable firms."[3] There were other instances where ironmongers obtained pattern books by opening an account for goods to be supplied but never placed an order, and when the account was closed the pattern books were not returned. In 1884, an ironmonger was charged with unlawfully detaining a pattern book, valued at £10, belonging to a brass founder.[3]

In a similar instance, J. Rabone & Sons, Birmingham rule makers, demanded the return of a pattern book. The defendant countered that the books had been sent abroad, and it was too expensive to get them returned. Rabone won the case.[3]

The Birmingham toy and tool trade

By the late seventeenth century, Birmingham and its immediate surrounding area had developed an extensive manufacturing trade in a variety of metal wares, despite the fact that there was neither iron nor coal there, and both had to be imported from Staffordshire. As a result of the high cost of fuel and materials, the Birmingham makers concentrated on small items of high value where the value was added by labour – swords, cutlery, guns, nails, jewellery, and those items known in Birmingham as "toys" being amongst the most prominent. The term "toys" in the eighteenth century did not mean children's playthings but small personal and household items. Toys did not have to be made of steel; there were silver, gold, and "tortoise" toys – the last made from tortoiseshell. Steel toys were divided into light steel toys: buckles, corkscrews, boxes, and small tools such as bits, compasses, etc.; and heavy steel toys that included larger tools such as edge tools – axes and adzes, chisels, plane irons, billhooks, – and hammers.

The metalworking trade in and around Birmingham continued to flourish and expand well into the nineteenth century, the network of canals being built from the 1770s helping with the transport of both the raw materials and the finished products. The introduction of steam power to the mills, forges, and workshops assisted in increasing this flourishing trade. Another factor in the growth was the increasing availability of brass; the invention, in 1769 by Richard Ford, of a means of fabricating brass items by rolling and stamping further advanced Birmingham's position. Indeed, by the end of the eighteenth century, the only other towns that could compete with Birmingham in manufacturing were London and Sheffield.

W. & C. Wynn

For a number of reasons, to be discussed later, it is likely that the pattern book reproduced here was issued by W. & C. Wynn.

In 1797, two brothers, William & Cornelius, established their firm, W. & C. Wynn, in Caroline Street, Birmingham as buckle makers. Their father, also Cornelius, was listed in the directories as a buckle maker in Constitution Hill from 1791, although it is very likely that he was in business well before this date. He married his wife, Mary Cook, in 1763 and their son William was born in 1765, with Cornelius following in 1768. It would be logical to assume that the two boys learned their trade from their father before setting up on their own, possibly when their father either retired or died as he ceased to be listed after 1798.

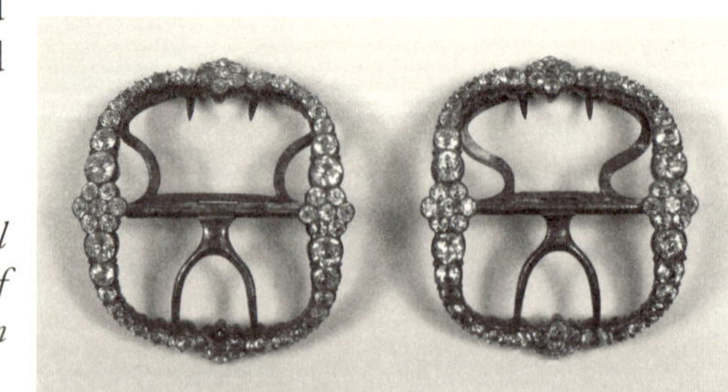

A pair of nineteenth century steel shoe buckles. This is the type of buckle that Cornelius Wynn senior would have made.

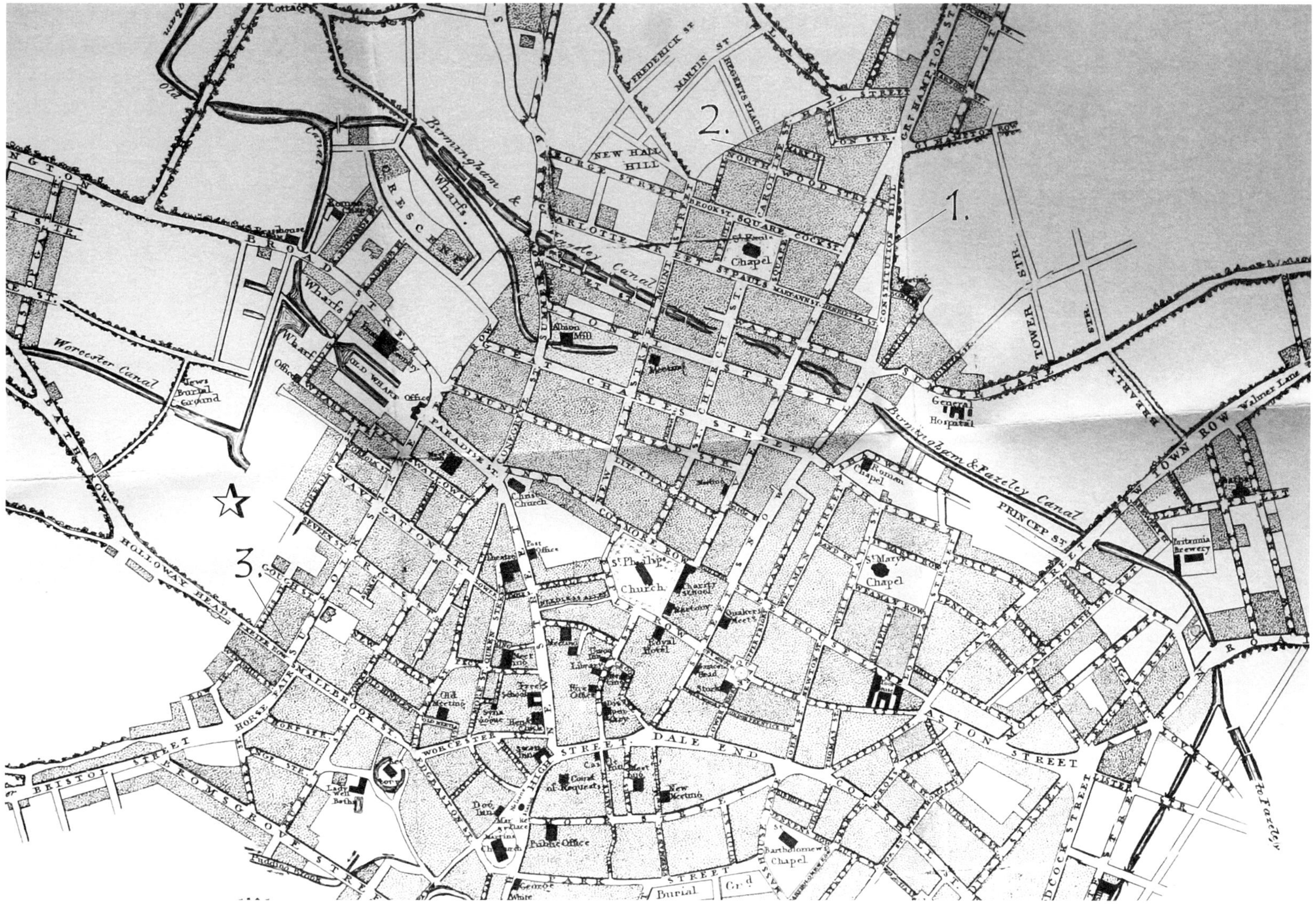

Map of Birmingham from Wrightson's Triennial Directory for 1818. Cornelius Snr.'s premises were located in Constitution Hill, (no. 1 on the map); the two brothers, William and Cornelius Jnr. set up in Caroline Street, (no. 2) in 1797, remaining there until 1813, when they moved to Suffolk Street on the corner of Exeter Row (no. 3). The approximate position of the future Commercial Street premises is indicated by the star.

In 1800, William and Cornelius added "steel toy makers" to the description of their business and continued with this description until 1808. The buckles, previously their staple product, were shoe buckles, but with the fickleness of fashion, by the end of the eighteenth century, laces had ousted buckles as a means of fastening shoes. The Birmingham manufacturers tried hard to turn this trend round – even to the extent of petitioning the Prince of Wales to encourage the wearing of buckles at Court – but fashion prevailed. The buckle makers had to look to other goods to manufacture.

From 1812, W. & C. Wynn started listing a much wider range of goods in the trade directories, adding gentlemen's tool chests, pincers, and compasses. However, they probably had been offering these for some time before that date as their 1810 *List of Prices* (reprinted with this book) includes all these as well as a wide range of other tools and household goods, from hammers and braces and bits to corkscrews, dental instruments, and skates.

In 1813, the firm moved to Suffolk Street, on the corner of Exeter Row, where they were to remain until 1872. The premises consisted of the works at No. 142 and William Wynn's house at No. 143. To what extent W. & C. Wynn actually made the goods they sold and how much they bought in – undoubtedly a proportion was in the latter category – is not known but throughout their occupation, No. 142 was called a "works," implying that at least some manufacturing was undertaken.

Cornelius died in 1833 at the age of 65 years and William in 1838 at the age of 73 years. After William's death, the house at No. 143 was disposed of but the business was continued by John Wynn (probably William's son) and other family members. In 1872, new premises were built in Commercial Street, which in 1897 were renamed "Century Works."

Previous to this, in 1889, W. & C. Wynn amalgamated with Richard Timmins & Sons, another prominent Birmingham firm that described itself as pincer, compass, and heavy steel toy makers. Timmins claimed to have started in business in 1790, but the earliest verifiable records date from 1795.

The resultant firm, Wynn, Timmins & Co., continued to occupy Century Works in Commercial Street until 1969. It became a limited company in 1892 when the directors were named as William Henry Wynn, John Henry Wynn, and Charles Henry Wynn. This firm also continued to issue lists of goods for sale into the twentieth century, although they were no longer described as pattern books. A careful inspection of the 1901 edition of their *Illustrated Book of Steel Toys* shows sixteen pages that have been printed using all or part of the same copper plates used in the circa 1820 volume reproduced here. The plates reused from this book are

Early nineteenth century socket chisel, ¾ in. wide, by WYNN *with left, a detail of the maker's mark. Chisels would have been classed as heavy steel toys. There are none shown in this pattern book, which shows only light steel toys.*

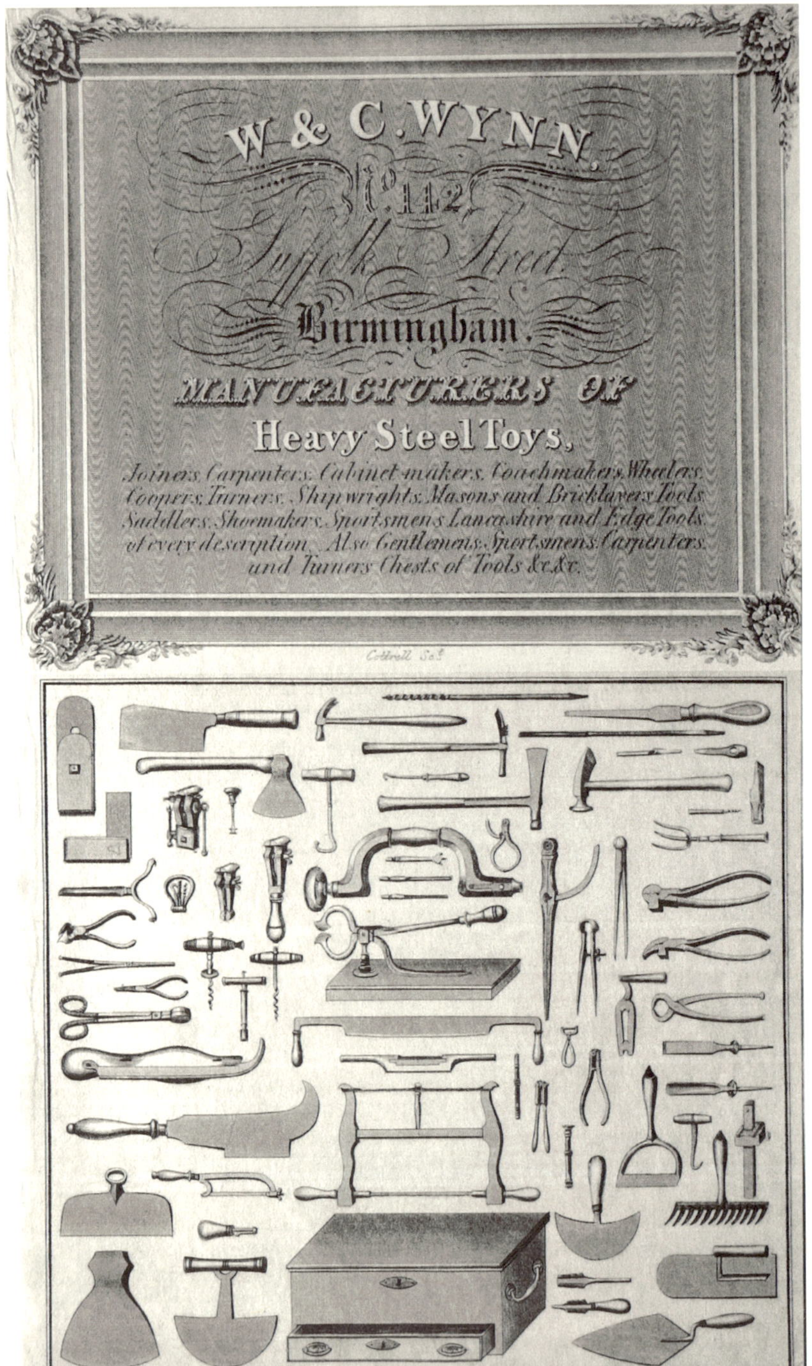

nos. 13, 16, 17, 22, 23, 27, 28, 29, 29½, 34, 35, 36½, 53, 59, 61 and 64½.

Two pages are identical in both books, the only variation being that in 1901, the prices of the articles have been engraved on the plates rather than added by hand. These are Plate 29, the Scotch brace and bits and Plate 34, showing plyers. The plate of nail nippers (clippers) (Plate 13) has the outer four patterns removed but is otherwise identical and Plate 27 (bits), in the 1901 list, has had the modern names added. On four pages, Plate 16 (kitchen utensils), Plate 17 (sugar nips), Plate 28 (bits) and Plate 64½ (Lancashire tools), the majority of the tools shown in 1820 are still in the 1901 list. Of these four, Plate 28 is of particular interest as the bedstead, sash, and table bits have been removed and replaced with two brace bits – a reflection of the fact that these three earlier types of bit were no longer in use at the beginning of the twentieth century. In the remaining seven plates, a variable number of items have been retained, for instance, the majority of the saw sets in Plate 29½ are still shown, but in Plate 23, only the top set of sugar cleavers is still used.

A comparison of the prices is also of interest. In eight plates, the prices remain unchanged; in three plates, the prices have been increased; in three plates, the prices have been reduced; and in one plate, the prices bear no resemblance to the 1820 prices. It is also interesting to note that all those items that remain in the 1901 list still have the same stock numbers.

Some tools in this 1901 book are shown with a maker's mark, the majority being marked "W & C Wynn" with only a few marked "Wynn Timmins," which would suggest that W. & C. Wynn considered themselves the dominant part of the partnership.

Wynn, Timmins & Co. Ltd. was dissolved in 1969 following its acquisition by Balfour Darwins Ltd. of Sheffield, and the premises in Commercial Street were vacated after almost 100 years of occupation.

The pattern book reproduced herein

This pattern book is undated, but the paper is watermarked 1818, which is therefore the earliest possible date. It is likely to have been published shortly after that date around 1820.

The range of goods made and sold as "toys" was extensive. This pattern book covers mainly light steel toys, tools, household goods, and sporting items but does not include edge tools or many heavy steel toys. It consists of eighty-two plates illustrating a wide variety of woodworking tools, garden tools, kitchen utensils, sewing tools, table wares, skates, boot hooks, curling irons, dentists' instruments, corkscrews, gun tools, saddlers' tools, Lancashire tools, watch and clock makers' tools, upholsterers' tools, and many others.

All the plates are numbered consecutively, although there are some additional "¼" and "½" plates indicating that there was a previously issued pattern book.

All the items are also numbered consecutively with the exception of the added-in "¼" and "½" pages and a few pages at the end of the book. The first seven plates show a variety of chests, with contents, and sets of tools. Plates 8 to 26 show a range of household goods followed by 16 plates of tools including braces, bits, hammers, saw sets, turnscrews (an alternative eighteenth and early nineteenth century name for screwdrivers), plyers and pincers. Plates 43 to 50 show personal items, the next four plates, corkscrews and then four plates of gun tools (guns and gun tools were a very important and extensive part of the manufacturing trade

Left: Trade card of W. & C. Wynn from Wrightson's Triennial Directory of 1821. Although the trade card describes W. & C. Wynn as "Manufacturers of Heavy Steel Toys" at this date the description of the firm in the directory covers both heavy and light steel toys and both these are shown on this trade card.

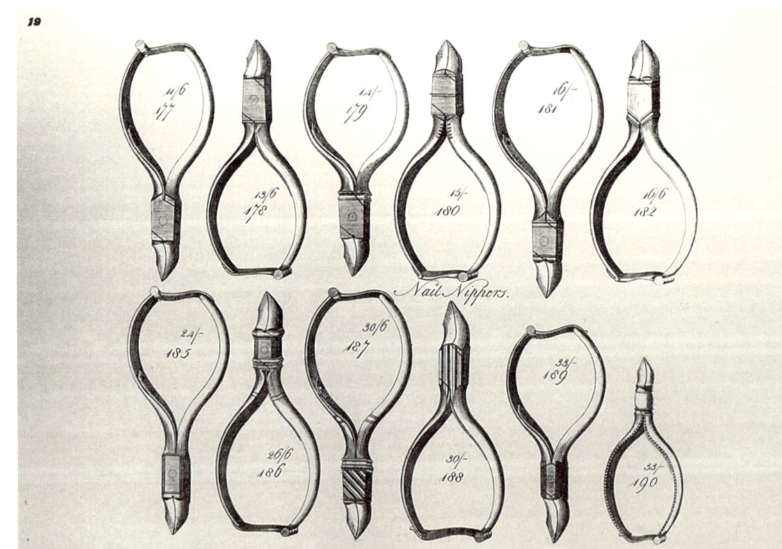

Page 19 from the 1901 Wynn, Timmins & Co. Ltd. Illustrated Book of Steel Toys *showing the range of nail nippers on offer. Comparison with Plate 13 of this pattern book shows that, although the four outer nippers have been omitted, the remainder are identical, printed from the same plate. Even the prices have remained unchanged.*

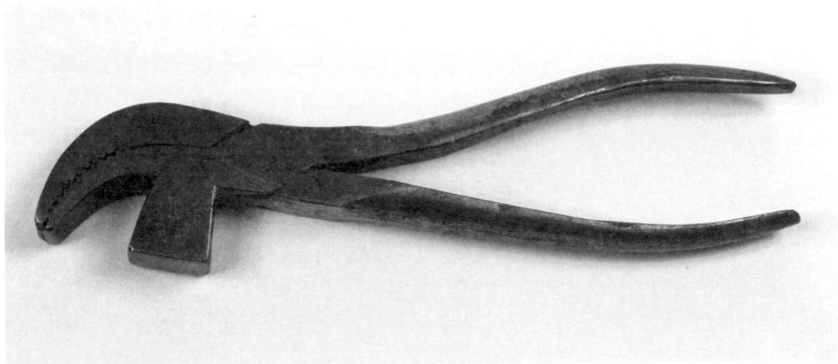

A pair of shoe plyers marked W. & C. WYNN WARRANTED STEEL[D] HAMMERS *with a "2" in the centre of the mark, indicating the size. They are also marked* "★ ENGLAND."

in Birmingham). The remaining plates, numbered 50 to 70, show specialist tools for the saddler and leatherworker, followed by compasses, dividers, and, finally, more hammers.

Most tools in this pattern book were made of some ferrous alloy. Larger tools that required wear-resistant or sharpened working surfaces, such as hammer faces, cutting edges, or the points of compasses, often were made of wrought iron, with a piece of steel welded to the surface that needed to be hardened. Many of the smaller tools and toys were made entirely of steel (the saddler's knife illustrated in Plate 60 even states the type, "Cast Steel"). This resulted in an entire tool that could be hardened, both to improve its function and also to receive a higher polish. Some items may have been made of wrought iron and then case-hardened, a process that converted the surface into steel. The designation "hard" indicates that the object, or at least its surface, had been heat-treated. In several instances, there are brass items or components. At least one box, likely made of sheet iron or tin-plated iron, was "Japan'd"– painted with a black varnish. Nutcrackers, skewers, and forks could be had "Best Plated…all over on steel," that is, silver plated.

Many of the plates appear to have large numbers of similar items; for instance Plates 9, 10, and 11 are all given over to nutcrackers, of which there are forty-three different patterns with some patterns being repeated but with a different finish. W. & C. Wynn wanted to insure that they not only offered a variety of designs to appeal to different tastes, they also offered a range of qualities to appeal to a variety of pocketbooks. Items offered as "black" were sold pretty much as they came from the forge, with only the minimum filing or grinding required to make them functional. The surfaces of "bright" items were filed, ground, or polished to reveal bare metal. Tools of superior construction, finish, or elaborate decoration were designated as "Fine," "Best," and even "Extra Best." One interesting description can be found in Plate 61 where the more superior key rings are faceted. These are described as "dyed," the decoration having been produced in a die.

One of the most interesting illustrations in the pattern book is the steel plane, item No. 28 shown in Plate 6. Steel smooth planes have been recorded made by Robert Towell, a metal plane maker working in London, probably from the 1830s, but the planes made by Towell have steel stocks infilled with a wooden stuffing. The plane illustrated here appears from the engraving to be made completely of steel, including the wedge. From the illustration it would seem to be a small plane, perhaps a thumb plane, but there are no dimensions given so it is not possible to verify this.

Plate 7 is also of interest. It shows a selection of garden tools, all designed to screw onto a jointed staff, 5 ft. 6 in. (1.68 m.) long. This would provide a long-handled bill hook, a long-handled pruning saw, and an unusually shaped fruit knife. There also appears to be a shaped cutting or stirring tool, named a paddle, the use of which is not known.

Plate 13 shows a pen engine for cutting quills to shape for pens. By the late 1820s, John Mitchell of Birmingham had introduced a machine-made steel pen nib and the use of quill pens rapidly declined and pen engines were no longer required.

Of the household articles included, many will be familiar to today's reader, though often now known by a different name, but there are a number the use of which is no longer part of our life today. Of the former,

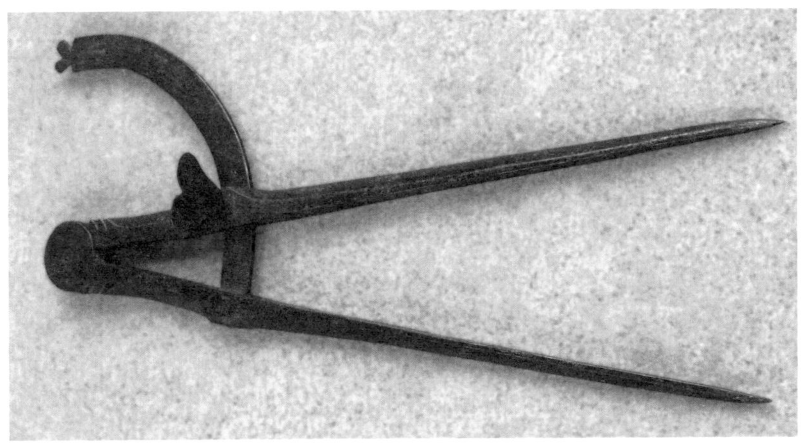

Pair of calipers marked W & C WYNN. *The design of the wing nut and the decoration near the joint suggests that these date from the early years of the nineteenth century.*

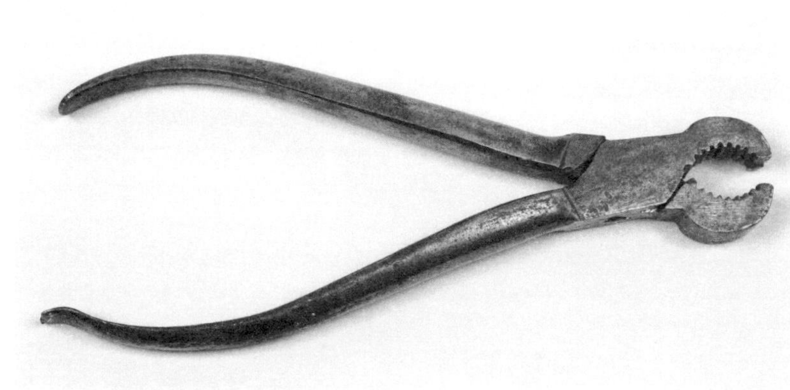

A pair of gas plyers by W. *&* C. WYNN *with turnscrew. These are not included in this pattern book but were available from the 1840s.*

Plate 16 shows an apple and a potato scope and a lemon racer, in modern terminology, an apple corer, a potato baller, and a lemon zester. Of the latter, Plates 17, 18, and 19 show sugar nippers and Plate 23, sugar cleavers; in the eighteenth and early nineteenth centuries, sugar was bought in large cones which needed to be broken up into manageable sized pieces.

The large selection of toasting forks in Plates 20 and 21 is a reminder that toast was made by holding slices of bread in front of an open fire. The bread rasp, in Plate 21, was logical when bread was baked in a bread oven, heated by means of faggots laid on the oven floor and the resulting ash on the bottom of the loaf needed to be removed.

Plates 26 and 26½ show a range of bed wrenches, necessary to take apart and re-assemble beds; these were used to turn the bolts that attached the side rails of the bed to the head and foot boards. Plate 26 also shows an Italian iron; these consisted of cylindrical slugs that were heated in the fire and then placed inside a tube on a stand used to form frilled trimmings to shirts or collars, the material being moved over the iron rather than *vice versa.*

Among the tools, there are also some that are no longer required: Plate 28 includes sash bits, needed in the making of sash windows when jointing the profiled bars; and bedstead bits, probably used when assembling the sides, head, and foot of wooden framed beds; and table bits. The use of these is not certain; R.A. Salaman in his *Dictionary of Tools* suggests that they were either for boring through the rails to secure the table top or for drilling the knuckle joint used in drop leaf tables.[4] Also in this plate are shown wimble bits. A wimble was, even then, an archaic term, dating from around the twelfth century, for a gimlet or auger, particularly one that threw out the waste material as it bored. W. & C. Wynn appear to be the only manufacturer to use this term.

Plate 31 (Plate 30 in the price list) shows two seals. The price list gives the explanation for these; seals were used for pressing down or marking the wafers used to seal letters and documents. (A wafer was a small disk of flour mixed with gum, or sometimes gelatin.)

In Plate 32, one of three plates of turnscrews, nos. 432 and 433 have an added notation "made to shift in the handles." This term means that the bit or blade is reversible or replaceable. In the case of turnscrews, this can mean a blade with a different sized bit at each end or a single bit at one and a notched bit at the other.

Plate 33½ is an example of an additional plate that has been introduced to include a variety of items neither related to each other nor numbered sequentially. In this plate, the labeling of the punch plyers as either for shoe makers or for marking lamb's ears may seem a strange combination of uses to modern ears but as a tool for cutting out shaped notches, the combination of applications is more logical that it first appears.

The same could also be said for the pair of plyers, no. 475 in Plate 36, sold for either bell hanging or bottling, but as both required the use of wire the two uses are perhaps not as incongruous as it would first seem. (The bells referred to are household bells that were controlled by a system of wires run round the house; the bottling reference is to the wires that are used to secure the corks in bottles of sparkling wine, Champagne, etc.) The wine coopers' nippers, no. 479, in the same plate are also of interest, combining as they do a pair of pincers with two different styles of timber scribe, perhaps for marking casks.

A shoe punch marked W & C. WYNN *with a detail of the mark. A wide range of sizes of these punches are shown on page 59 of this pattern book. This punch is now 4¼ in. long but was probably 4½ in. originally. The end of the punch has been turned over by constant hitting with a hammer.*

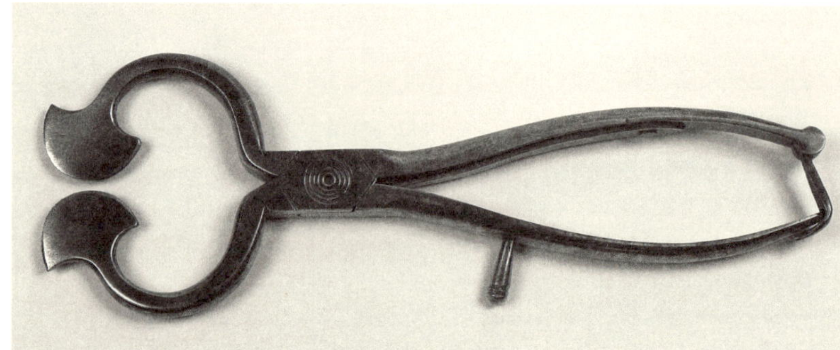

A pair of sugar nips, marked W & C. WYNN. *They are shown in Plate 17 of this pattern book and this pair is 9 in. long.*

Plate 38 illustrates a further wide range of timber scribes. They were used by a variety of people connected with the timber trades, from merchants marking the logs or trees they had purchased to carpenters assembling timber frame buildings.

Fashion dictated the need for curling tongs and pinching and craping irons (Plates 46, 47, and 48) (craping irons, which today would be known as crimping irons, were used to produce ringlets), still used today by those aspiring to fashionable hair styles, but long superceded by appliances powered by electricity, and the boot and button hooks, shown in Plates 45 and 48, were aids to ease dressing in the days before zip fasteners and Velcro.

Many of the tools were intended for the tradesman rather than for household use. Into this category fall the range of saddlers' and shoe tools illustrated in Plates 59 to 61 and the wide range of watch, clock, and Lancashire tools (Plates 62 to 64½).

There are six plates of tools made in Lancashire. This is an area in the northwest of England where the clock and watch trade was concentrated in the eighteenth and nineteenth centuries, particularly centered around Liverpool and Prescot and that was known for its superior quality tools designed for those trades. Those illustrated include a variety of designs of plyers, dividers, callipers, and compasses. There are screw plates and draw plates (for forming wire) and various styles of vices, both hand and bench. There are also to be had further hand vices, shown in Plate 40, no doubt made in Birmingham but described as "....Black of a Superior Quality nearly equal to Lancashire."

Comparison with 1810 List of Prices

Also reproduced in this publication is a price list issued by W. & C. Wynn in 1810. The prices are given, with a very few exceptions for larger items, per dozen, indicating that this was intended for the wholesale rather than the retail trade. It is likely that the actual prices paid would have been less than those shown as discounts for preferred customers and larger orders were common.

Although dating from at least eight years before the pattern book, a comparison of the price list plate numbers and stock numbers (excluding the additional "¼" and "½" numbered plates) very closely matches those in the pattern book. All the prices in both the price list and the pattern book are given in shillings and pence (before decimalisation, there were 20 shillings to the pound and 12 pence to the shilling), even when the price exceeded one pound, for example pen engines in Plate 13 are 45*s* a dozen, 33*s* a dozen and 84*s* a dozen. The only exception is the price of Gentlemen's Chests of Tools in Plate 1, which are shown in the price list and written into the pattern book in £. *s. d.* and the Mahogany Chests with Sportsmen's Implements, which are priced in pounds and shillings in the price list (but not written thus in the pattern book).

A pair of goffering irons marked W & C. WYNN. *Goffering irons do not appear in either this pattern book or the list of prices, though they are found in other pattern books dating to the mid-nineteenth century. However, they were offered in the 1901 Wynn, Timmins & Co. Ltd.* Illustrated Book of Steel Toys.

Many of the prices did not change in the years between the publication of the price list and the pattern book; nutcrackers, spinet hammers, nail clippers, bits of all kinds, saw sets, and turnscrews all remained static.

Some, however, do differ; and, unlike today, many of the prices are lower in 1820 than in 1810. The price of sugar nippers has gone down by between 6*d* and 6*s* 0*d,* and Scotch braces have been reduced by 2*s* 0*d.* Similarly, smiths' braces have been reduced by several shillings.

Other prices have increased; fruit tongs, in Plate 44, have increased in price by between £7 and £14, a considerable increase, the greatest in the book. The prices of some of the corkscrews shown in Plates 52 and 54 have increased by two or three shillings, although many have remained at the 1810 price.

There are fourteen additional plates, three numbered as "¼" plates and eleven as "½" plates. The stock numbers of the items included in these additional plates run on consecutively from the last stock number in the price list, a Tylers Hatchet, no. 1065, with a best quality iron brace, no. 1066 and best steel punches, no. 1067, on Plate 33½. This plate is not the first additional plate in the book, but the two previous to this, Plates 26½ and 33¼, were inserted immediately after plates showing the same goods, bed keys and turnscrews. Two items in Plate 6, the vice, no. 27, and steel plane, no. 28, do not appear in the price list.

There are three instances where the arrangement of the plates in the pattern book and price list vary. Plate 30 is missing from the pattern book, but the contents match the description of Plate 31 in the price list and Plate 29½ in the pattern book matches the description of Plate 31 in the price list. The plate numbered 60½ in the pattern book, appears to be Plate 61 in the price list with Plate 61 in the pattern book being an additional plate with key rings and prickers with stock numbers in the 1100s. Plates 69 and 70 have been interchanged. However, it should be noted that the plates in the pattern book are numbered by hand in the top corner so there is a margin for human error. It is not possible to determine at what date the plate numbers were added or when the additional plates were included.

Three harness makers' pinking irons, marked W & C. WYNN, *with a detail of the mark. The top two are for pinking straps finished with a "Cathedral window" end and the bottom is a straight pinking iron. Pinking irons are not offered in this pattern book.*

A saw set marked W & C. WYNN. *A variety of saw sets of a similar style were offered in this pattern book but this design was not offered.*

Surviving pattern books

One of the largest collections of early English pattern books is in the library of the Peabody Essex Museum in Salem, Massachusetts, and this is where the original of this reprint is housed.

The pattern book chosen is unnamed but is almost certain to have been issued by the Birmingham toy and tool manufacturers, W. & C. Wynn. As previously noted the paper is watermarked 1818 and the book probably dates to circa 1820. The copy of *A List of Prices to Pattern Book of Articles* issued by W. & C. Wynn in 1810, and also reprinted in this publication, were both printed by J. Belcher & Sons, High Street, Birmingham.

A number of factors contributed to the attribution. First and foremost is the considerable semblance between the named price list and the pattern book and that both were printed by the same printer. The continued use of the plates from this book in the 1901 Wynn Timmins & Co. Ltd. catalogue, with identical stock numbers, is another strong clue. Finally, the known W. & C. Wynn tools that correspond exactly with those shown in the pattern book, and are illustrated in this introduction, endorse this attribution. This evidence leaves little doubt that, although unnamed, this pattern book was issued by W. & C. Wynn.

A number of other pattern books and catalogues have been reprinted in the past, notably the John Wyke *Catalogue of Tools for Watch and Clock Makers* which dates from circa 1760,[5] the pattern book of Richard Timmins, circa 1845[6] and Joseph Smith's *Explanation or Key to the Various Manufactories of Sheffield*[7] but none are now in print. This is the first facsimile reprint of a Birmingham pattern book at full size.

Pattern books such as this are an invaluable source of pictorial information documenting the variety and design of the goods produced by the firms they represent. The breadth of the material included will give this book considerable appeal within many collecting areas. It will be of interest to all who are involved in researching American and English material culture in all its facets and also those interested in the history of the trade between England and America.

Notes

1. Jane E. Norton, *Guide to the National and Provincial Directories of England and Wales*, London, 1950.
2. Jane E. Norton, *Ibid.*
3. From a selection of scrapbooks collected by John Rabone & Sons from the late 19th century onwards, now in the Hawley Collection, University of Sheffield, England.
4. R.A. Salaman, *Dictionary of Woodworking Tools c. 1700–1970 and Tools of Allied Trades,* revised edition, London, 1989.

W. & C. Wynn's Birmingham wire gauge with detail of mark. The gauges are used to measure steel wire to the Birmingham Standard. Until 1847, when Holtzapffel defined the sizes and published them in his work Turning and Mechanical Manipulation, *the Birmingham Wire Gauge was a variable measure. Holtzapffel published a table of 40 sizes from 0000 (= 0.454 in.) to 36 (=.004 in.). It is interesting to note, however, that in the 1893 Wynn Timmins & Co. catalogue, the sizes of Wynn's Birmingham Wire Gauges differed from the standard B.W.G. by a factor of between 1% and 5%, so it would appear that W. & C. Wynn were still using their own standard although the gauge was marked Birmingham!*

5. John Wyke, *A Catalogue of Tools for Watch and Clock Makers*, Liverpool, c. 1760. Reprinted by Henry Francis du Pont Winterthur Museum, Virginia, and the Early American Industries Association, 1978. Introduction by Alan Smith.
6. There have been two reprints of the pattern book of Richard Timmins and Sons, c. 1845: Ken Roberts, *Tools for the Trades and Crafts*, Fitzwilliam, New Hampshire, 1976. In this reprint the plates from the pattern book were reduced by twenty-five percent.
   Philip Walker, *The Victorian Catalogue of Tools for Trades and Crafts*, London, 1994. In this reprint the plates were reduced by fifty percent.
7. Joseph Smith, *Explanation or Key to the Various Manufactories of Sheffield*, Sheffield, 1816. Reprinted by the Early American Industries Association, 1975. Introduction by John Kebabian.

A folding hoof pick marked W & C WYNN. *This pattern does not appear in this pattern book, although other styles of folding hoof picks are shown.*

The Hale and related gifts to the Peabody Essex Museum

Elton W. Hall

The Peabody Essex Museum in Salem, Massachusetts, has one of the most extensive collections of pattern books and related material that has survived. Part of the collection, and possibly all or most of it, was the gift of Henry Appleton Hale, a second generation hardware importer and dealer of Salem. The gift books of the Peabody Essex Museum record that on September 4, 1908, Hale gave five volumes of hardware catalogs of John Francis of Birmingham. (It has not been possible to identify John Francis.) While the volume reproduced here is not one of those five, it is very closely related, sharing many of the same plates. It is the association with the Hale family that makes this collection particularly useful.

Henry Hale, father of the donor, was born in Salem February 18, 1808. When Henry's father, Joseph Hale, became a British prisoner of war, his mother moved back to her native Byfield, Massachusetts, where Henry eventually attended Governor Dummer Academy. In 1824, he returned to Salem and became a clerk for Coleman & Johnson in their crockery store. Three years later, John Derby began the development of Derby Square off Essex Street. Taking an interest in young Hale, he leased him a store on the corner of Essex Street and Derby Square and provided the capital for Hale to go into the hardware business as an importer as well as a dealer, both wholesale and retail. The *Salem Gazette* of February 5, 1828 announced the formation of a partnership consisting of Henry and his brother Joseph under the name of J. & H. Hale. He appears to have prospered in that trade, and when Derby died, Hale bought the property and carried on.[1]

Salem was the shopping center of Essex County during the Colonial period and on through the Civil War. With its fine harbor and well-established trade, it was a great crossroads for the import, export, and exchange of goods. Consequently, Hale was well positioned to carry on a successful business, and although he was not the only hardware dealer in Salem, he survived all the others. During the 1830s, he was in partnership with Samuel Stickney, advertising a wide variety of hardware and household goods in both the *Salem Gazette* and the Salem directories. Joseph Hale, who may have been out of the firm for a while or managing a branch of it in an adjacent building, was listed at the same address as Henry in the 1842 directory. Their advertisement in that volume styled them as "importers and dealers in hard ware goods and cutlery, foreign and domestic, house keeping articles, and fancy goods, agricultural tools & ploughs, plough castings, friction rollers & cranks, iron and copper pumps and Lead Pipe, Camphene, Camphene Lamps, Hanging, Side, and Astral, a great variety of styles, cut glass, Britannia, Brass, Bronze, and Mantle Lamps, Carpenters' Tools & House Trimmings, Shoe Makers' Tools, Nails, Thread & Pegs, boiler doors and Oven Mouths, Furnaces, Cast Iron Hollow Ware, Tubs, Pails, Mats, Cut Nails, Emery, Zinc, Lead, & C & C. No. 215 Essex St."

In 1866, Major Henry Appleton Hale returned from the Civil War, joined his father as junior partner, and eventually took over the business, carrying it on until about 1896. By then, he had become president of the Salem Five Cents Savings Bank, and subsequently served as president of the Salem Gas Light Company and the Salem Athenaeum. He died in 1927.[2]

The gift of Birmingham pattern books to the Essex Museum came twelve years after he sold the family hardware business. Yet, even at that early time in the history of preservation in the United States, Hale recognized their importance and took the prudent step to ensure their survival.

Notes

1. Henry Hale's obituary appeared in the *Salem Evening News* on July 8, 1890.
2. Henry Appleton Hale's obituary appeared in the *Salem Evening News* on August 9, 1927.

A shoe hammer marked "WYNN" *and* "2". *The mark is the same as that used to mark the chisel shown on page 3. Although this pattern of shoe hammer does not appear in this pattern book, it is shown in the 1901 Wynn, Timmins & Co. Ltd.* Illustrated Book of Steel Toys.

A Pattern Book of Tools and Household Goods

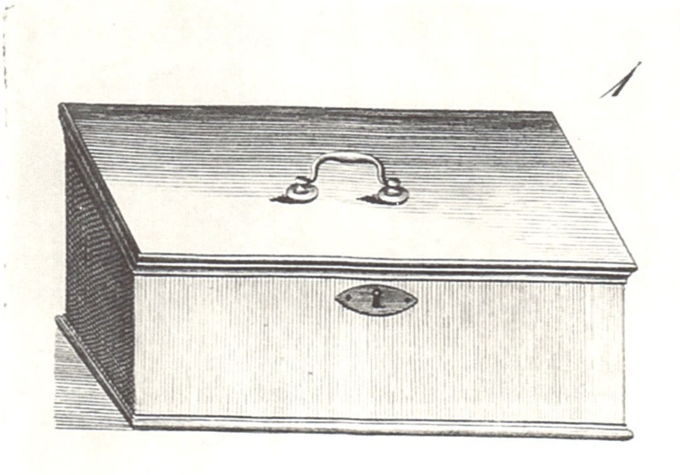

Gentlemen's

£. s.

OAK CHEST, No. 1, contains

A hammer, hatchet, saw, pair of bright pincers, two-foot rule, three gimblets sorted, two brad awls, one turnscrew, mallet, one file, one rasp, two firmers, one gouge, one brad punch, and a key hole saw - - - - - - - - -

If Mahogany Chest - - - - - - - -

OAK CHEST, No. 2, contains

A hammer, hatchet, saw, pair of bright pincers, pair of bright plyers, two-foot rule, small plane, six gimblets sorted, two brad awls, one turnscrew, pair of steel compasses, mallet, one file, one rasp, two firmers, one gouge, one brad punch, one key hole saw, and a row of wood partitions containing nails, wood-screws, &c. - - - - - - - -

If Mahogany Chest - - - - - - - -

OAK CHEST, No. 3, contains

A hammer, hatchet, saw, hand-vice, pair of bright pincers, pair of bright plyers, two foot rule, small plane, six gimblets sorted, two brad awls, two turnscrews, pair of steel compasses, one file, one rasp, mallet, two firmers, one gouge, one brad punch, one saw set, one key hole saw, and a row of wood partitions containing nails, wood-screws, &c. - -

If Mahogany Chest - - - - - - - -

OAK CHEST, No. 4, contains

A hammer, hatchet, saw, hand vice, pair of bright pincers, pair of bright plyers, two-foot rule, small plane, six gimblets sorted, two brad awls, mallet, pair of steel compasses, two turnscrews, two files, one rasp, three firmers, one gouge, one brad punch, one saw set, one bright chissel, one key hole saw, and sundry partitions containing an assortment of clasp and other nails, wood-screws, brads, tacks, brass work, &c. - - - - -

If Mahogany Chest - - - - - - - -

OAK CHEST, No. 5, contains

In the chest, a hammer, pair of bright pincers, pair of bright plyers, table vice, two-foot rule, pair of steel compasses, two brad awls, two turnscrews, six gimblets sorted, one brad punch, two files, one rasp, three firmers, one gouge, one saw set, one bright chissel, one key hole saw, and sundry partitions containing an assortment of clasp, clout, trunk, and other nails, wood-screws, brads, tacks, brass work, &c &c. In a drawer is contained a hatchet, best saw, mallet, oil stone in a wood case, a jack plane, and a smoothing plane - - -

If Mahogany Chest - - - - - - - -

OAK CHEST, No. 6, contains

In the chest, a hammer, pair of bright pincers, pair of bright plyers, table vice, two-foot rule, pair of steel compasses, three brad awls, three turnscrews, six gimblets sorted, three files, one rasp, three firmers, two gouges, one bright chissel, one claw wrench, one brad punch, one saw set, one key hole saw, and sundry partitions containing an assortment of clasp, clout, trunk and other nails, woodscrews, brads, tacks, brass hooks, brass knobs, screw rings, &c. &c. In a drawer is contained a hatchet, best saw, mallet, oil stone in a wood case, a jack plane, and a smoothing plane - - - - - - - -

If Mahogany Chest - - - - - - - -

OAK CHEST, No. 7, contains

In the chest, a hammer, table vice, hand vice, pair of bright pincers, pair of bright plyers, two-foot rule, pair of steel compasses, six gimblets, two brad awls, two turnscrews, two files, one rasp, three firmers, two gouges, one bright chissel, one claw wrench, one brad punch, one saw set, and sundry partitions containing an assortment of nails, woodscrews, brads, tacks, brass work, &c. Likewise underneath the lid is a till, containing a best hand saw, best dove tail saw, and a key hole saw. In a drawer is contained a hatchet, mallet, oil stone in a wood case, jack plane, smoothing plane, and a hand pad, with six bits sorted - -

If Mahogany Chest - - - - - - - -

OAK CHEST, No. 8, contains

In the chest, a hammer, pair of bright pincers, pair of bright plyers, two-foot rule, pair of steel compasses, four brad awls, three turnscrews, six gimblets sorted, one bright chissel, one claw wrench, one saw set, one brad punch, one striking knife, and sundry partitions containing a great variety of nails, wood-screws, brads, tacks, brass work, &c. &c. In a drawer is contained a best table vice, hand vice, bick iron, four firmers, two gouges, four files, one rasp, two mortice chissels, one bevil, one square, one key hole saw, and a line and roller. In another drawer is contained a best hand saw, best dove tail saw, an oil stone in a wood case, glue pot, jack plane, smoothing plane, hatchet and a mallet - - - - - - -

If Mahogany Chest - - - - - - - -

4. Payment Book 1697 J. S. & Son

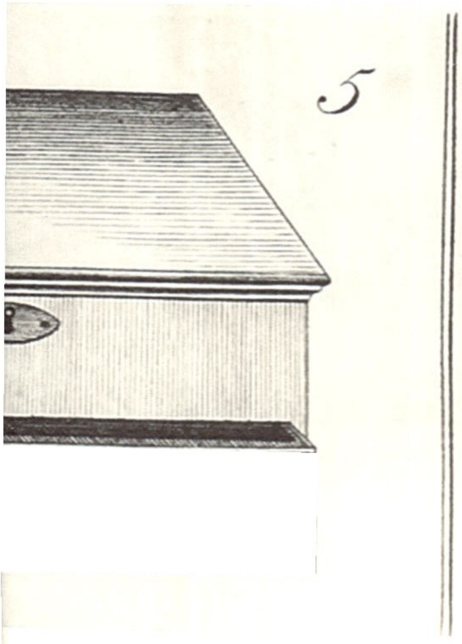

5

8

Chests of Tools.

	£.	s.	d.
Oak Chest, No. 9, contains			
In the chest, a hammer, best table vice, hand vice, pair of bright cutting nippers, pair of bright plyers, pair of bright pincers, pair of steel compasses, six gimblets sorted, four brad awls, three turnscrews, two-foot rule, one bright chissel, one claw wrench, one striking knife, one saw set, one brad punch, and sundry partitions containing a great variety of nails, wood-screws, brads, tacks, brass work, &c. &c. In a drawer is contained a brace, with twelve bits, a line and roller, a bevil, a square, bick iron, four firmers, two gouges, two mortice chissels, four files, one rasp, and a key hole saw. In another drawer is contained a best hand saw, best dove tail saw, hatchet, mallet, jack plane, smoothing plane, glue pot, and an oil stone in a wood case	3	15	6½
If Mahogany Chest - - - - - - -	6	15	
Oak Chest, No. 10, contains			
In the chest and in two drawers are the same tools, nails, wood-screws, &c. &c. as in No. 9. In another drawer is contained a set of garden tools, as follows: a saw, a rake, a hook bill, a fruit knife with hook, a paddle, a hoe, these six articles are made to screw into a terule, which is fixed on a jointed staff; also a jointed staff, five feet six inches long, a fork, a pruning knife, a pair of shears, a pair of scissars, a garden line, reel and peg, and some list -	7	1	6
If Mahogany Chest - - - - - - -	8	15	
Oak Chest, No. 11, contains			
A hammer, hatchet, table vice, pair of bright pincers, pair of bright plyers, two-foot rule, six gimblets sorted, three brad awls, two turnscrews, two files, one rasp, three firmers, one gouge, one brad punch, one saw set, one bright chissel, mallet, plane, pair of steel compasses, and sundry wood partitions, containing an assortment of nails, wood-screws, brads, tacks, brass work, &c. Likewise underneath the lid is a till, containing a best hand saw, best dove tail saw, and a key hole saw - - - - - - - - - -	2	1	6
If best Mahogany Chest, and extra. best Tools with best Walnut Handles to correspond - - - - - -	3		
Oak Chest, No. 12, contains			
In the chest a hammer, table vice, hand vice, pair of bright pincers, pair of bright plyers, six gimblets sorted, three brad awls, two-foot rule, pair of steel compasses, three turnscrews, three files, one rasp, four firmers, two gouges, one brad punch, one saw set, one bright chissel, one bright claw wrench, and sundry wood partitions containing an assortment of nails, wood-screws, brads, tacks, brass work, &c. &c. Likewise underneath the lid is a till, containing a best hand saw, best dove tail saw, and a key hole saw. In a drawer is contained a gentleman's best brace, with twelve bright bits, hatchet, mallet, glue pot, jack plane, smoothing plane, and an oil stone in a wood case - - - - - - - - - -	1	7	6
If best Mahogany Chest, and extra. best Tools with best Walnut Handles to correspond - - - - - -	3	3	–
Oak Chest, No. 13, contains			
In the chest, a claw hammer, rivetting hammer, best table vice, table bick iron, hand vice, pair of bright pincers, pair of bright cutting nippers, pair of bright flat nose plyers, pair of bright round nose plyers, two-foot rule, pair of steel compasses, pair of best rack compasses, six gimblets sorted, three brad awls, three turnscrews, one saw set, one brad punch, one bright chissel, one bright claw wrench, and sundry partitions containing a great variety of nails, wood-screws, brads, tacks, brass work, &c. &c. Likewise underneath the lid is a till, containing a best hand saw, best dove tail saw, and a key hole saw. In a drawer is contained a gentleman's best brace, with eighteen bright bits, a spoke shave, wood gauge, line and roller, a bevil, a square, six firmers, two gouges, two mortice chissels, four files, and one rasp. In another drawer is contained a hatchet, mallet, glue pot, oil stone in a wood case, a jack plane, and a smoothing plane - - - - - - - - - -	7	3	
If best Mahogany Chest, and extra. best Tools with best Walnut Handles to correspond - - - - - -	8	15	–

N. B. Any of the above Tool Chests may be had with an extra. Drawer, containing a Set of Garden Tools, as in No. 10, for extra.

Great Variety of GENTLEMEN's OAK & MAHOGANY CHESTS, with Carpenter's and Turning Tools, from £. 9 9 0 to £. 10 10 0 and upwards.

Carpenters' Large Deal Chests

May be had with Carpenters' and Joiners' Tools compleat, in great Variety, from £. 8 8 0 to £. 31 10 0 and upwards.

Printed by J. Belcher and Son, High-street, Birmingham.

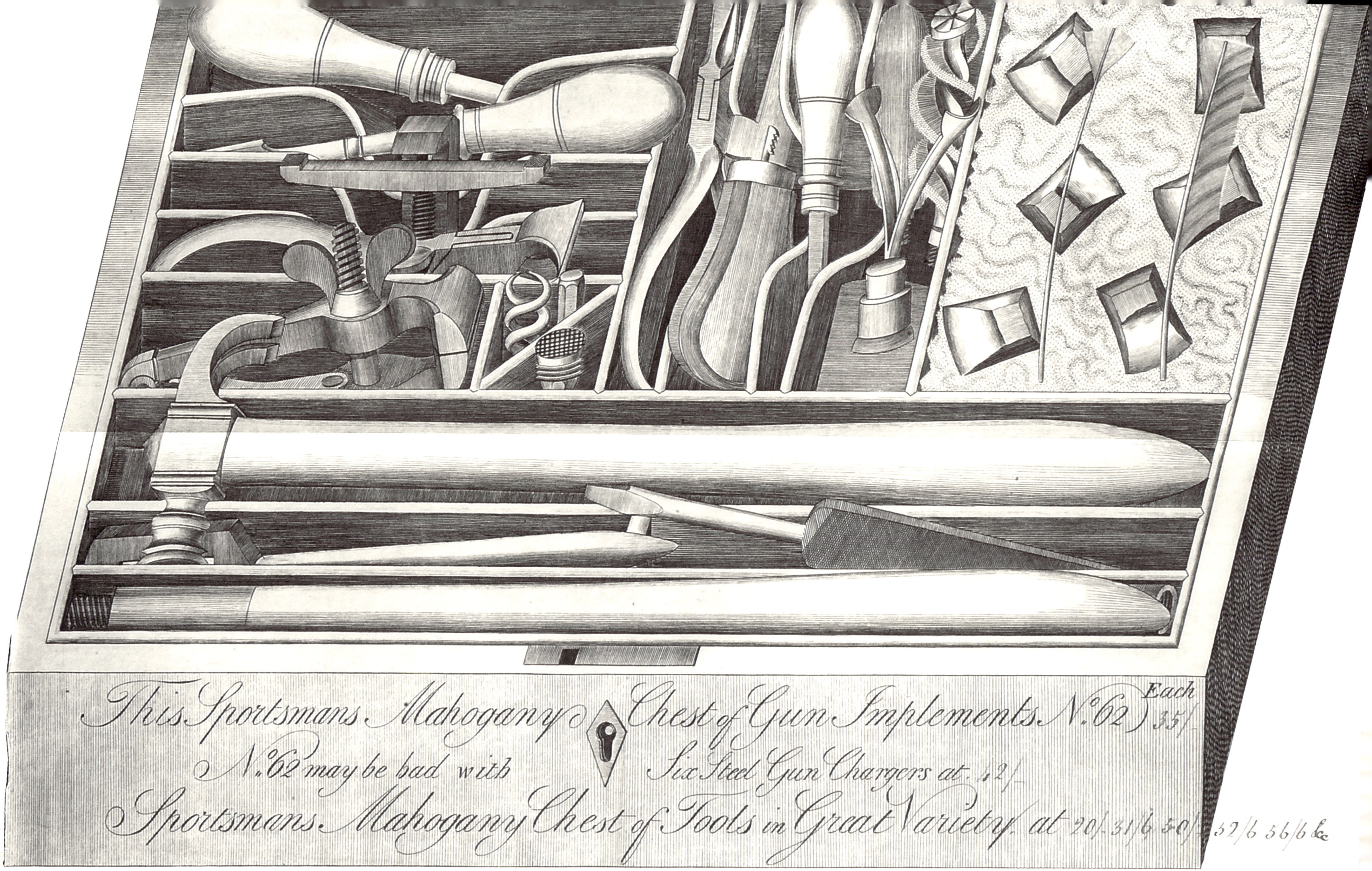
This Sportsmans Mahogany Chest of Gun Implements N.o 62 Each 35/-
N.o 62 may be had with Six Steel Gun Chargers at 42/-
Sportsmans Mahogany Chest of Tools in Great Variety at 20/- 31/6 50/- 52/6 56/6 &c

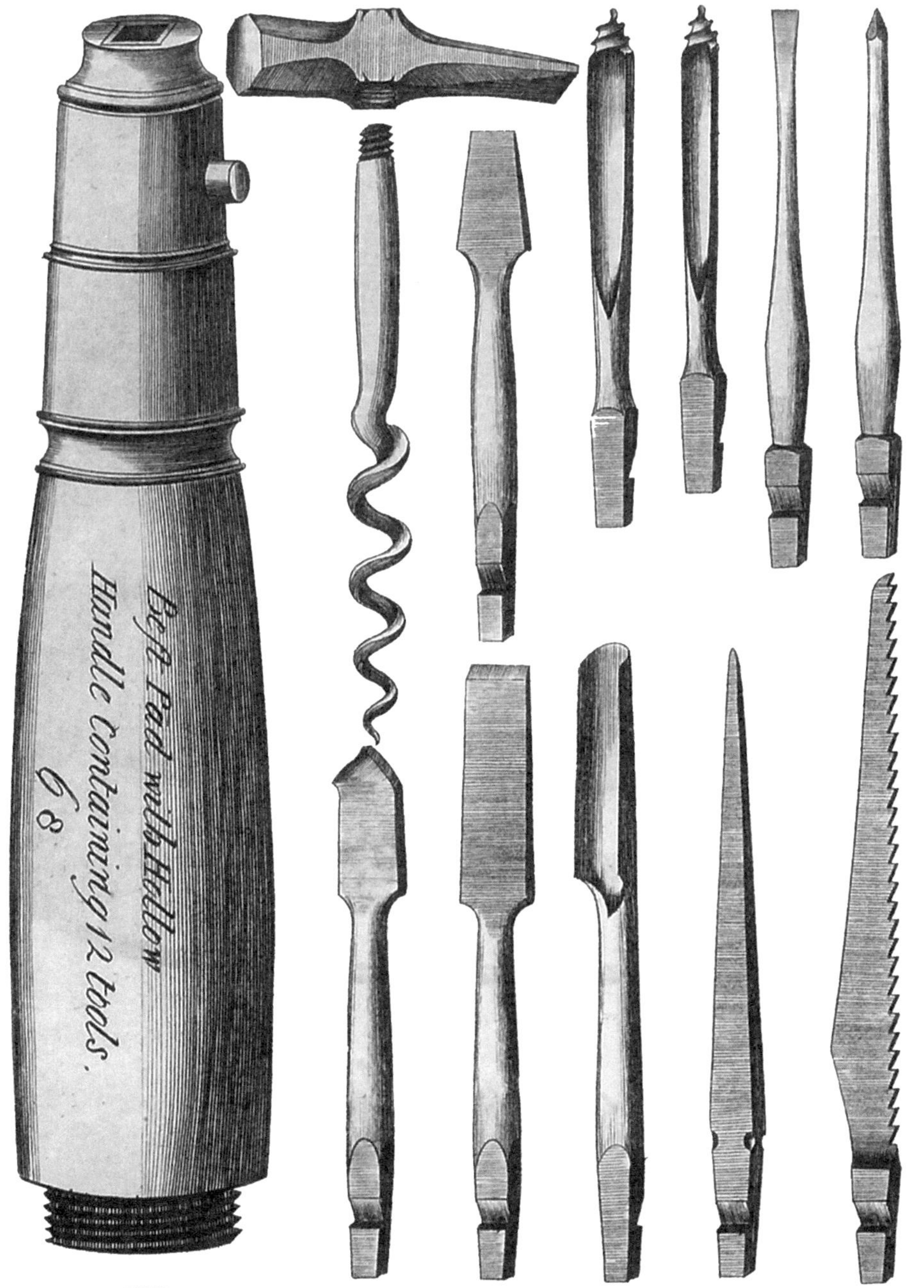

Each

Handle with 6 tools 66. 6/

with 9 tools 67 7 — with 12 tools 68 8

with 18 tools 69 10 — with 24 tools 70 12/6

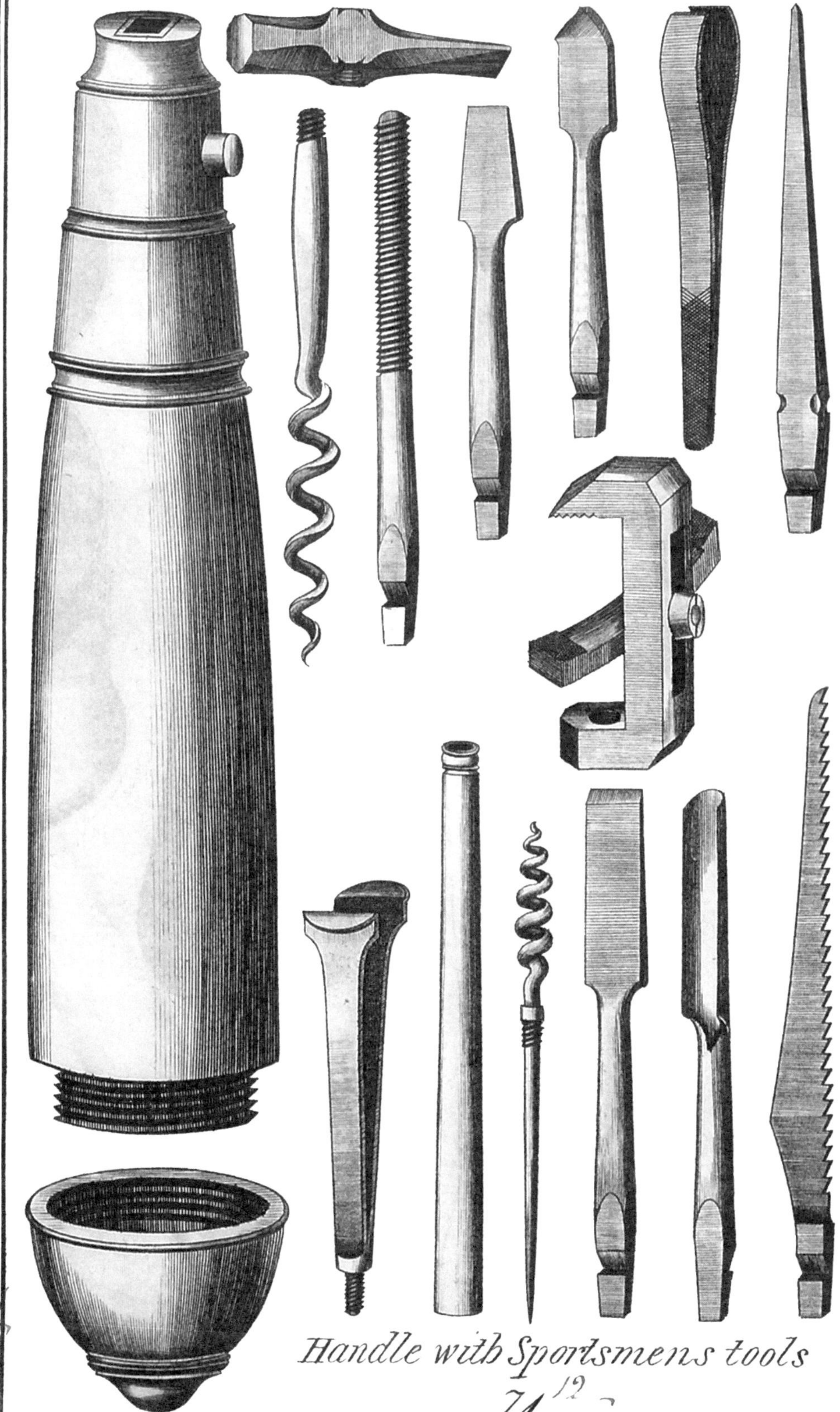

Handle with Sportsmens tools

71 12

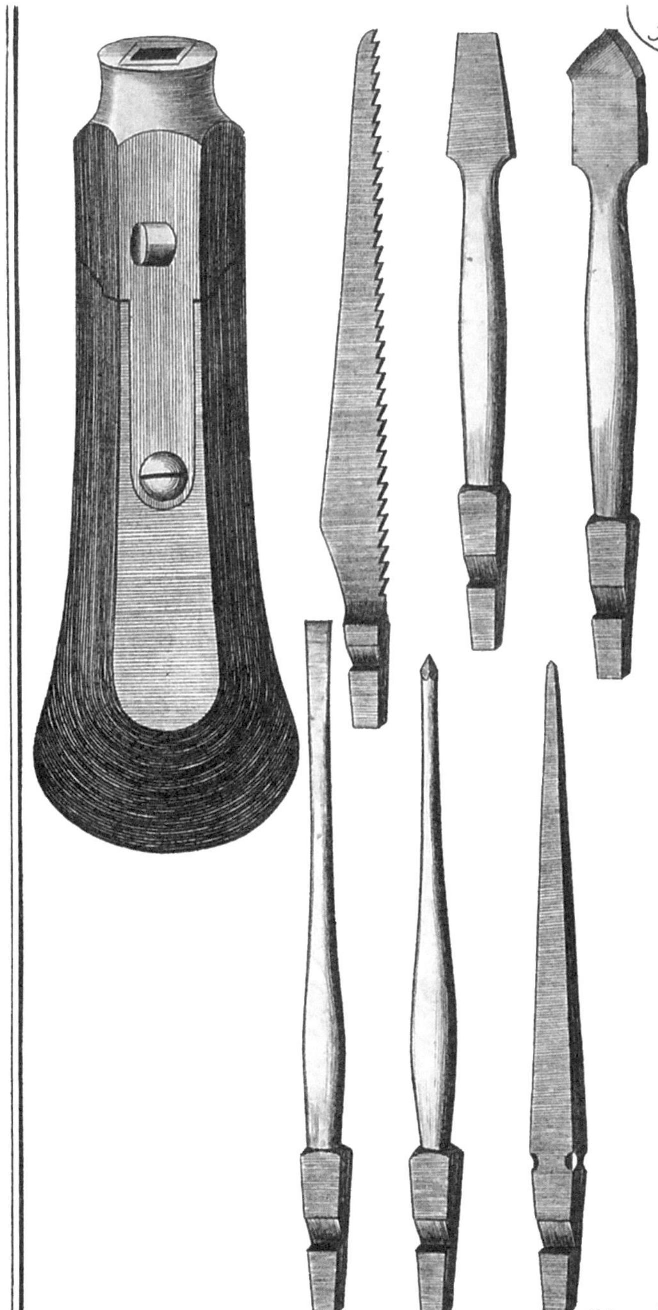

Each

Best Hand pad with 6 tools 72 5

d°. — d°. — 12 d°. — 73 8

d°. — d°. — 18 d°. — 74 12

d°. — d°. — 24 d°. — 75 15 6

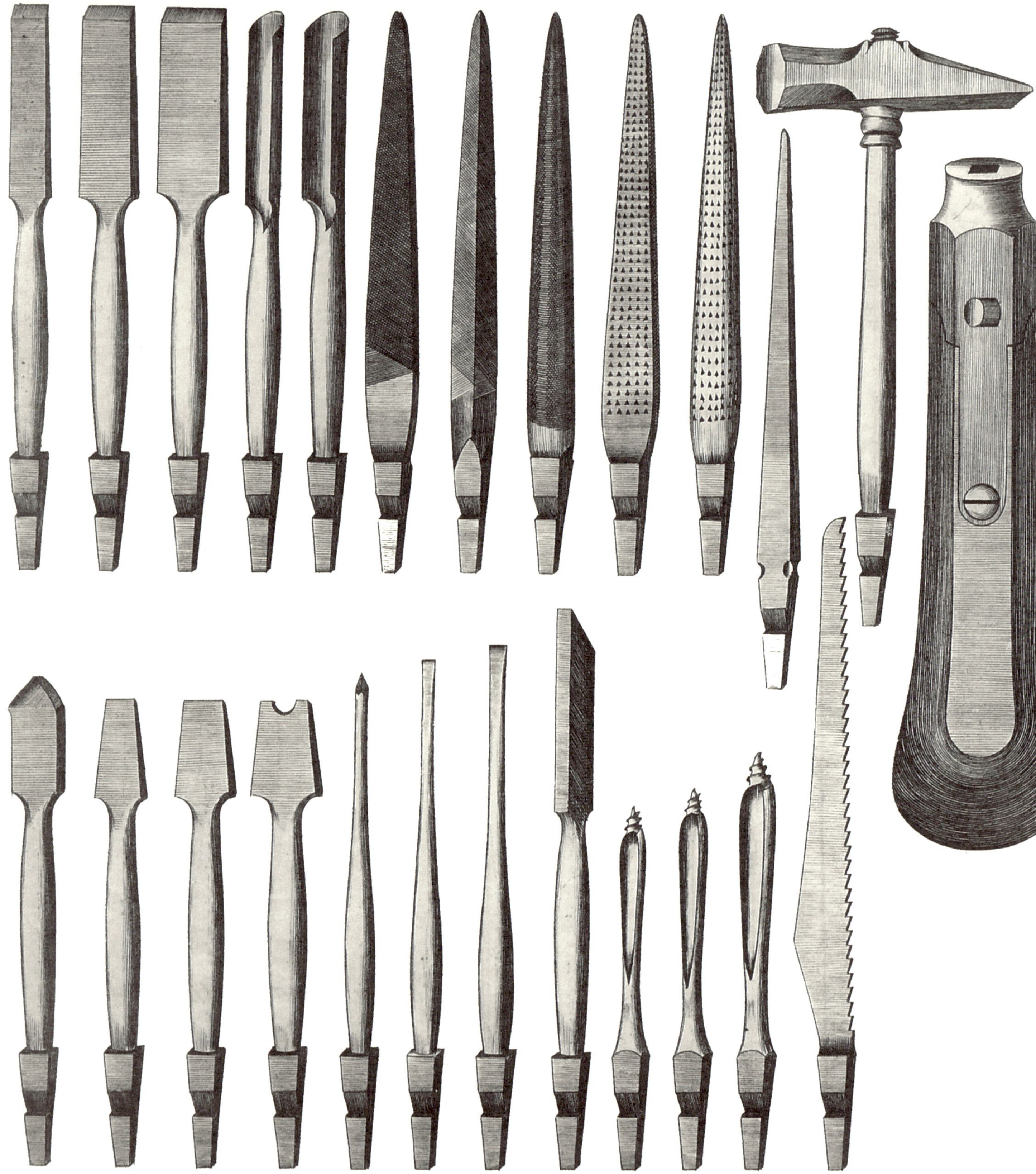

Each

Japan'd Box with 12 Tools 76 12/

d.o ___ d.o ___ 18 Tools 77 16/

d.o ___ d.o ___ 24 Tools 78 21/

d.o ___ d.o ___ 30 Tools 79 26/

May likewise be had of Larger Sizes

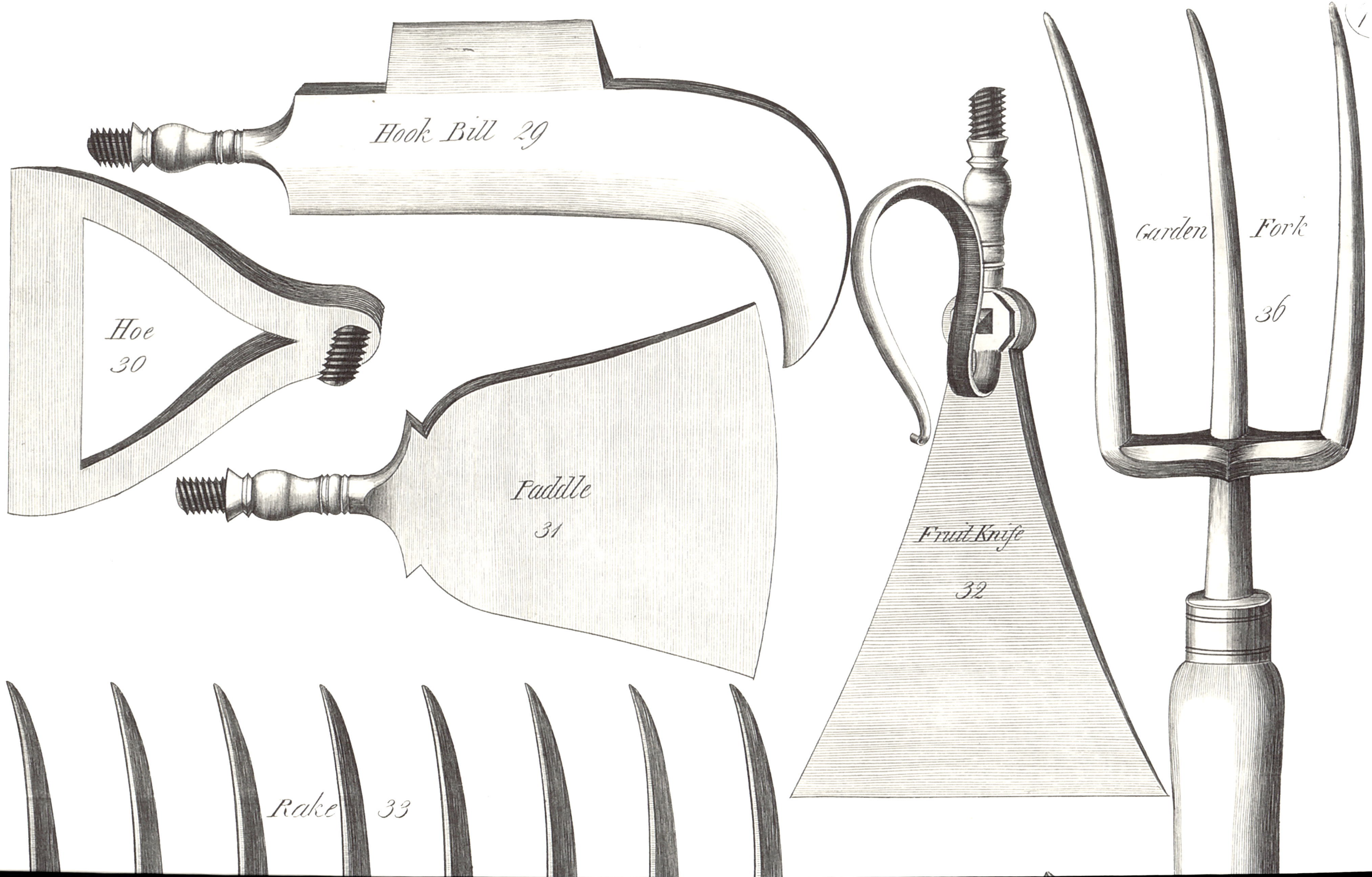
Hook Bill 29
Hoe 30
Paddle 31
Fruit Knife 32
Rake 33
Garden Fork 36

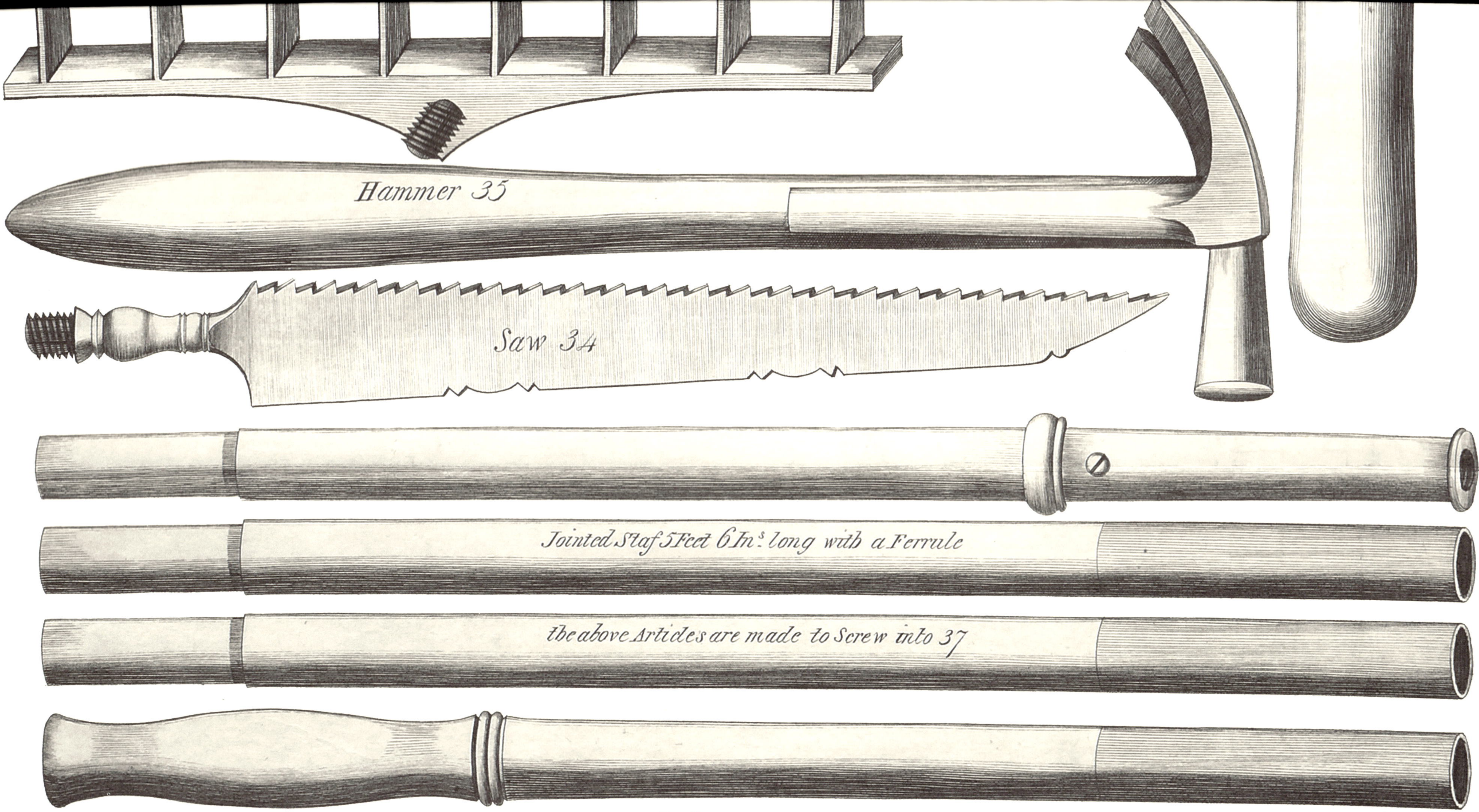

		L	S	D
N.o 100 a Gentlemans Oak Chest. Containing the above Garden Tools, a P.r of Sissars & a Partition, with Nails & lift	Each	1	11	6
101 Oak Chest Contains the Same Tools &c as N.o 100 with the addition of a Pruning Knife, P.r of Garden Shears & a Hatchet		2	3	–
102 Oak Chest Contains the Same Tools &c as N.o 101 with the addition of a Garden line, reel & Peg & 3 Gimblets		2	8	–
103 Oak Chest Contains the Same Tools &c as N.o 102 with the addition of a Small Hand Saw, Tinder Box, Flint & Fire Steel		2	14	–
104 a Sett of Garden Tools consisting of 29.30.31.32.33.34 & a Ferrule to fix upon a Staf — 16. — P.r Sett. 105 the Articles Size Smaller		–	13	6

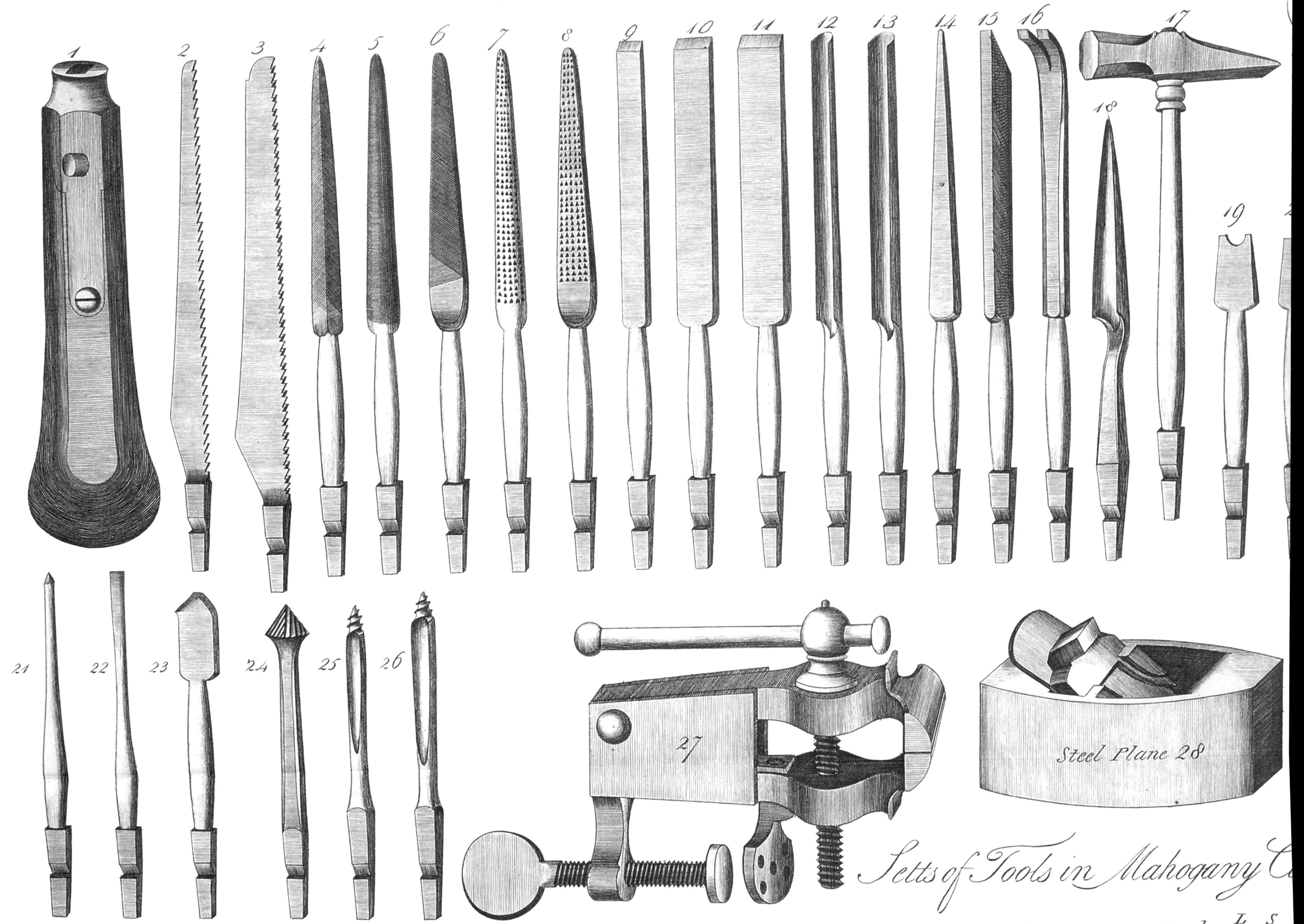

Setts of Tools in Mahogany Ca

	L	S
N.° 88 a Case 6 Inches long. contains Hand pad & Tools N.° 1 _ 2 _ 3 _ 10 _ 12 _ 14 _ 17 _ 19 _ 20 _ 21 _ 22 _ 23 _ 25 & 26 Each		14
89 a Case 8 Inches long. contains Hand pad & Tools N.° 1 _ 2 _ 3 _ 4 _ 5 _ 6 _ 7 _ 8 _ 9 _ 10 _ 12 _ 13 _ 14 _ 15 _ 17 _ 19 _ 20 _ 21 _ 22 _ 23 _ 25 _ 26	1	
90 a Case 8 Inches long. contains Hand pad & Tools. same as 89 with the addition of Table Vice 27	1	5
91 a Case 8 Inches long. contains Hand pad with Tools. Table Vice & Steel plane N.° 1 to 28	1	10
92 a Case 8 Inches long. contains Hand pad & Tools. as 91 with the addition of a Table Bick Iron. a P.r Pincers. & a P.r of Steel Compasses.	1	15
93 a Case 8 Inches long. contains Hand pad & Tools. N.° 1 _ 2 _ 4 _ 5 _ 6 _ 9 _ 11 _ 12 _ 14 _ 15 _ 16 _ 17 _ 18 _ 19 _ 20 _ 21 _ 22 _ 23 _ 24 _ 25 _ 26 Vice 27 likewise a Small Hand Vice. Table Bick Iron. Pair Plyers. 2 Warding files. 3 pick locks. a Jointed Drill Bow. Brest Plate. 3 Drills. Brad punch. prick Punch. & a Small Screw Plate with Taps	2	2

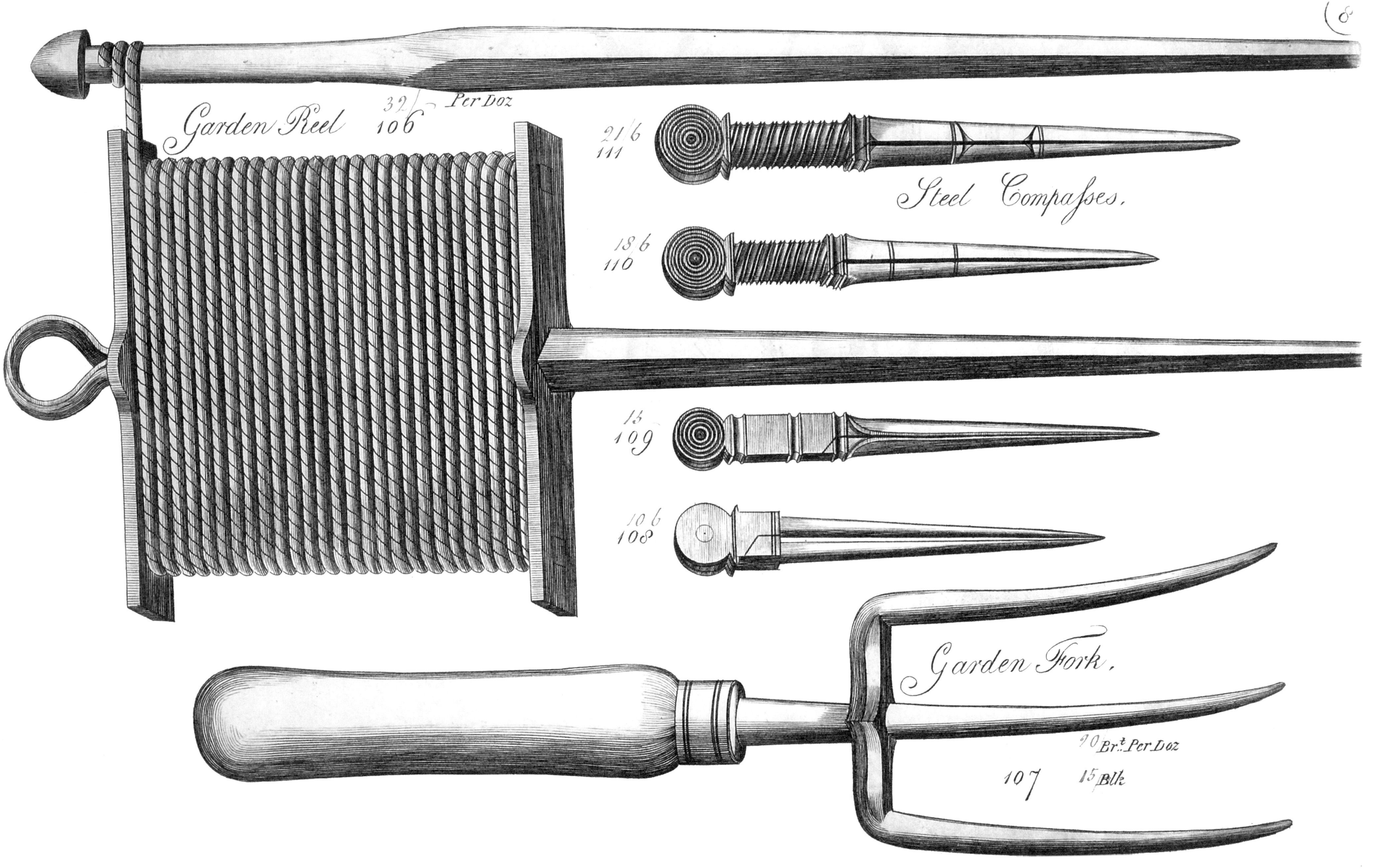
(8
Garden Reel
32/ Per Doz
106
21/6
111
Steel Compasses.
18 6
110
15
109
10 6
108
Garden Fork.
90 Brt. Per Doz
107
15 Blk

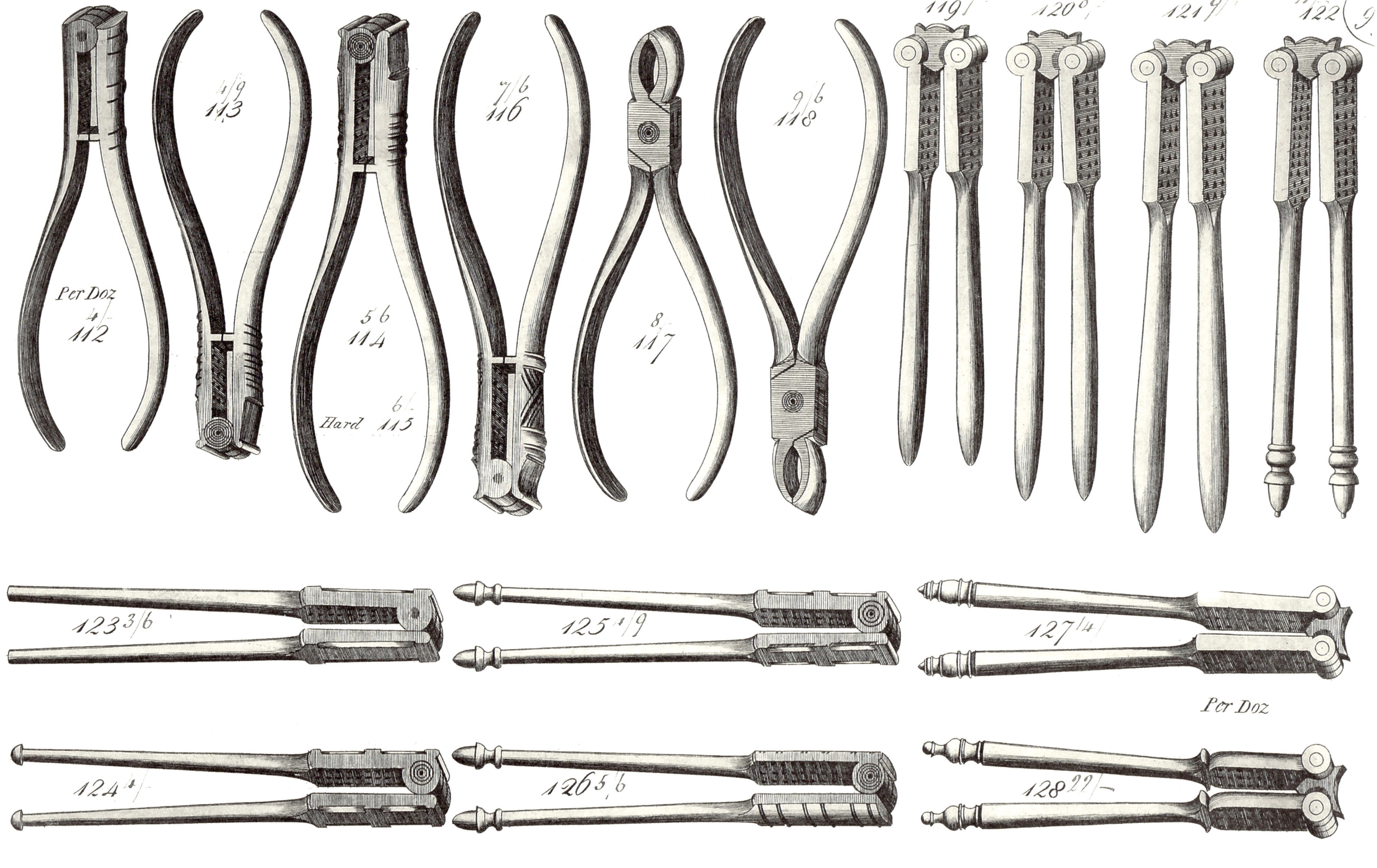
Per Doz
4/-
112
4/9
113
5 6
114
Hard
6/-
115
7/6
116
8/-
117
9/6
118
119 7/-
120 8/-
121 9/-
11/-
122
123 3/6
125 4/9
127 14/-
Per Doz
124 4/-
126 5/6
128 22/-

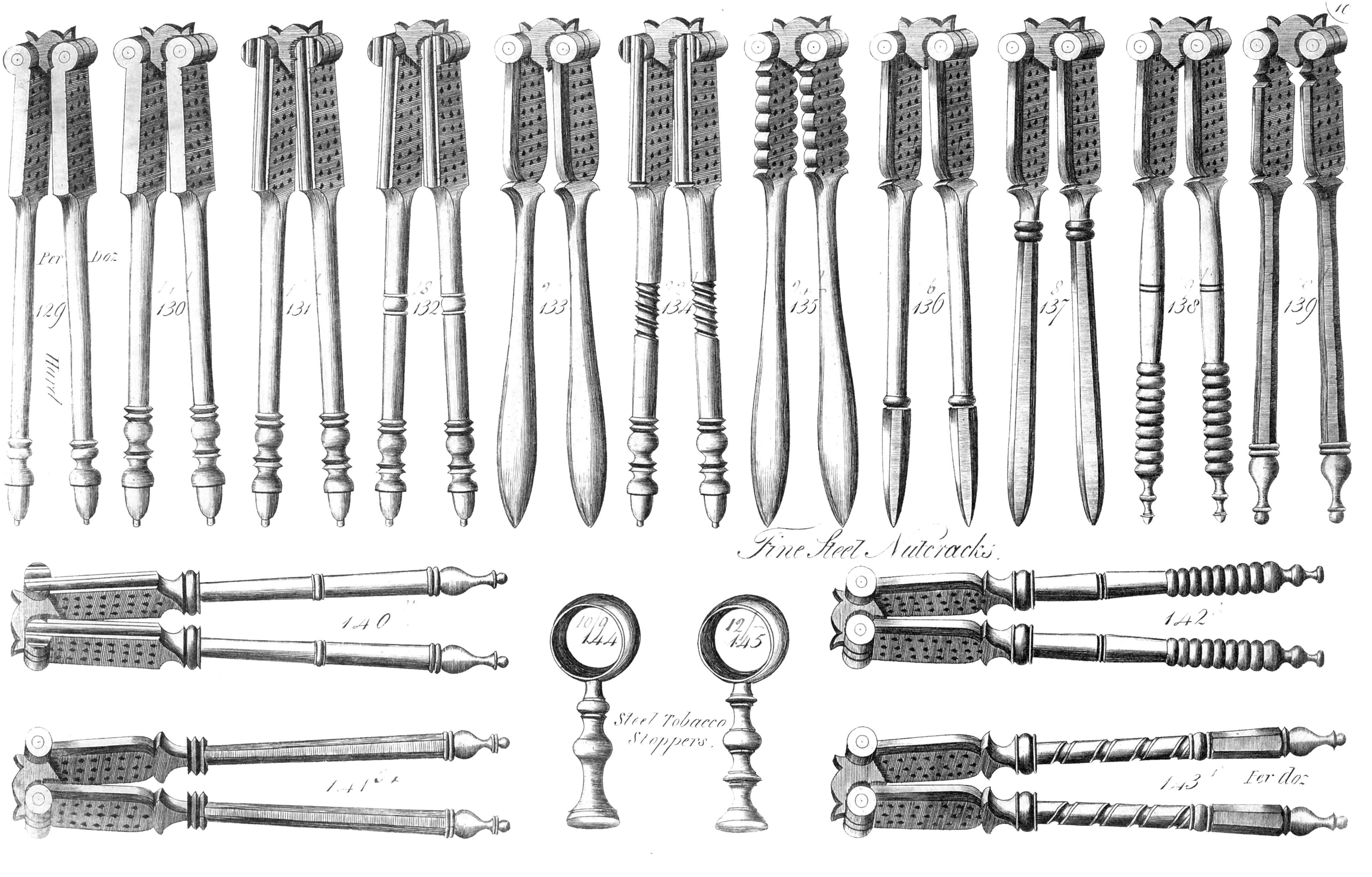

Fine Steel Nutcracks.
129
130
131
132
133
134
135
136
137
138
139
140
141
142
143
144
145
Steel Tobacco Stoppers.

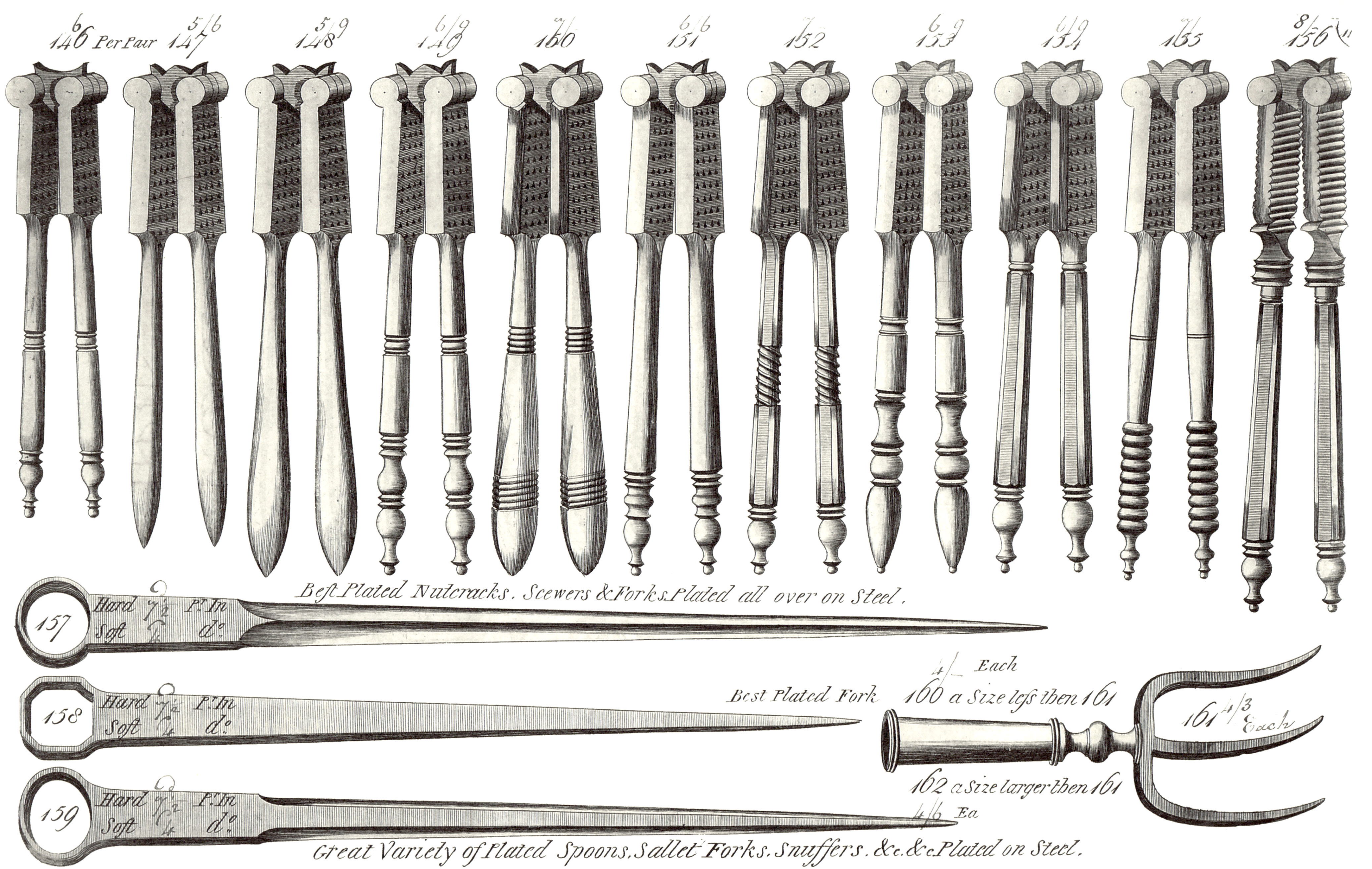

6
146 Per Pair
5/6
147
5/9
148
6/9
149
7/
150
6/6
151
7/
152
6/9
153
6/9
154
7/
155
8/
156
Best Plated Nutcracks. Scewers & Forks Plated all over on Steel.
157
Hard 7½ P. In
Soft d°
158
Hard 7½ P. In
Soft d°
159
Hard 7½ P. In
Soft d°
Best Plated Fork
4/ Each
160 a Size less then 161
161 4/3 Each
162 a Size larger then 161
4/6 Ea
Great Variety of Plated Spoons, Sallet Forks, Snuffers, &c. &c. Plated on Steel.

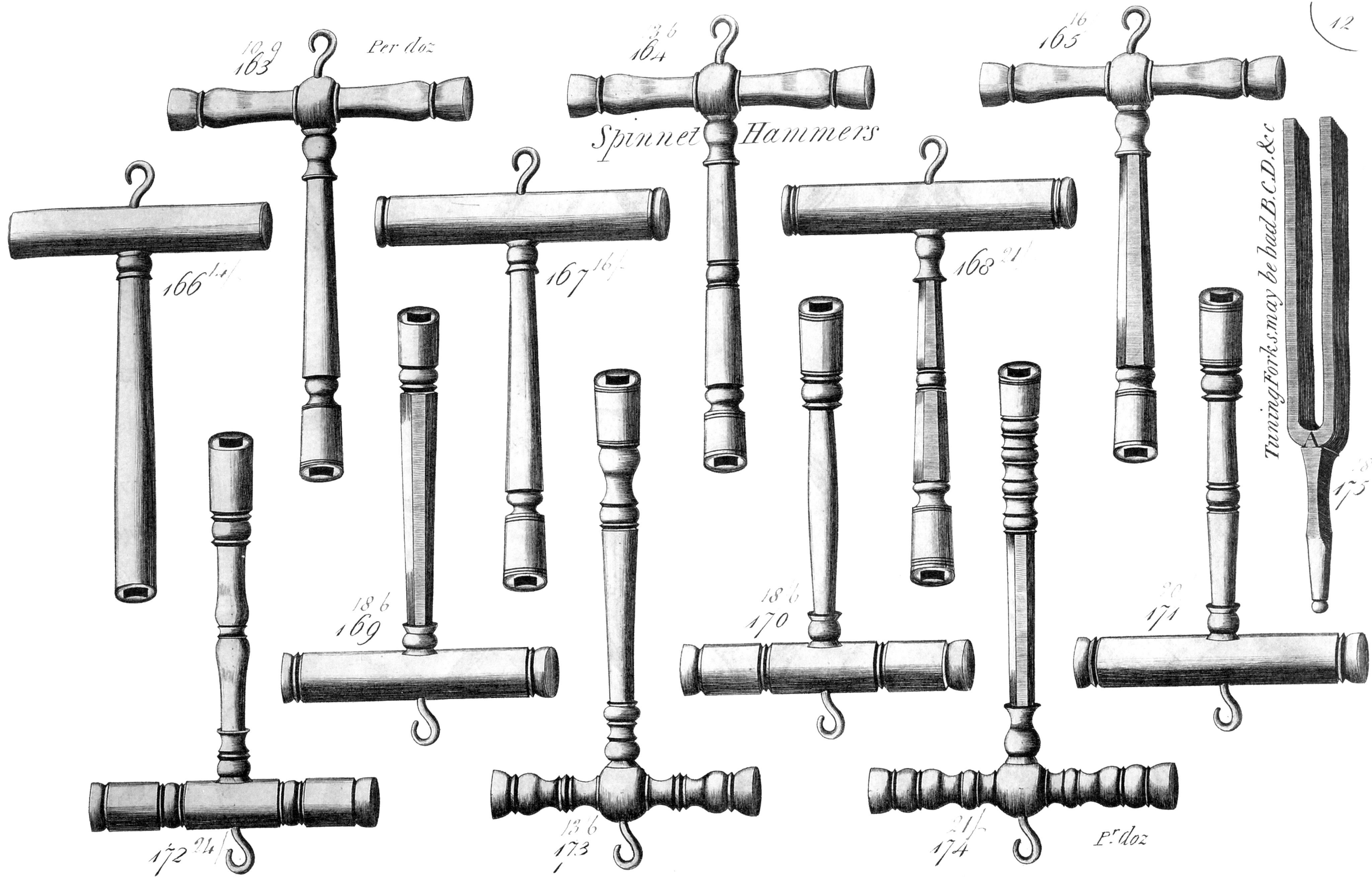
10 9
163
Per doz
3 6
164
16
165
Spinnet Hammers
166 14/
167 16/
168 21/
Tuning Forks may be had B.C.D.&c
18
175
18 6
169
18 6
170
20
171
172 24/
13 6
173
21/
174
Pr. doz

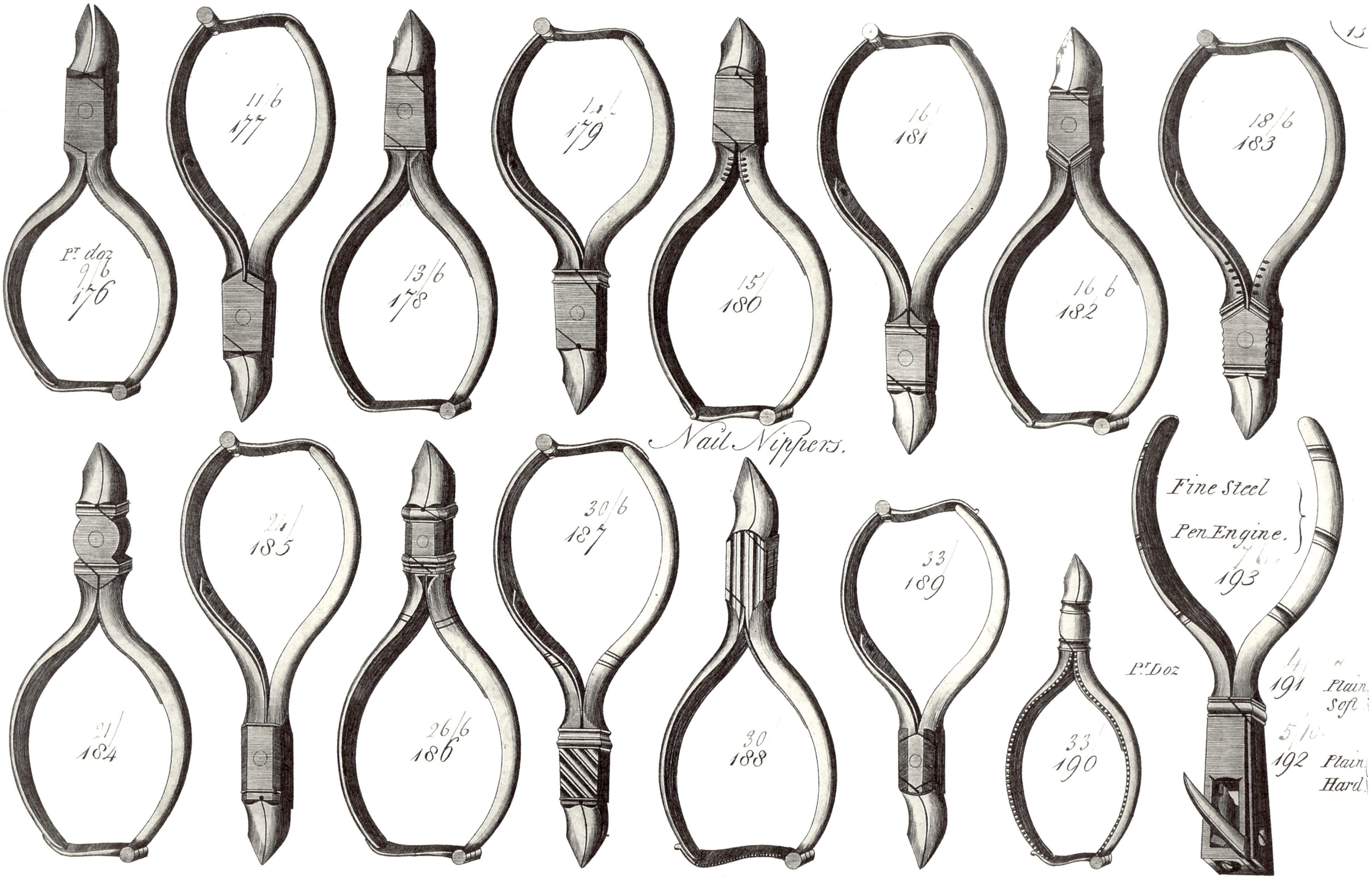
Pr doz
9/6
176
11/6
177
13/6
178
179
15/
180
16/
181
16/6
182
18/6
183
Nail Nippers.
21/
184
24/
185
26/6
186
30/6
187
30
188
33/
189
33/
190
Fine Steel
Pen Engine.
193
Pr Doz
4/
191
Plain
Soft
192
Plain
Hard

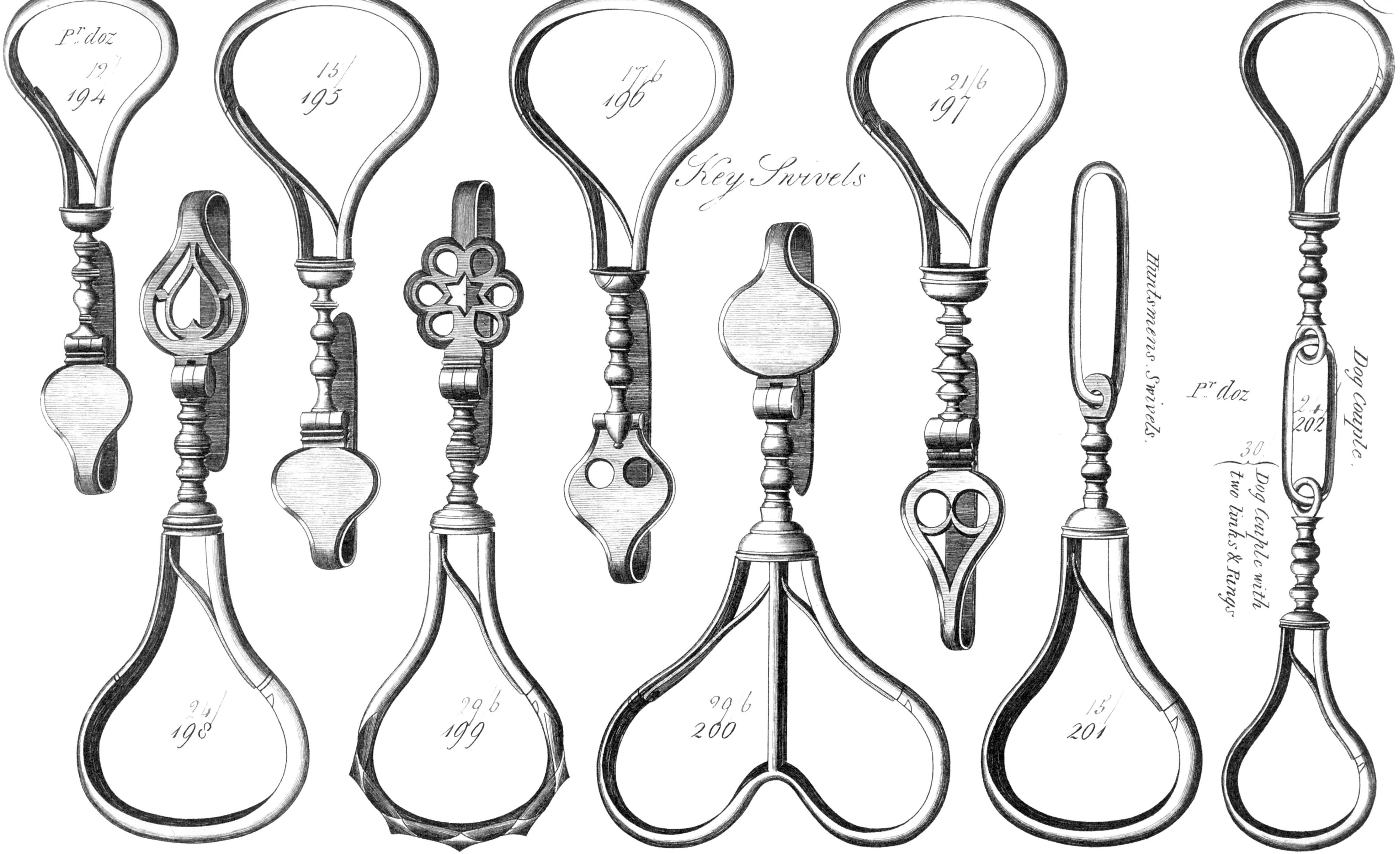
Pr. doz
12/
194
15/
195
17/6
196
Key Swivels
21/6
197
Huntsmens Swivels.
Pr. doz
24/
202
Dog Couple.
30/ Dog Couple with two links & Rings
24/
198
29/6
199
29/6
200
15/
201

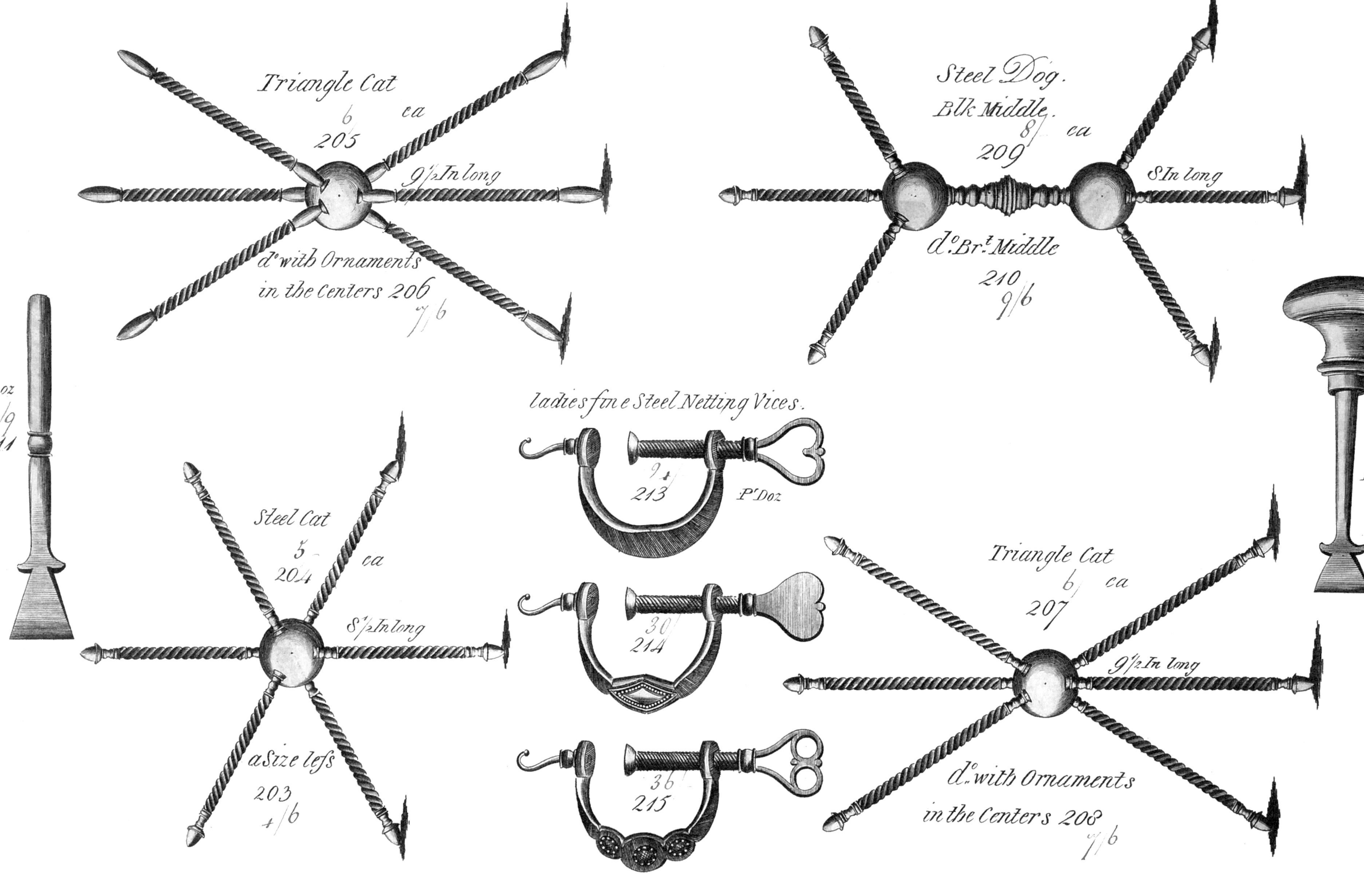
Triangle Cat
6 ca
205
9½ In long
dº with Ornaments
in the Centers 206
7/6
Steel Dog.
Blk Middle.
8/ ca
209
8 In long
dº Brt Middle
210
9/6
Pr Doz
4/9
211
ladies fine Steel Netting Vices.
9/4
213
Pr Doz
Steel Cat
5 ca
204
8½ In long
a Size less
203
4/6
30/
214
36/
215
212
6/
Pr Doz
Triangle Cat
6/ ca
207
9½ In long
dº with Ornaments
in the Centers 208
7/6

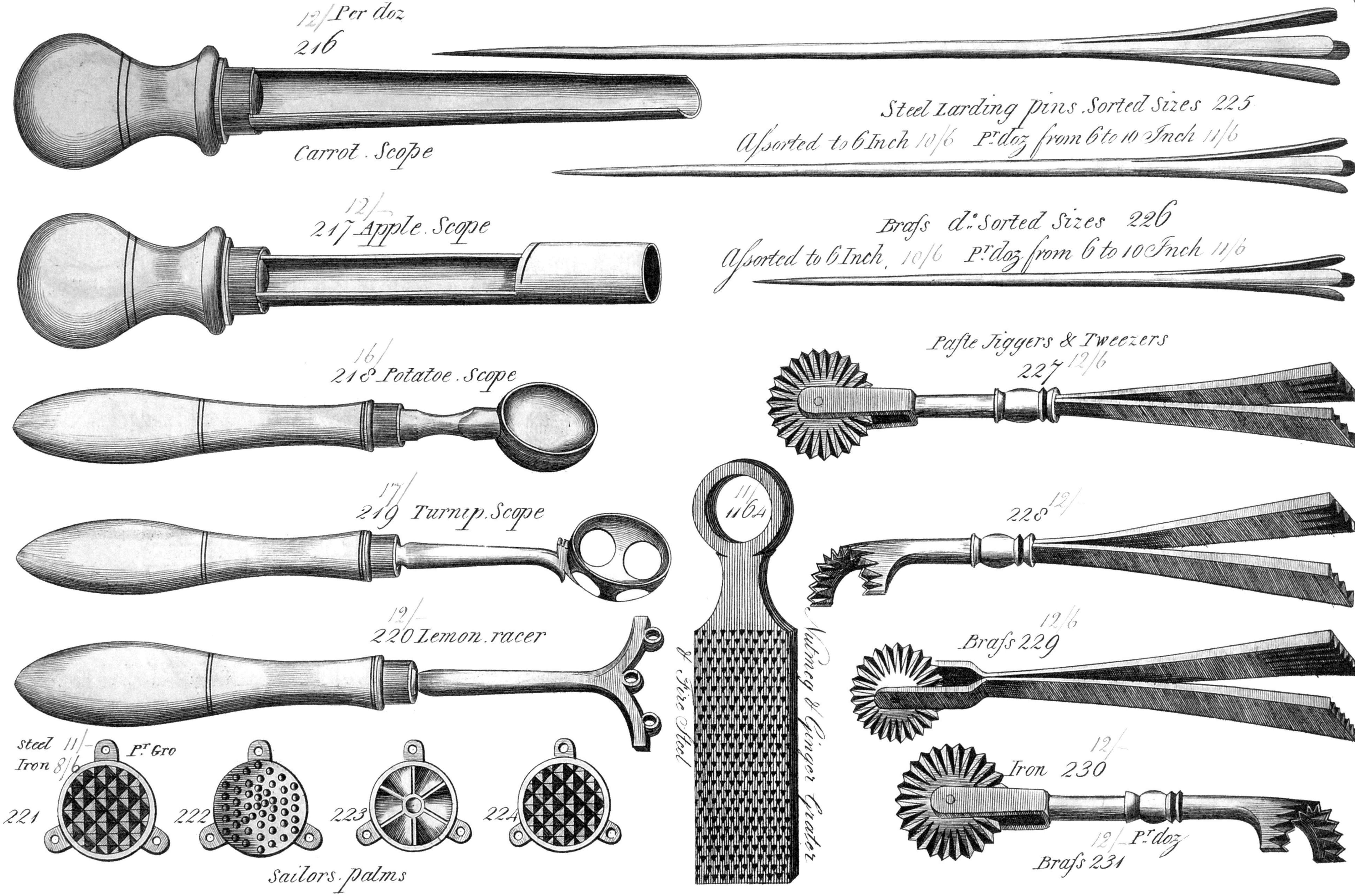
12/ Per doz
216
Carrot. Scope
Steel Larding pins. Sorted Sizes 225
Assorted to 6 Inch 10/6 Pr. doz from 6 to 10 Inch 11/6
12/
217 Apple. Scope
Brass do. Sorted Sizes 226
Assorted to 6 Inch. 10/6 Pr. doz from 6 to 10 Inch 11/6
16/
218 Potatoe. Scope
Paste Jiggers & Tweezers
227 12/6
17/
219 Turnip. Scope
11/
1164
Nutmeg & Ginger Grater
& Fire Steel
228 12/
12/
220 Lemon. racer
12/6
Brass 229
steel 11/ Pr. Gro
Iron 8/6
221
222
223
224
Sailors. palms
12/
Iron 230
12/ Pr. doz
Brass 231

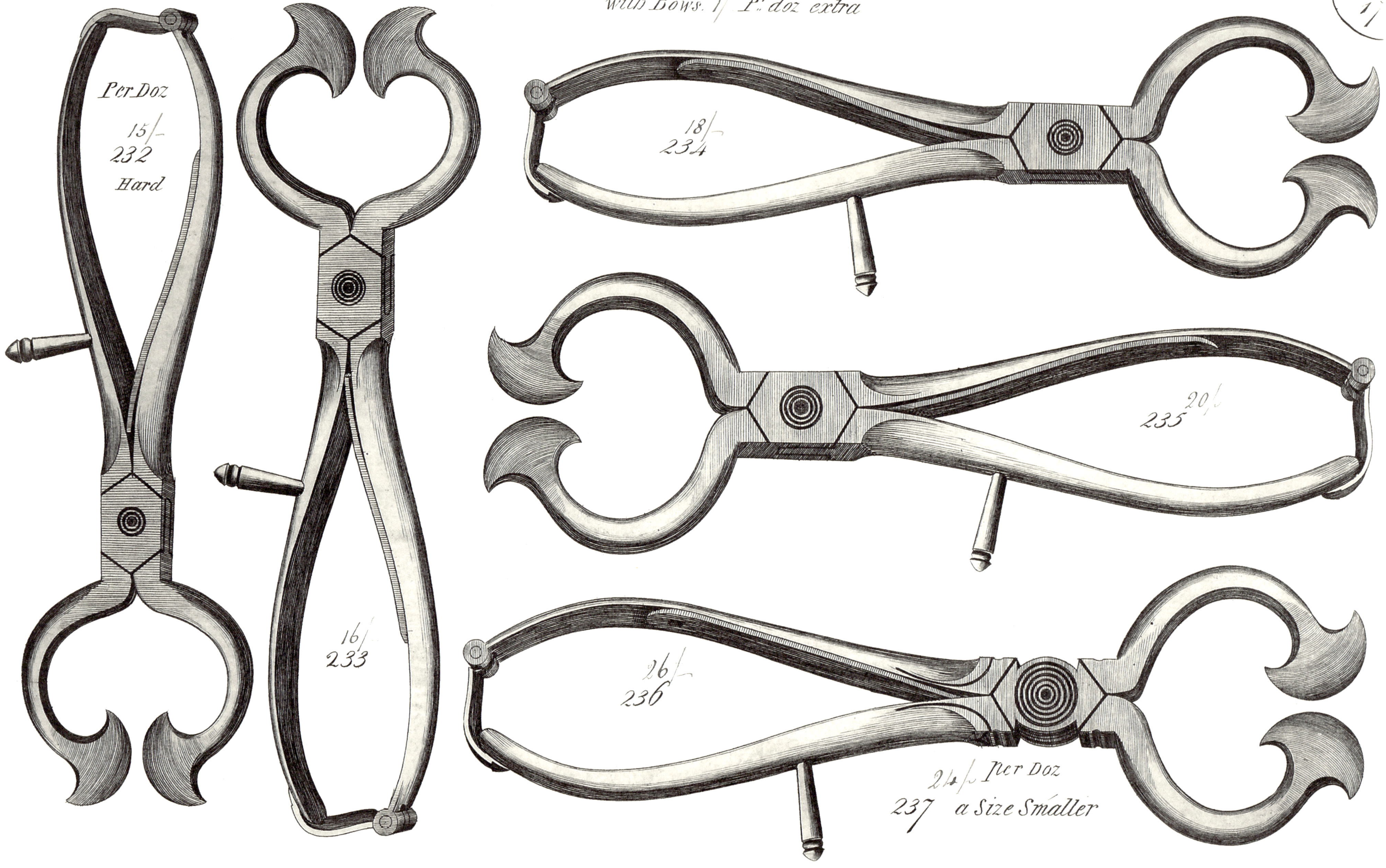
with Bows. 1/ Pr. doz extra
Per Doz
15/-
232
Hard
16/-
233
18/-
234
235 20/-
26/-
236
24/- Per Doz
237 a Size Smaller

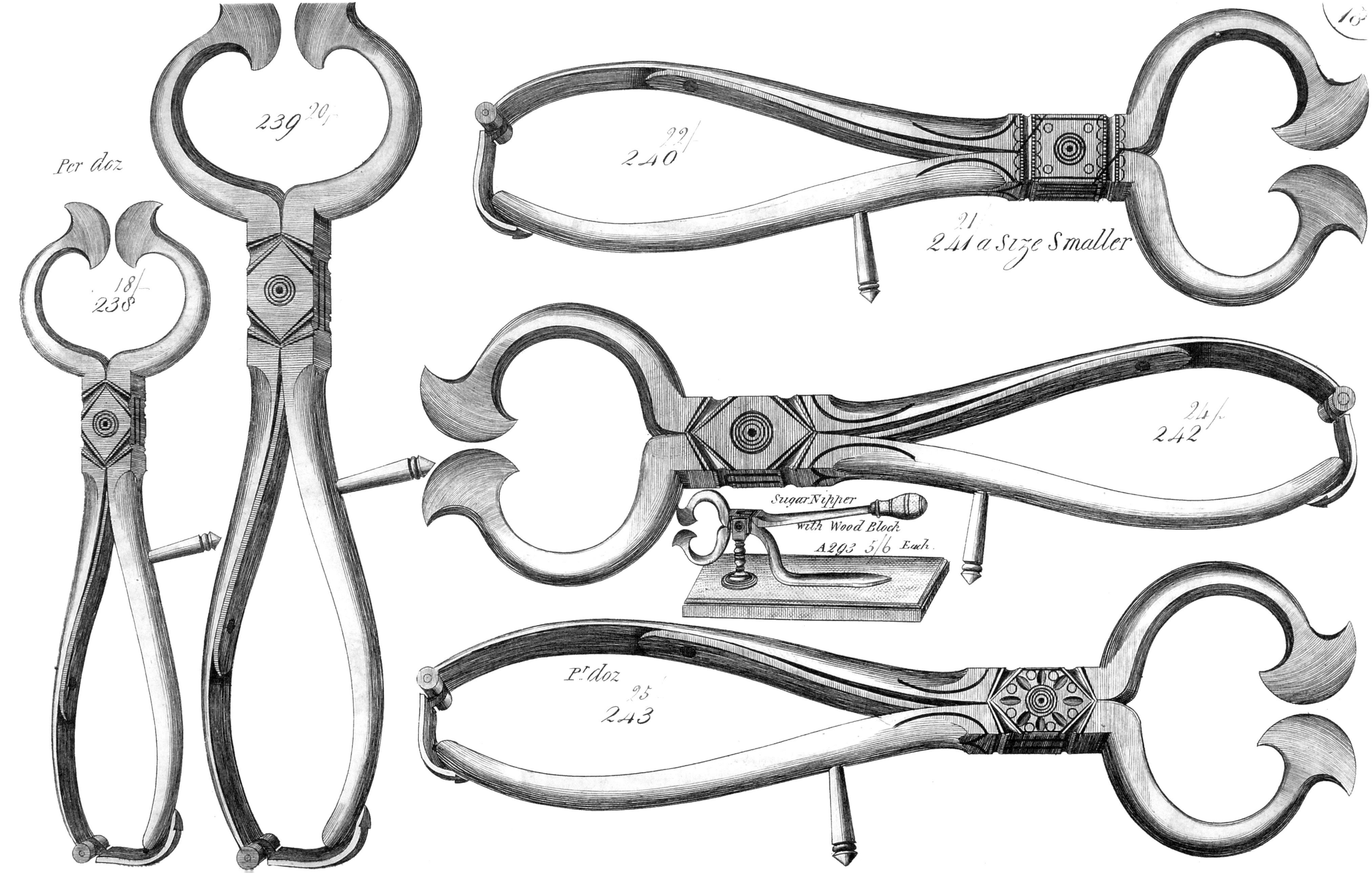
Per doz
18/
238
239 20/
22/
240
21/
241 a Size Smaller
24/
242
Sugar Nipper
with Wood Block
A293 5/6 Each.
Pr doz
25/
243

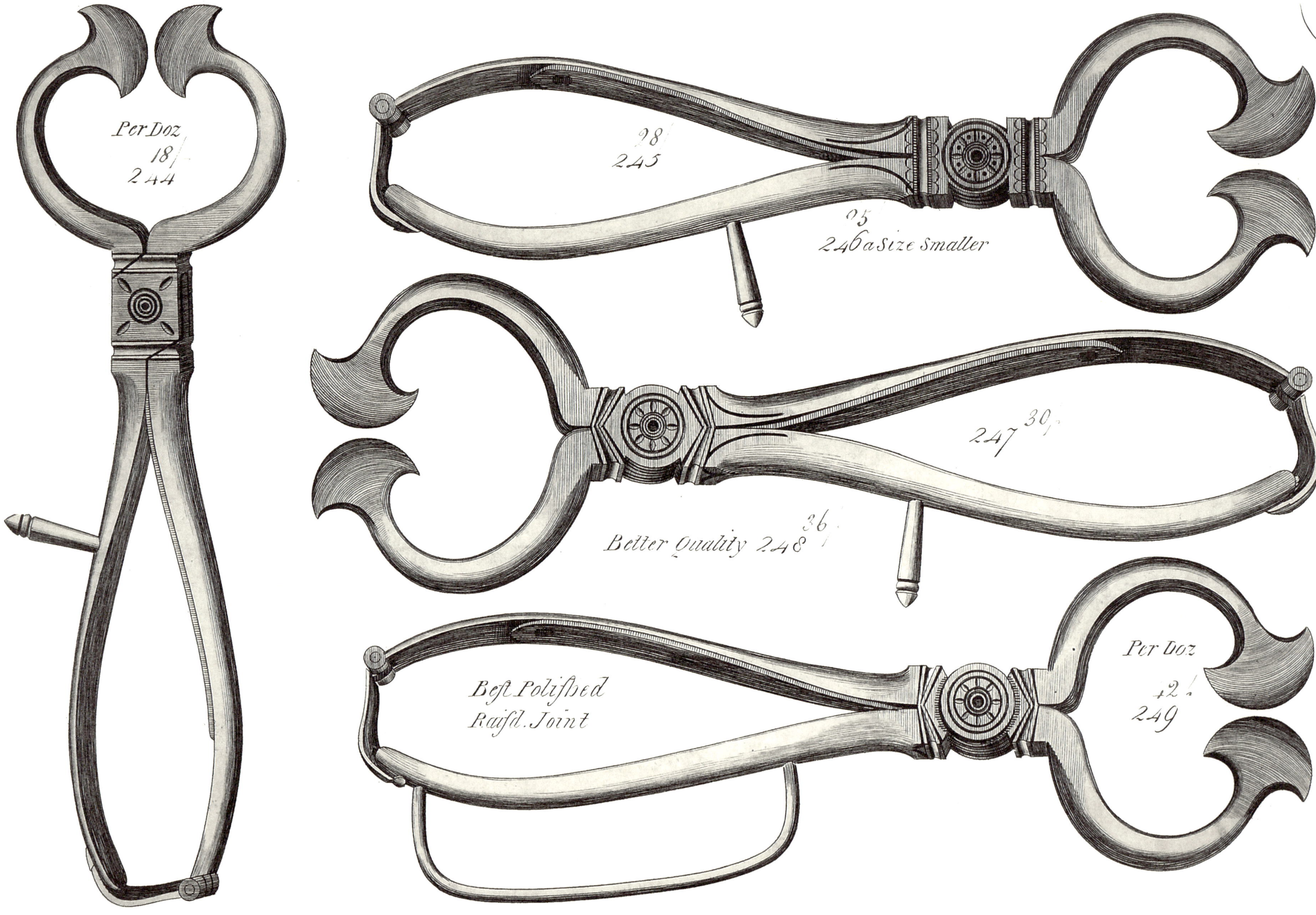
Per Doz
18/
244
98
245
95
246 a Size Smaller
247 30/
Better Quality 248 36/
Best Polished
Raisd. Joint
Per Doz
42/
249

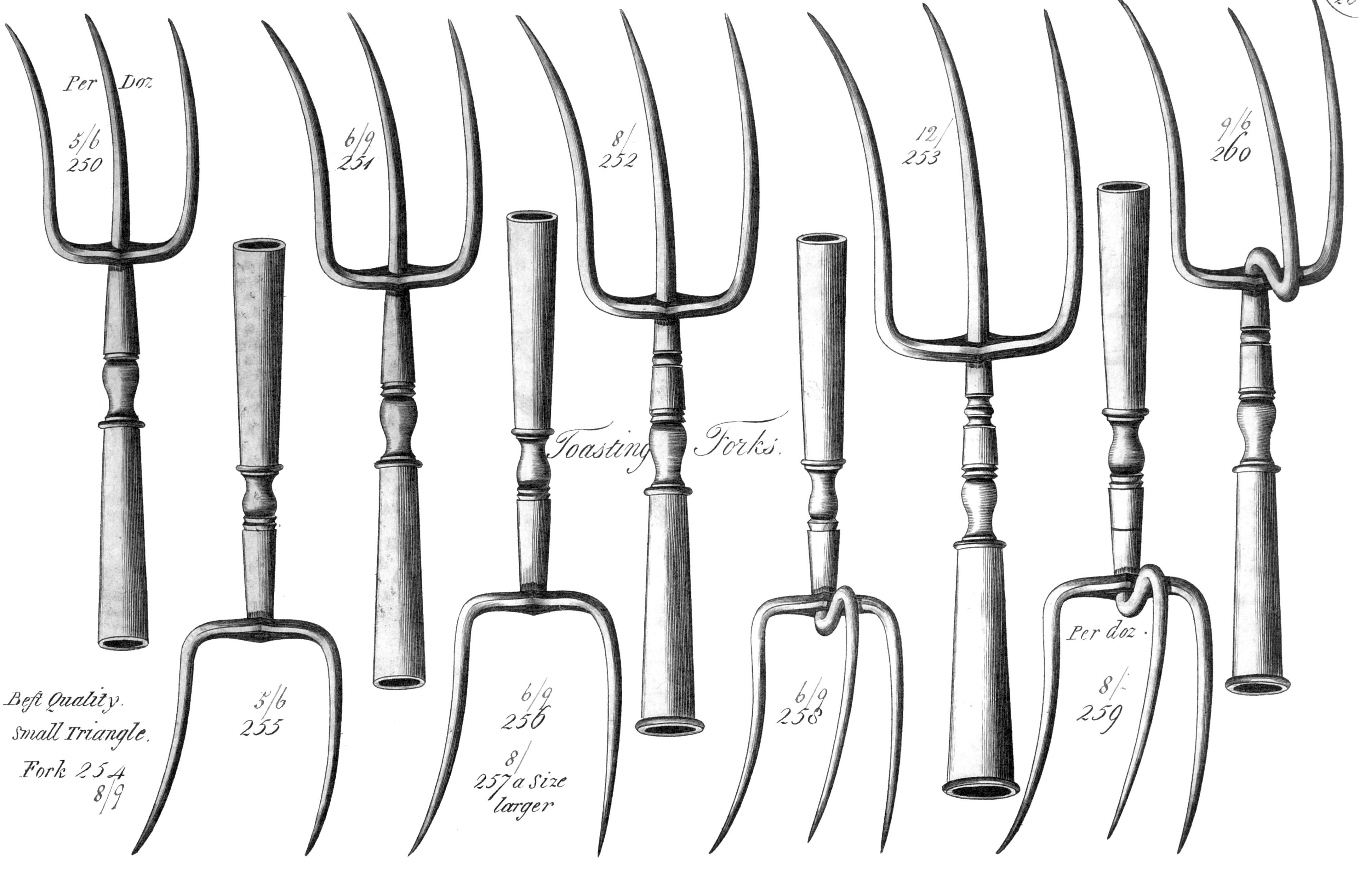
Per Doz
5/6
250
6/9
251
8/
252
12/
253
9/6
260
Toasting Forks.
Best Quality.
Small Triangle.
Fork 254
8/9
5/6
255
6/9
256
8/
257 a Size
larger
6/9
258
Per doz.
8/-
259

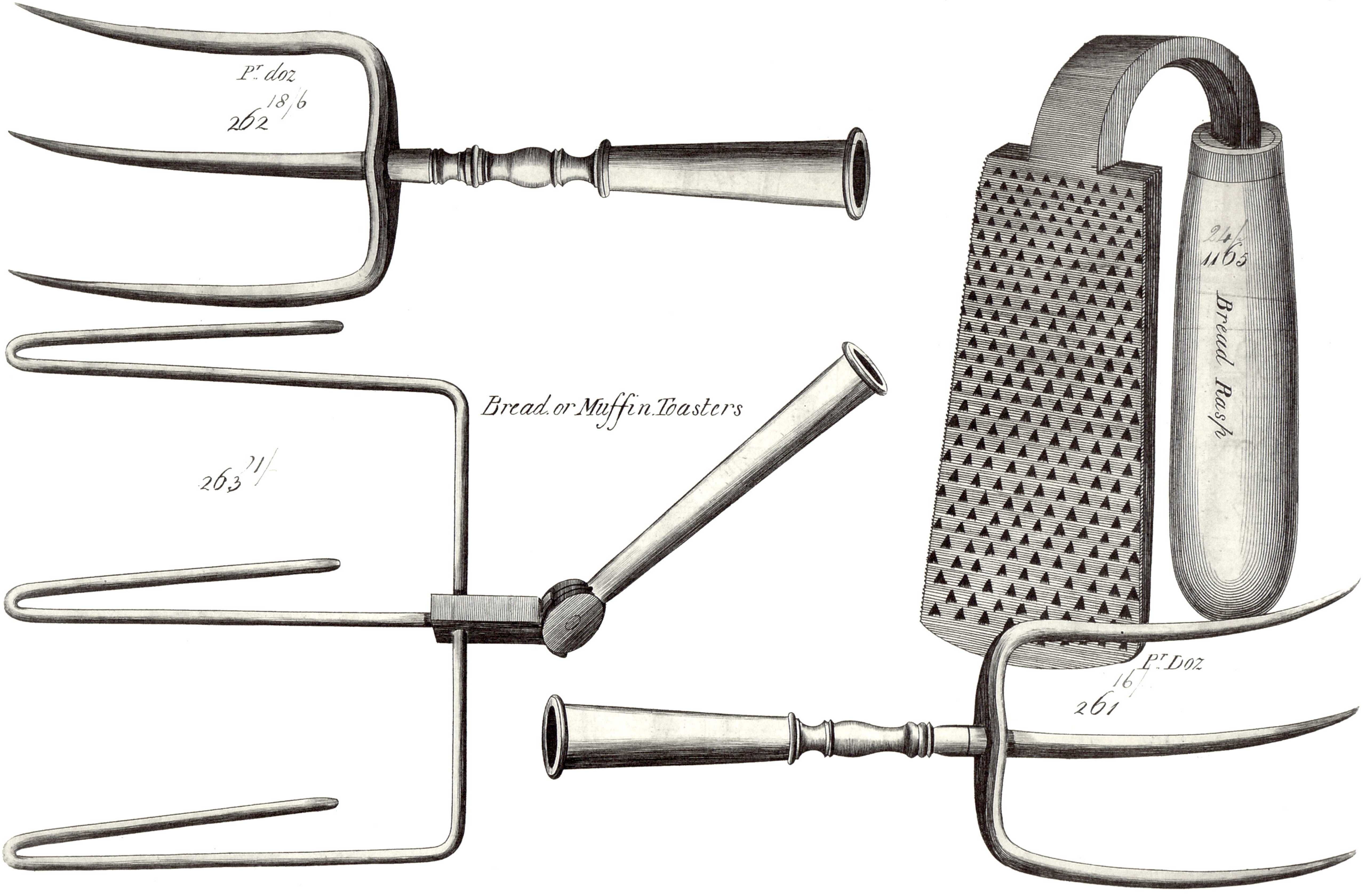

Pr. doz
262 18/6
Bread or Muffin Toasters
263 21/
1165 24/
Bread Rasp
Pr. Doz
261 16/

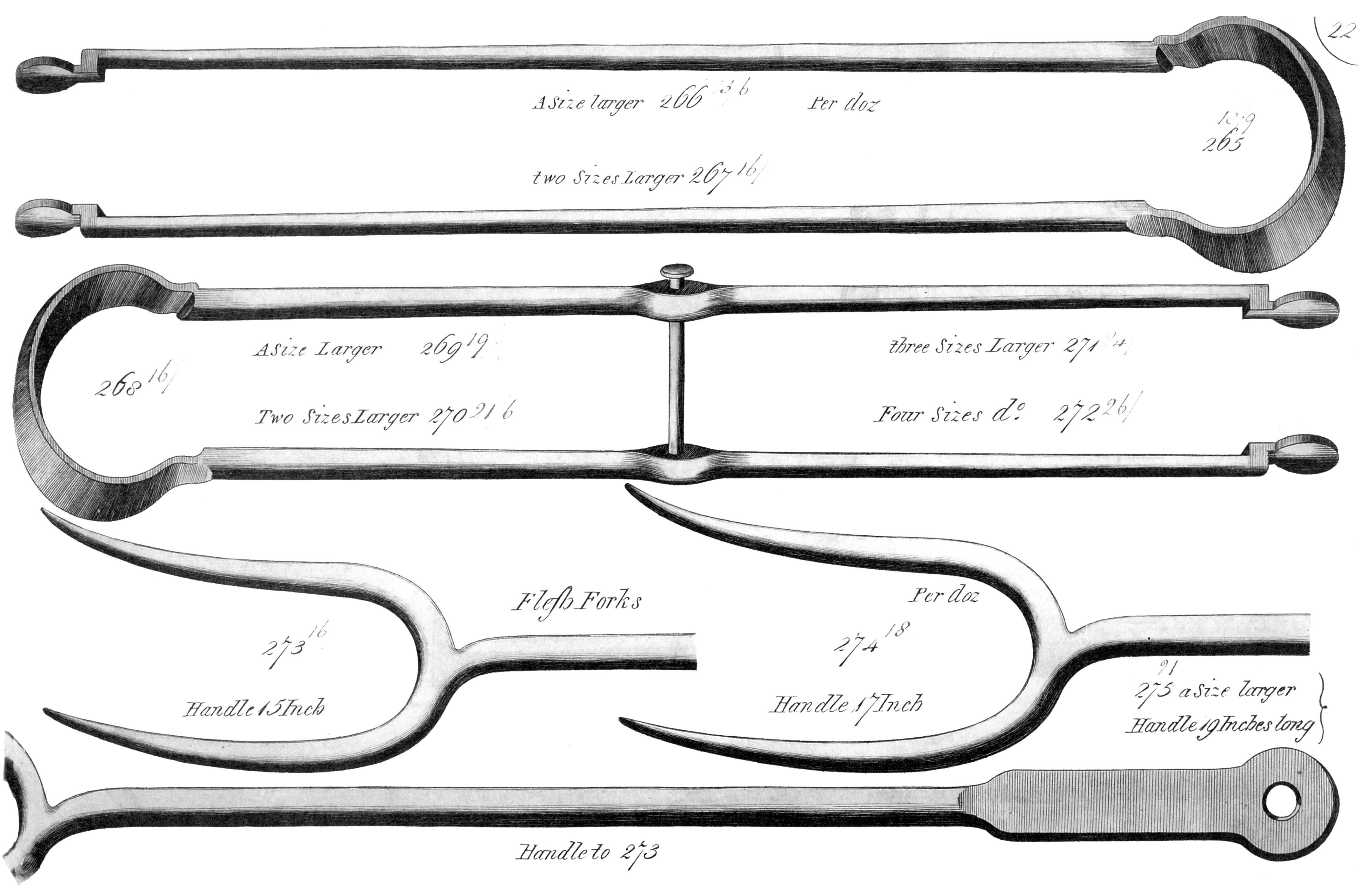
22
A Size larger 266 13/6
Per doz
10/9
265
two Sizes Larger 267 16/
A Size Larger 269 19/
three Sizes Larger 271 24/
268 16/
Two Sizes Larger 270 21/6
Four Sizes do. 272 26/
Flesh Forks
Per doz
273 16
274 18
Handle 15 Inch
Handle 17 Inch
91
275 a Size larger
Handle 19 Inches long
Handle to 273

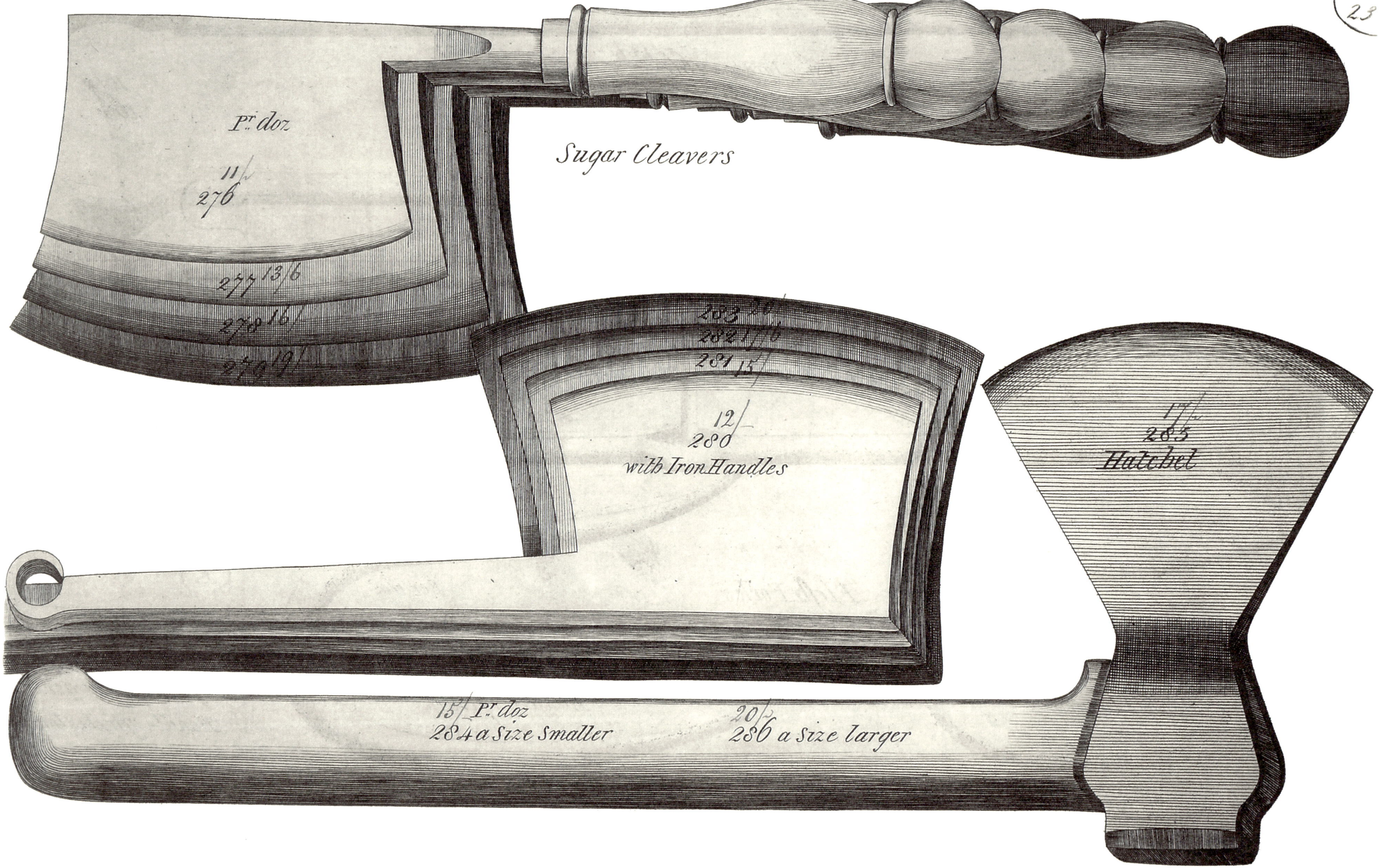
Pr. doz
11/-
276
Sugar Cleavers
277 13/6
278 16/-
279 19/-
283 20/-
282 17/6
281 15/-
12/-
280
with Iron Handles
17/-
285
Hatchet
15/- Pr. doz
284 a Size Smaller
20/-
286 a Size larger

Per doz

Fire Steels may be had better Quality

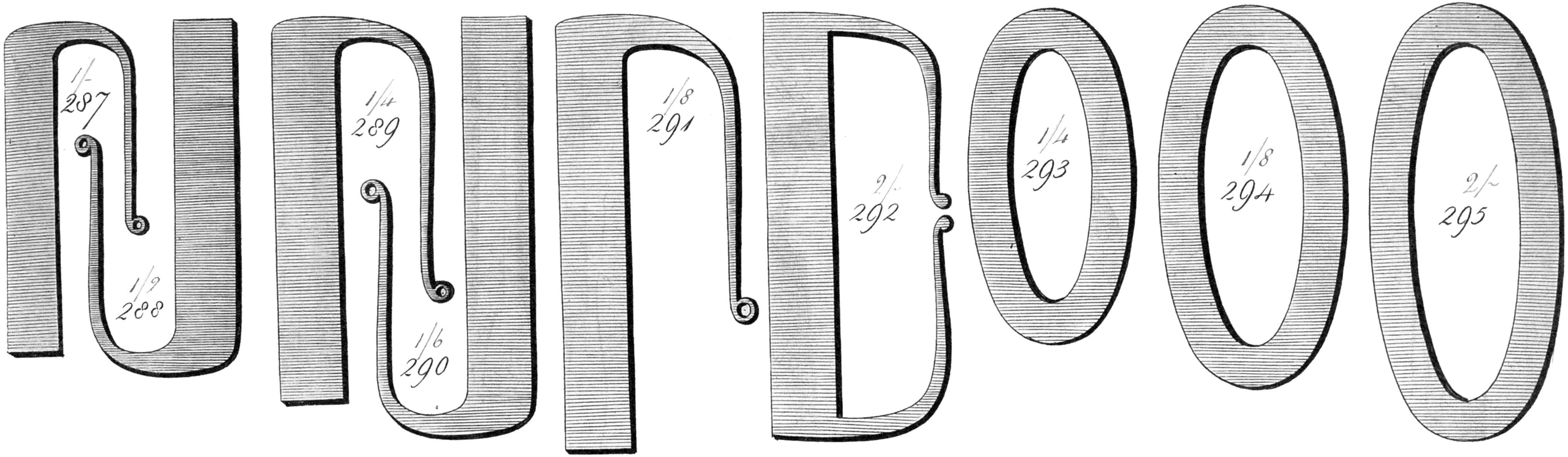

Fire Steels with Morocco Cases.

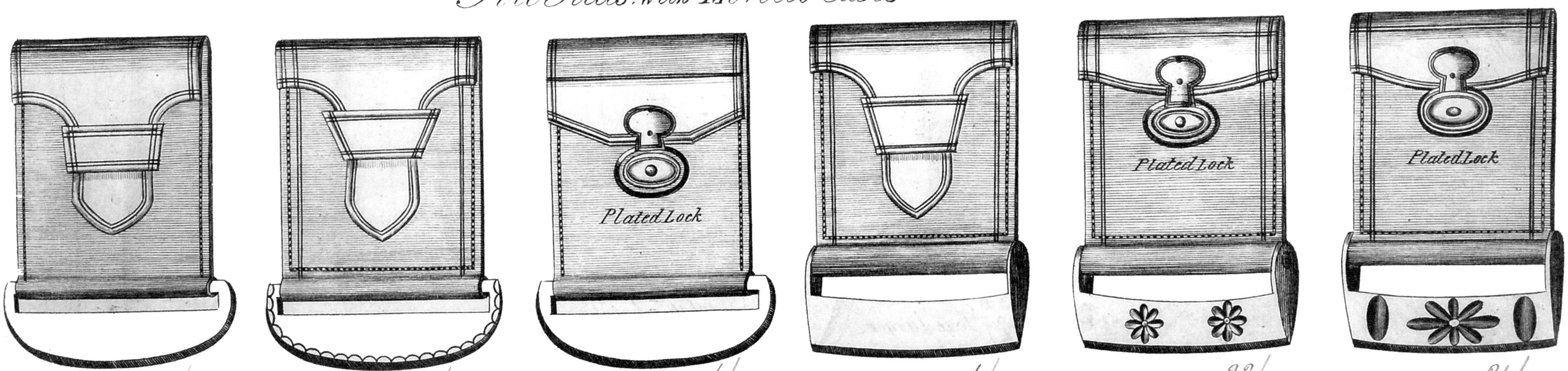

296 13/ 297 14/ 298 16/ 299 16/ 300 22/ Per doz 301 24/-

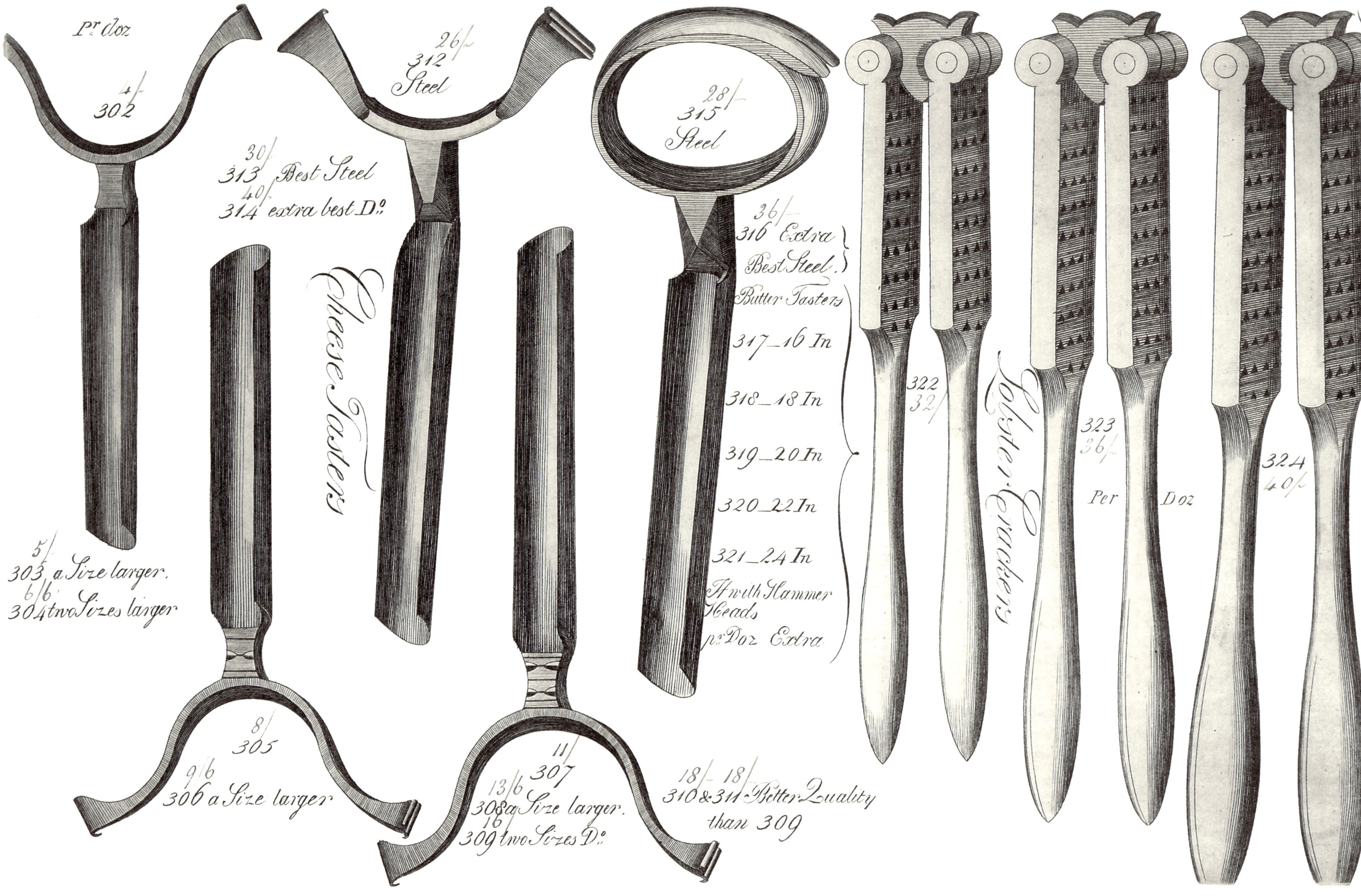
Pr. doz
4/
302
26/-
312
Steel
28/-
315
Steel
30/
313 Best Steel
40/
314 extra best Do.
36/-
316 Extra
Best Steel.
Cheese Tasters
Butter Tasters
317_16 In
318_18 In
319_20 In
320_22 In
321_24 In
If with Hammer
Heads
pr. Doz Extra
5/
303 a Size larger.
6/6
304 two Sizes larger
8/
305
9/6
306 a Size larger
11/
307
13/6
308 a Size larger.
16/
309 two Sizes Do.
18/- 18/
310 & 311 Better Quality
than 309
Lobster Crackers
322
32/
323
36/
Per Doz
324
40/

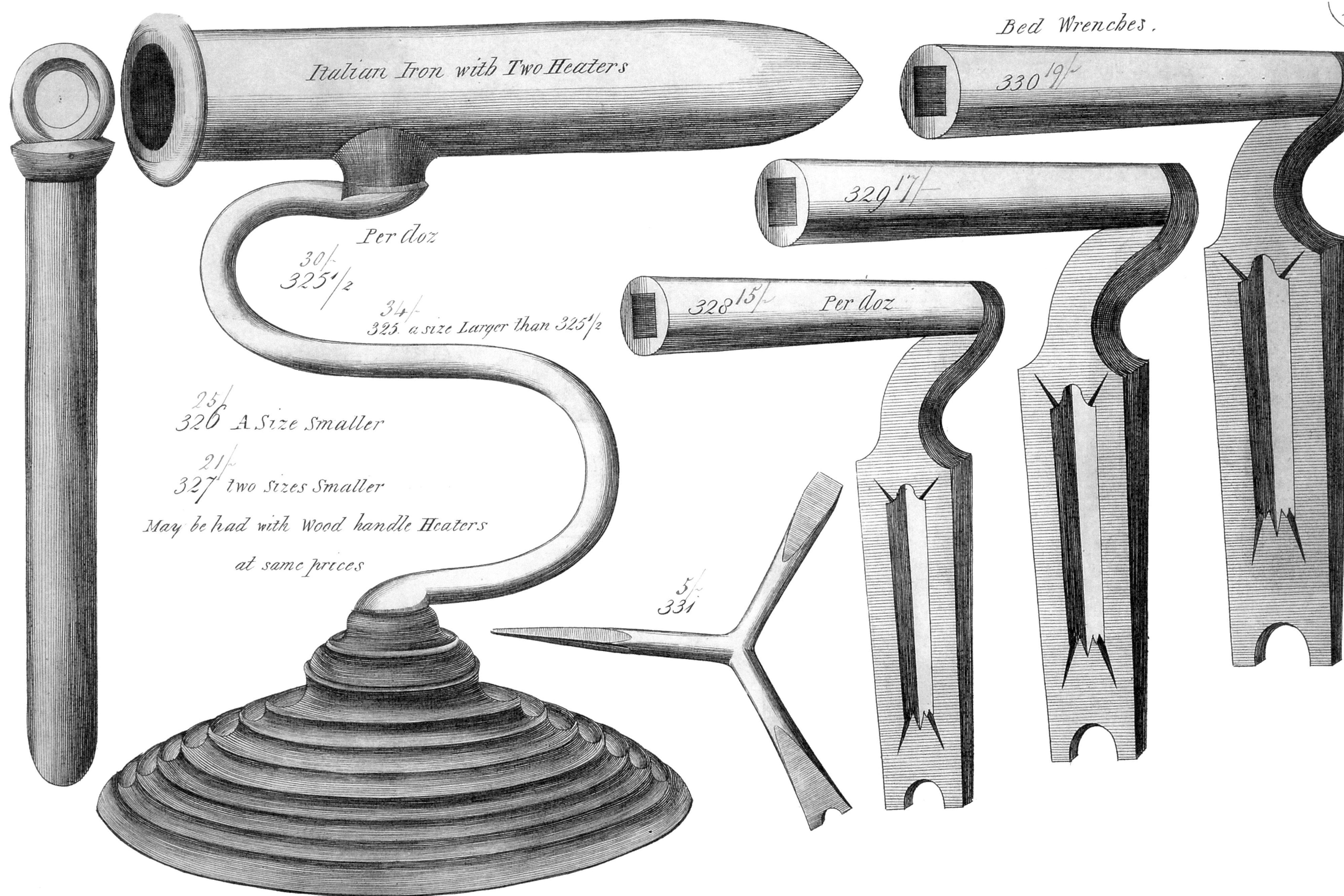
Italian Iron with Two Heaters
Per doz
30/- 325½
34/- 325. a size Larger than 325½
25/ 326 A Size Smaller
21/- 327 two Sizes Smaller
May be had with Wood handle Heaters
at same prices
Bed Wrenches.
330 19/-
329 17/-
328 15/- Per doz
5/- 331

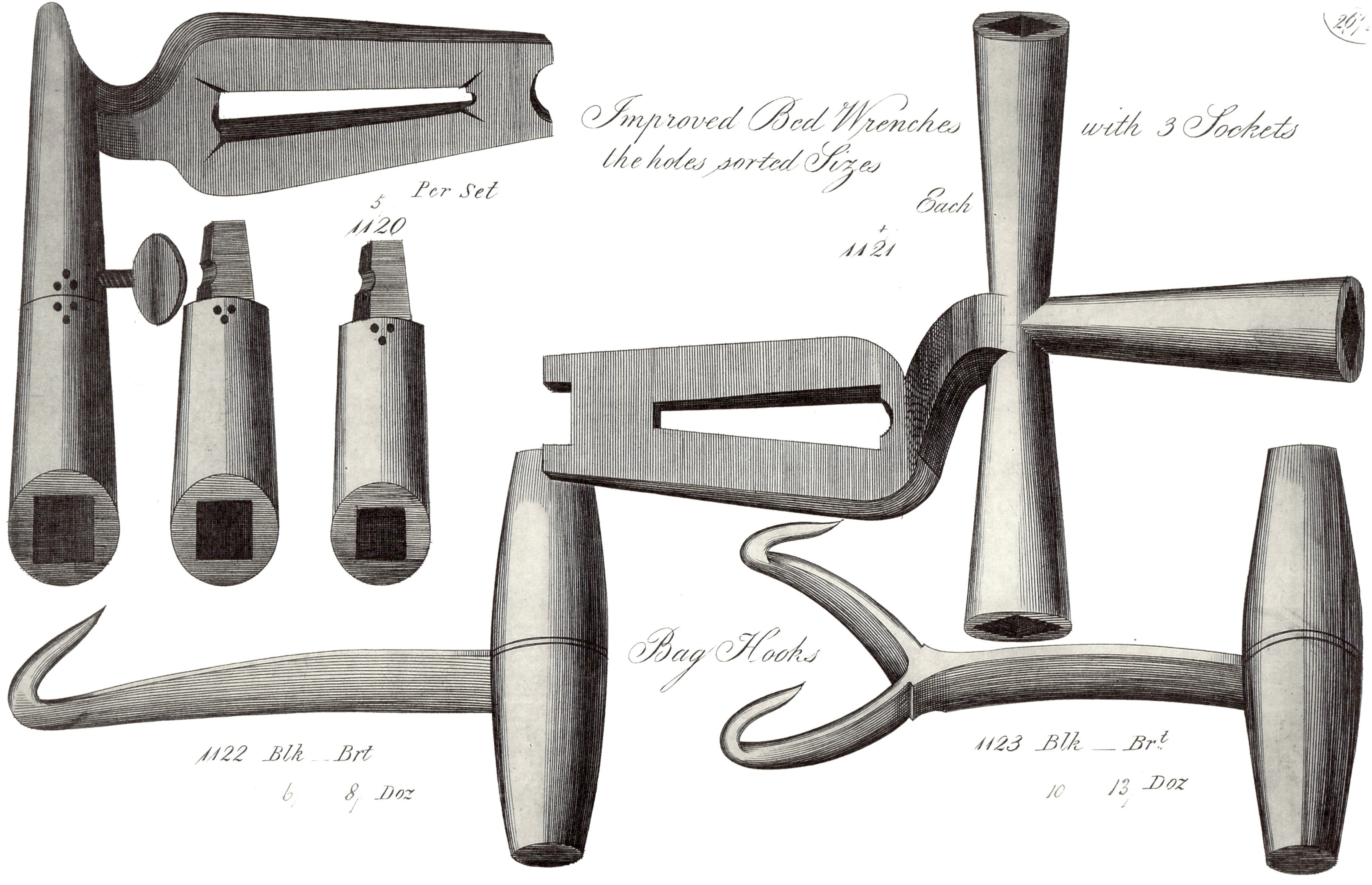
Improved Bed Wrenches with 3 Sockets
the holes sorted Sizes
Per Set
5
1120
Each
1121
Bag Hooks
1122 Blk _ Brt
6/ 8/ Doz
1123 Blk _ Brt
10 13/ Doz

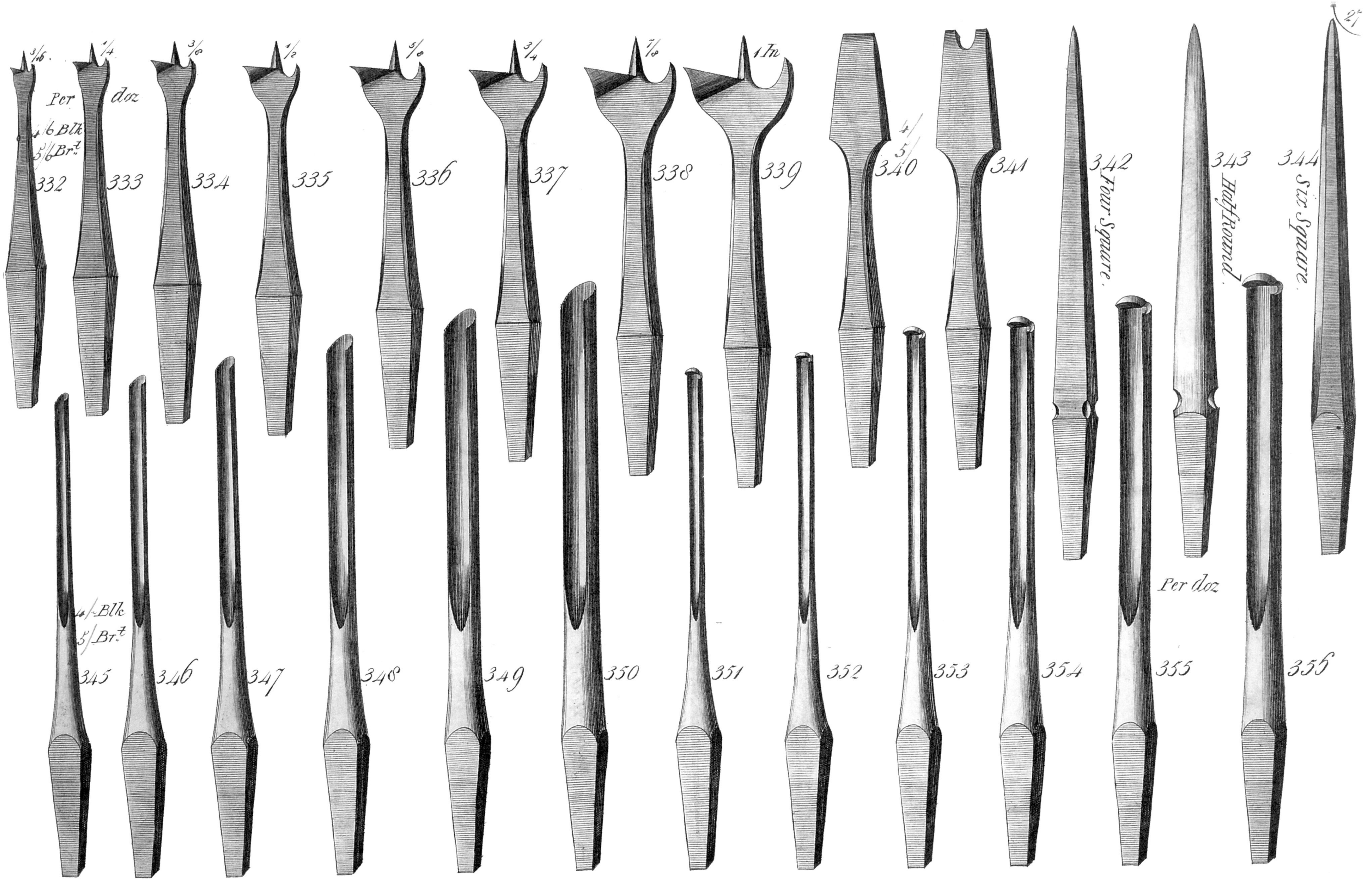
27
3/16
1/4
3/8
1/2
5/8
3/4
7/8
1 In
Per doz
4/6 Blk
5/6 Br.t
4/
5/
332
333
334
335
336
337
338
339
340
341
342
343
344
Four Square.
Half Round.
Six Square.
4/- Blk
5/ Br.t
Per doz
345
346
347
348
349
350
351
352
353
354
355
356

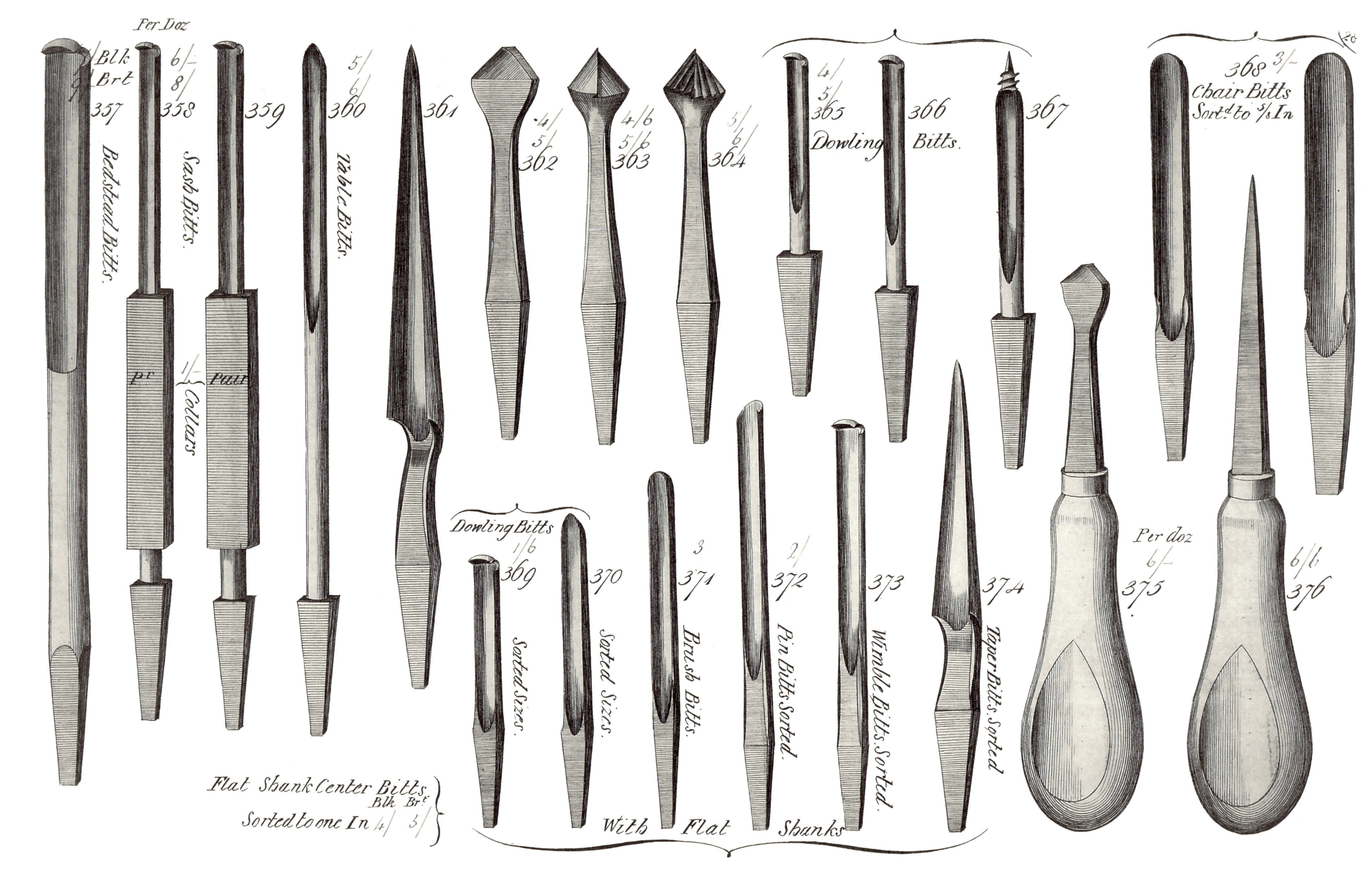
Per Doz
Blk
Brt
357
Bedstead Bitts.
6/-
8/
358
Sash Bitts.
Pr
Pair
1/-
Collars
359
5/
6/
360
Table Bitts.
361
4/
5/
362
4/6
5/6
363
5/
6/
364
4/
5/
365
Dowling Bitts.
366
367
368 3/-
Chair Bitts
Sortd to 5/8 In
Dowling Bitts
1/6
369
Sorted Sizes.
370
Sorted Sizes.
3
371
Brush Bitts.
2/
372
Pin Bitts Sorted.
373
Wimble Bitts Sorted.
374
Taper Bitts Sorted
Per doz
6/-
375
6/6
376
Flat Shank Center Bitts
Blk Brt
Sorted to one In 4/ 5/
With Flat Shanks

Per Set

378 Scotch Brace with 12 Blk Bitts. 13/

379 d°. with 18 Blk Bitts & Collars. 16/6

380 d°. with 24 d°. & d°. 19/

381 d°. with 30 d°. & d°. 21/6

382 d°. with 36 d°. & d°. 24/

With Common Mounted Brace.
Pr Set 2/ lower

Per Set

383 Scotch Brace with 12 Br^d Bitts. 14/

384 d°. with 18 d°. & Collars. 18/

385 d°. with 24 d°. & d°. 21/

386 d°. with 30 d°. & d°. 24/

387 d°. with 36 d°. & d°. 27/

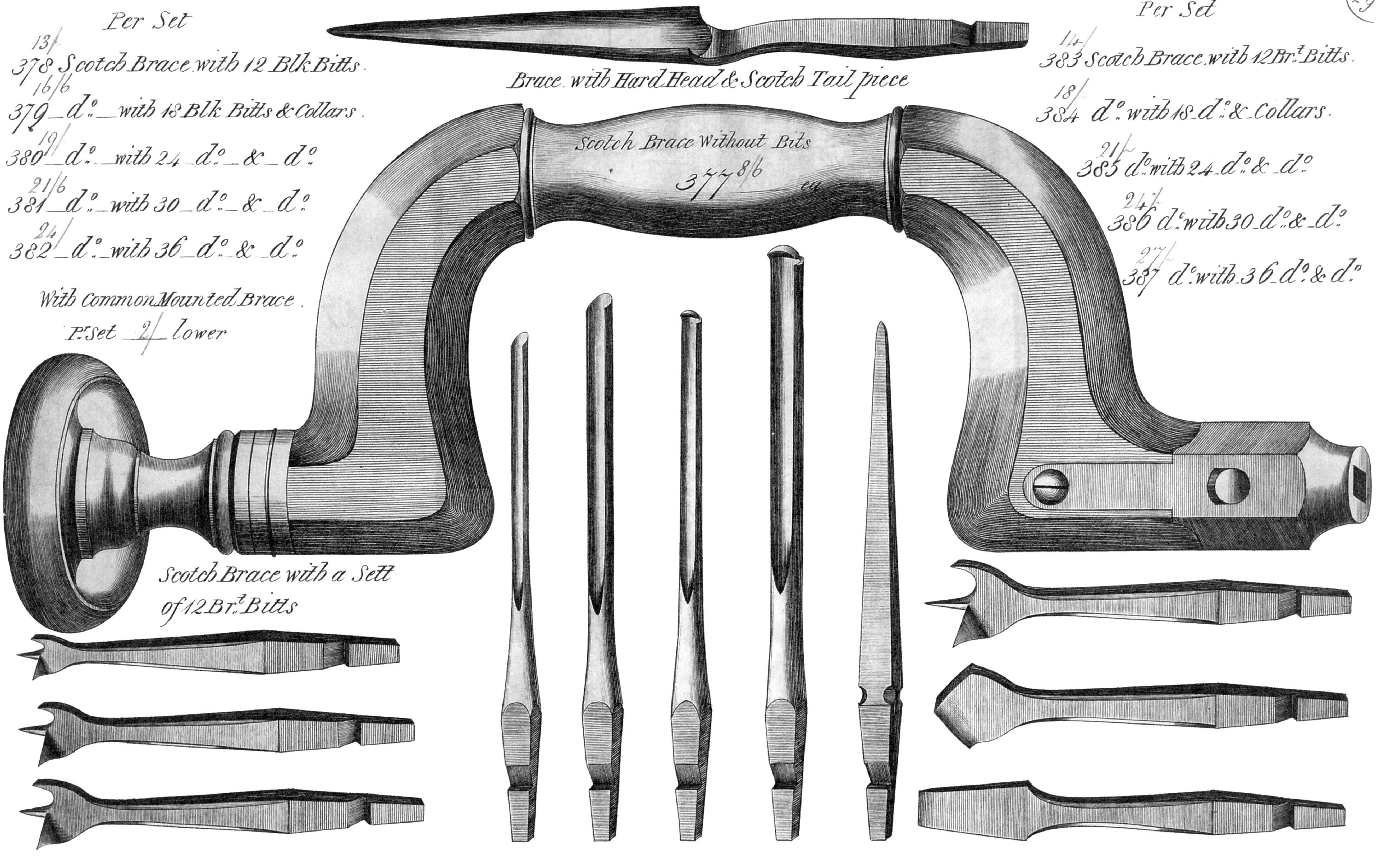

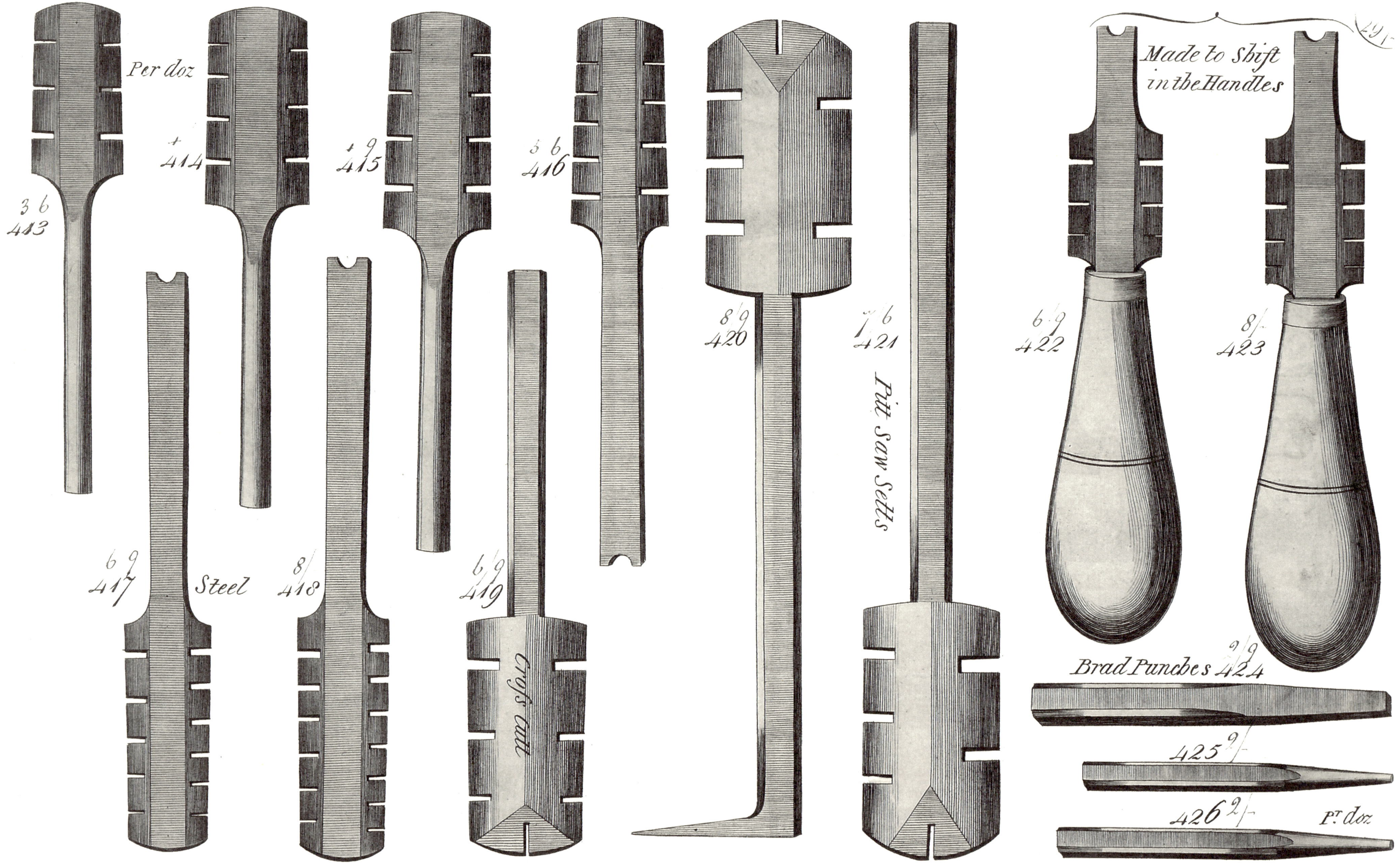
Per doz
3 6
413
4
414
4 9
415
3 6
416
6 9
417
Steel
8/
418
6/9
419
Crofs Cut
8/9
420
7/6
421
Pitt Saw Setts
Made to Shift
in the Handles
6/9
422
8/
423
Brad Punches 2/9 424
425 2/
426 2/
Pr doz

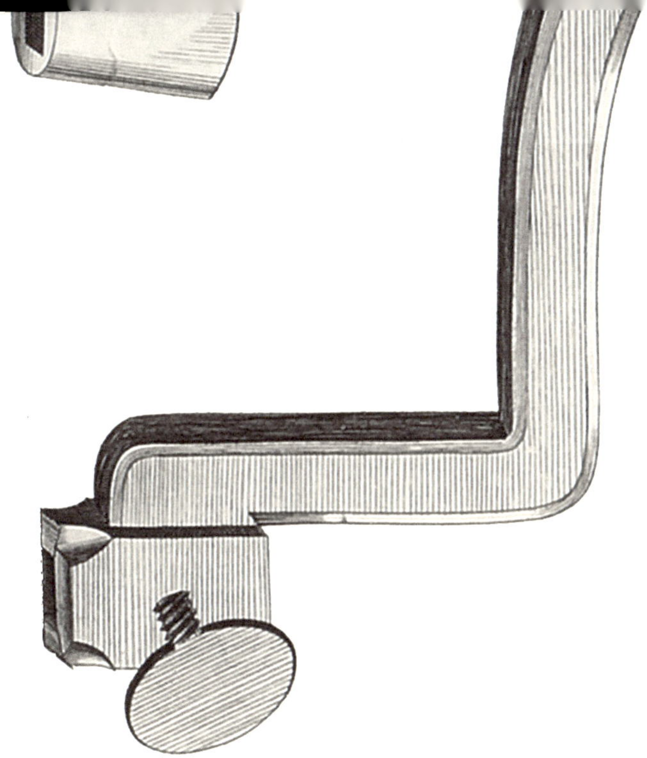

396 46/–

397 35/–

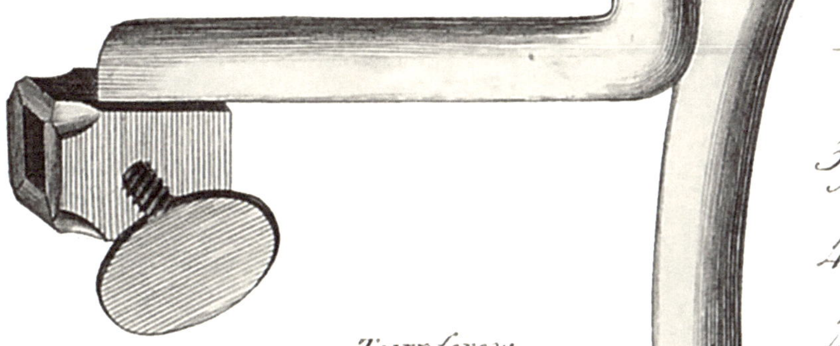

Per Doz

398 Size Larger than 397 – with Swan Neck as 396 — 42/

Gentlemens Iron Brace 397 with Sett of Bitts as Follows –

Per Set		Per Set	
7/3	399 Brace with 12 Blk. Bitts	8/3	404 Brace with 12 Brd. Bitts
9/9	400 – d°. – with 18 – d°. –	11/3	405 – d°. – with – 18 – d°. –
12/3	401 – d°. – with 24 – d°. –	14/3	406 – d°. – with – 24 – d°. –
14/9	402 – d°. – with 30 – d°. –	17/3	407 – d°. – with – 30 – d°. –
17/3	403 d°. with 36 – d°. –	20/3	408 d°. – with 36 – d°. –

Turnscrew 409 5/–

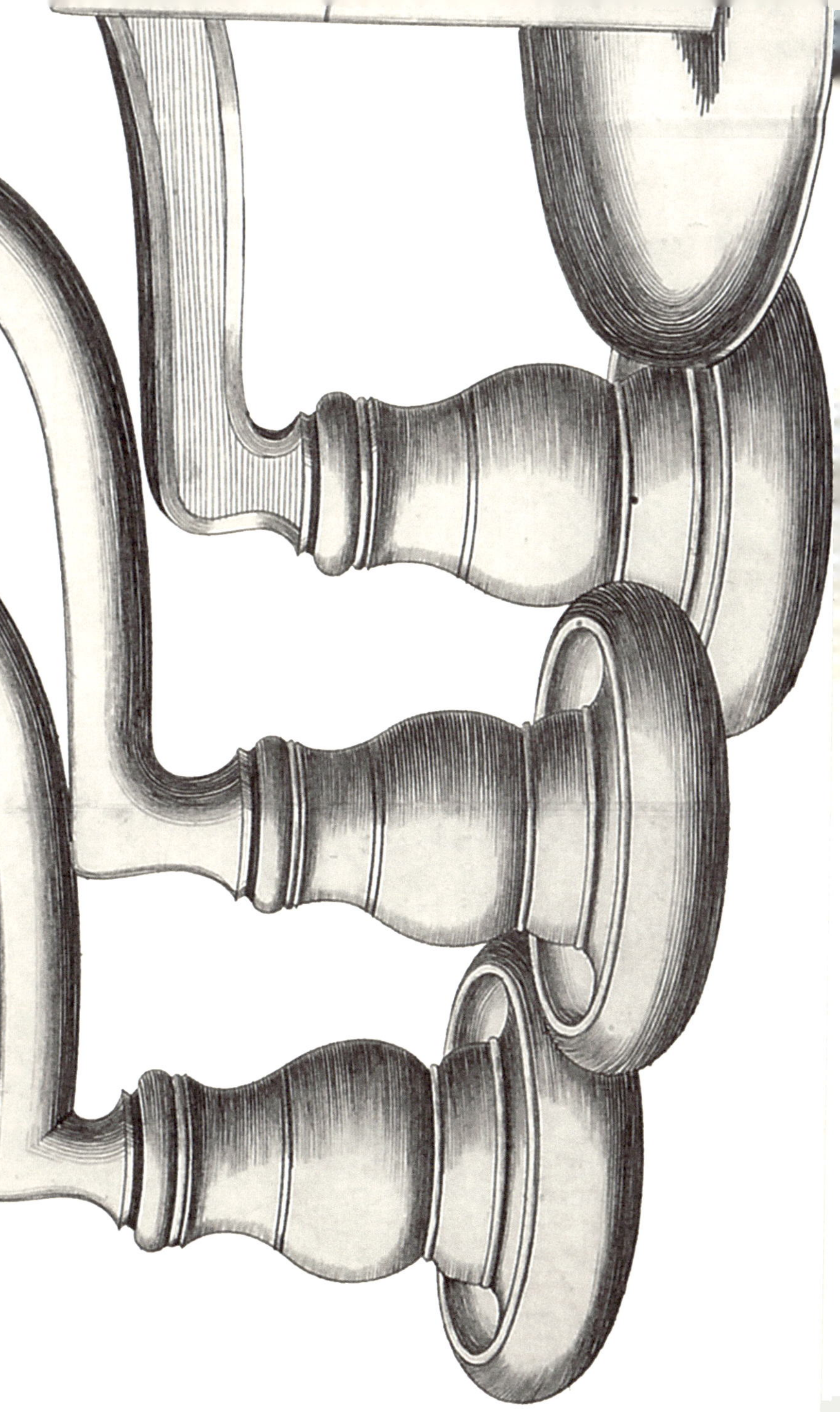

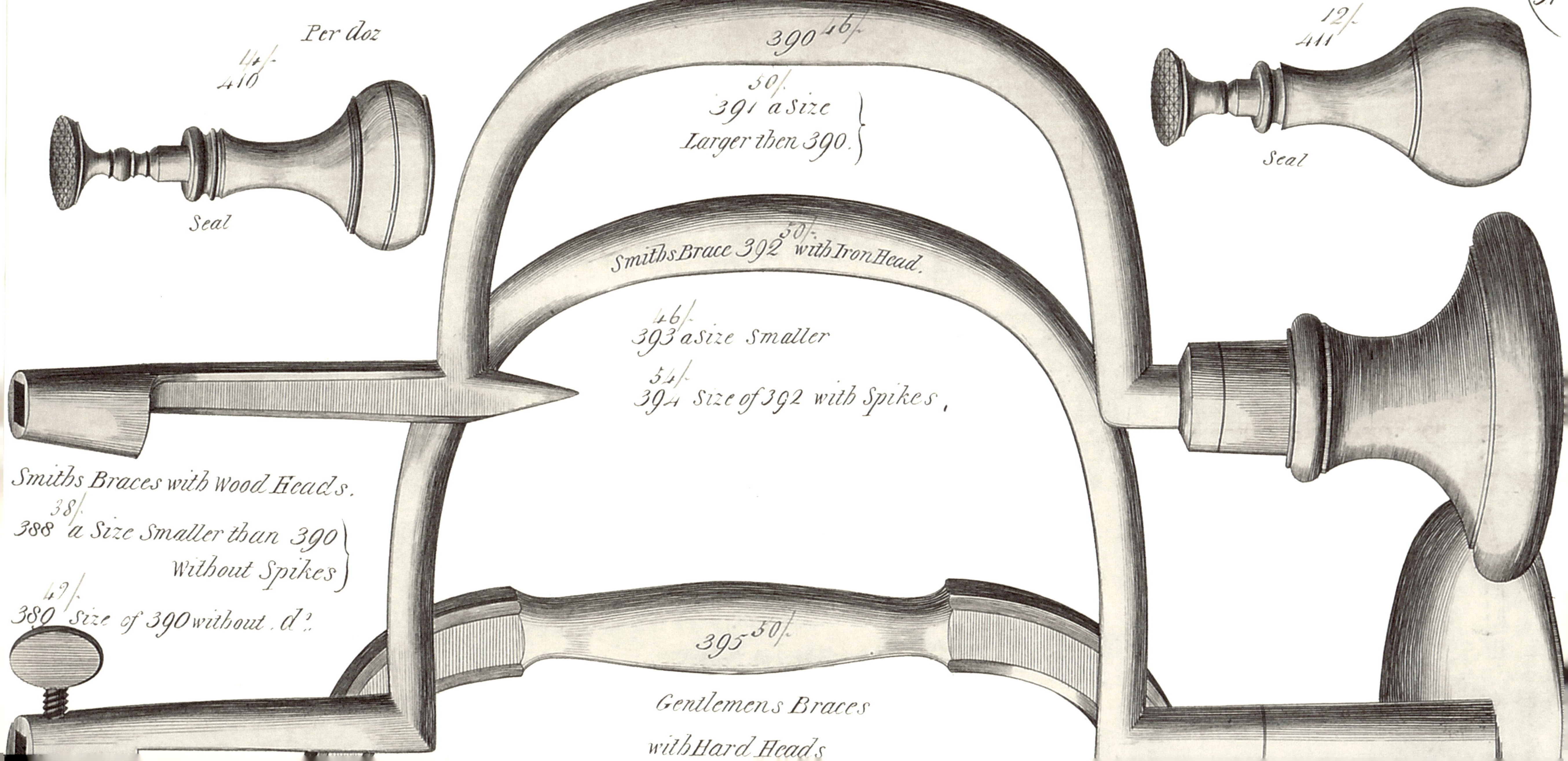
Per doz
14/-
410
Seal
12/-
411
Seal
390 46/-
50/-
391 a Size
Larger then 390.
Smiths Brace 392 50/- with Iron Head.
46/-
393 a Size Smaller
54/-
394 Size of 392 with Spikes.
Smiths Braces with Wood Heads.
38/-
388 a Size Smaller than 390
Without Spikes
49/-
389 Size of 390 without d°.
395 50/-
Gentlemens Braces
with Hard Heads

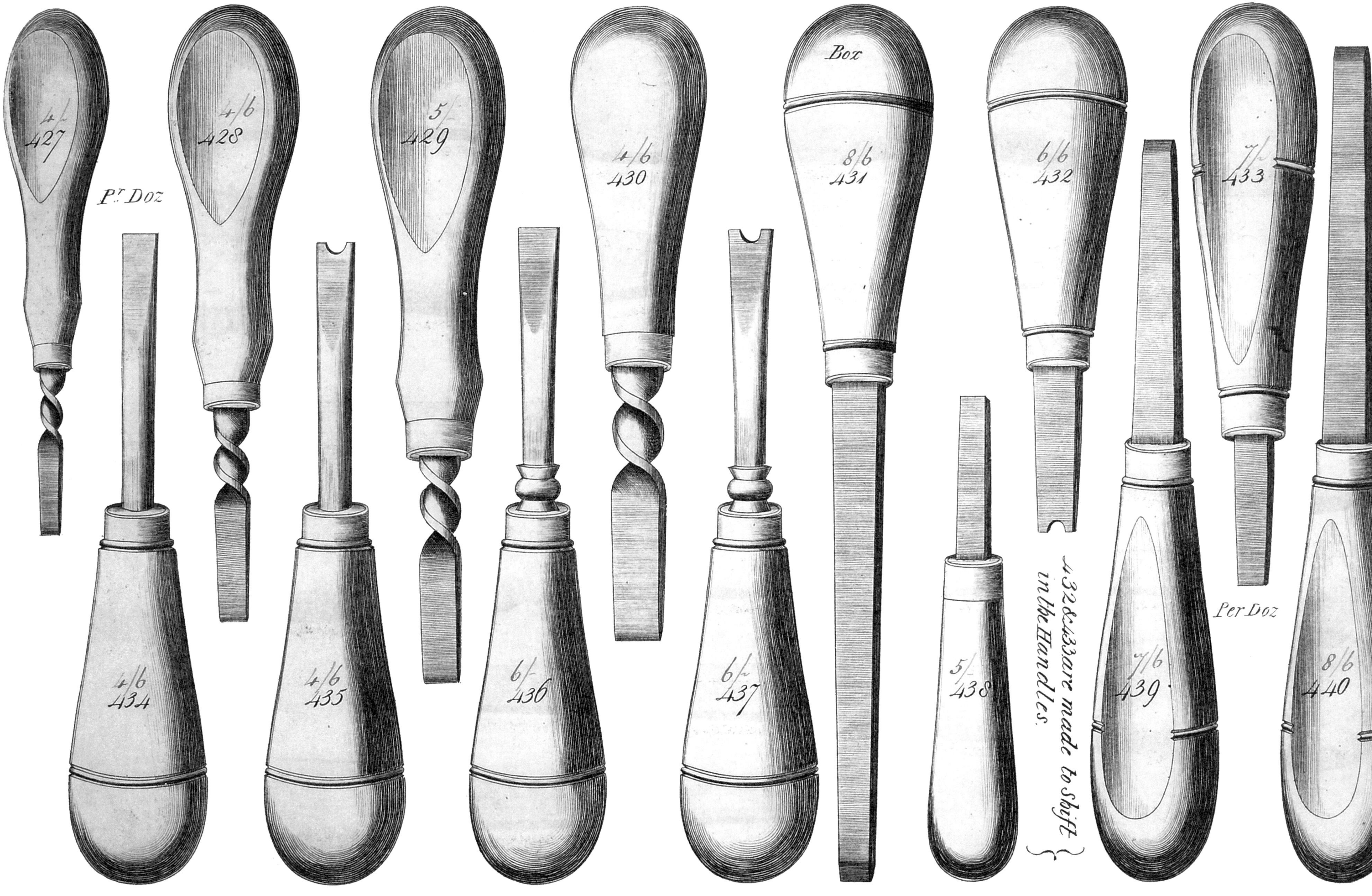
Pr. Doz
4/ 427
4/6 428
5/ 429
4/6 430
Box
8/6 431
6/6 432
7/ 433
4/6 434
4/6 435
6/ 436
6/ 437
5/ 438
432&433 are made to Shift in the Handles.
Per Doz
7/6 439
8/6 440

Best Black Turnscrews.

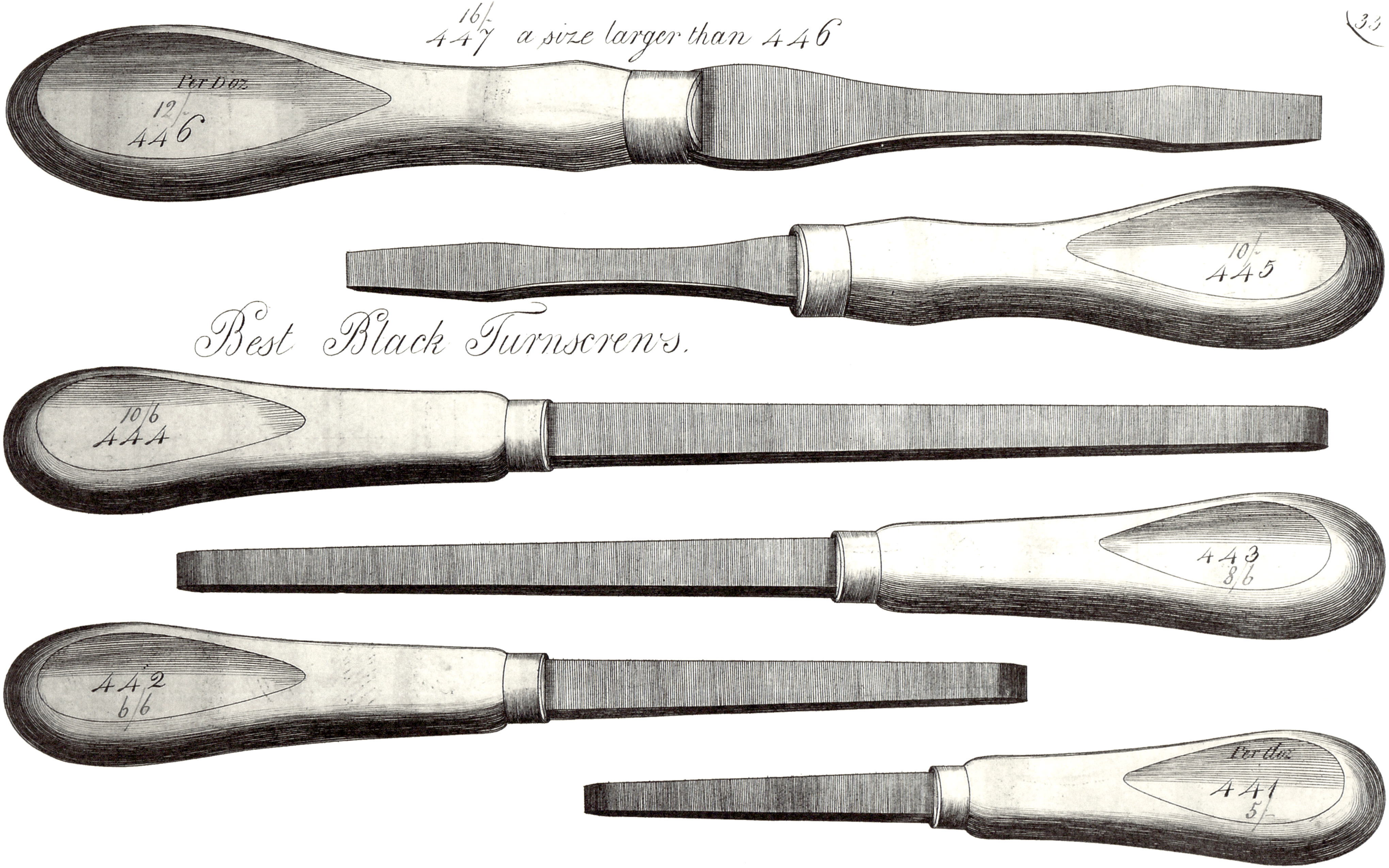

Best Bright Carpenters Turnscrews

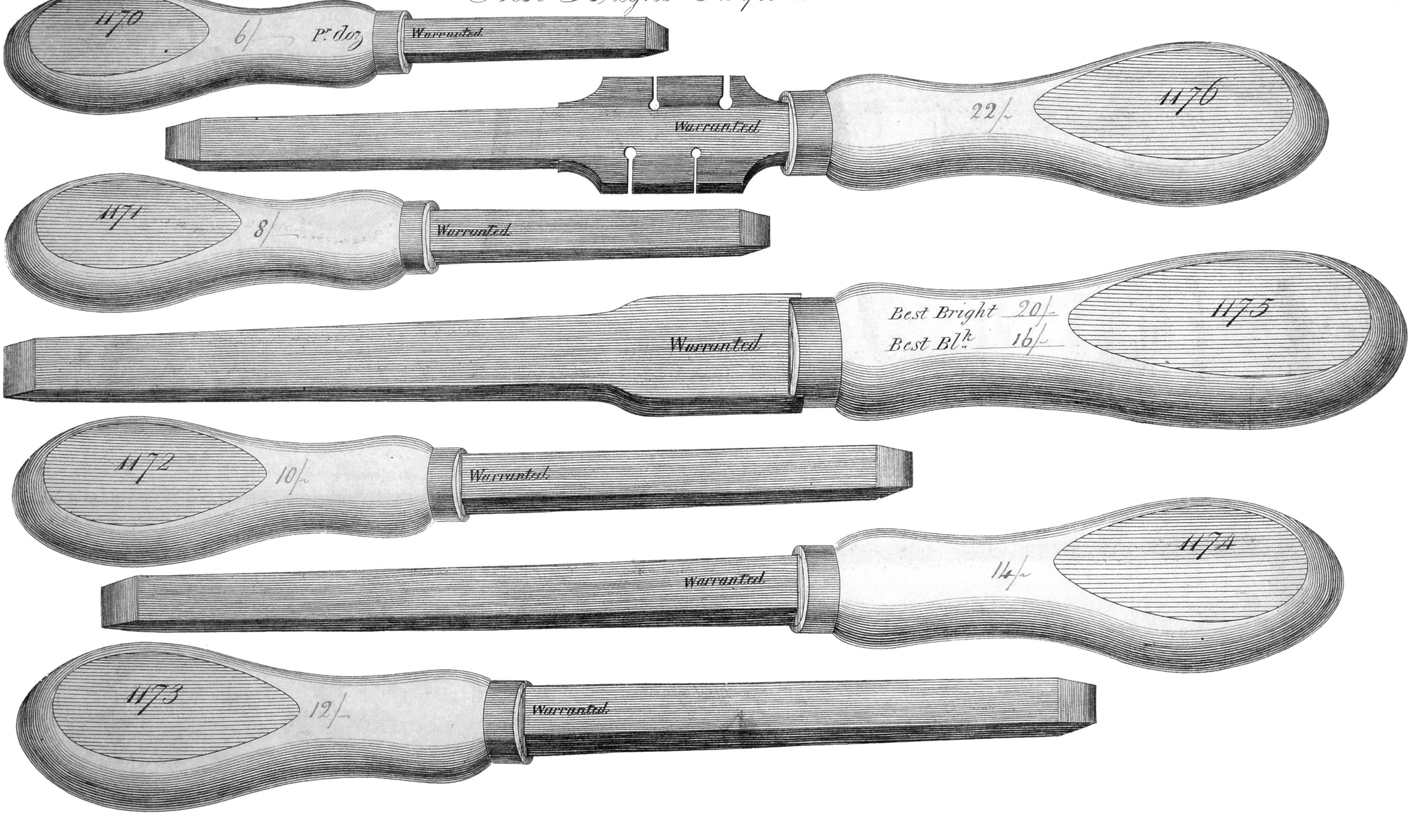

1067 11/6 Pr doz

Best Steel Punches Drilled out of the Solid

1066 7/-

Best Quality Iron Brace

1166 48/ Pr doz

commoner finished 42/

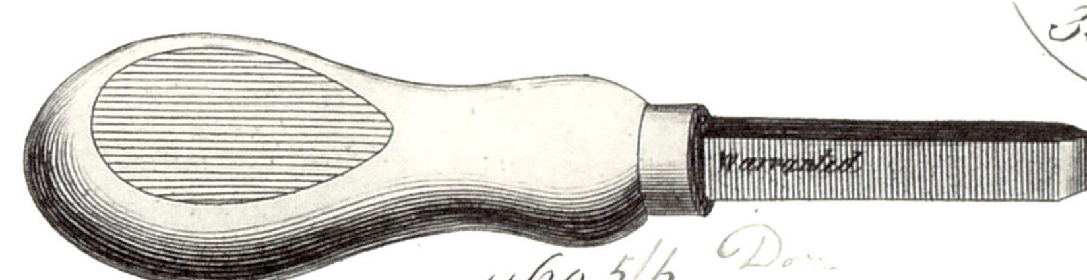

1169 5/6 Doz

1168 5/-

Butter & Flour Tryers

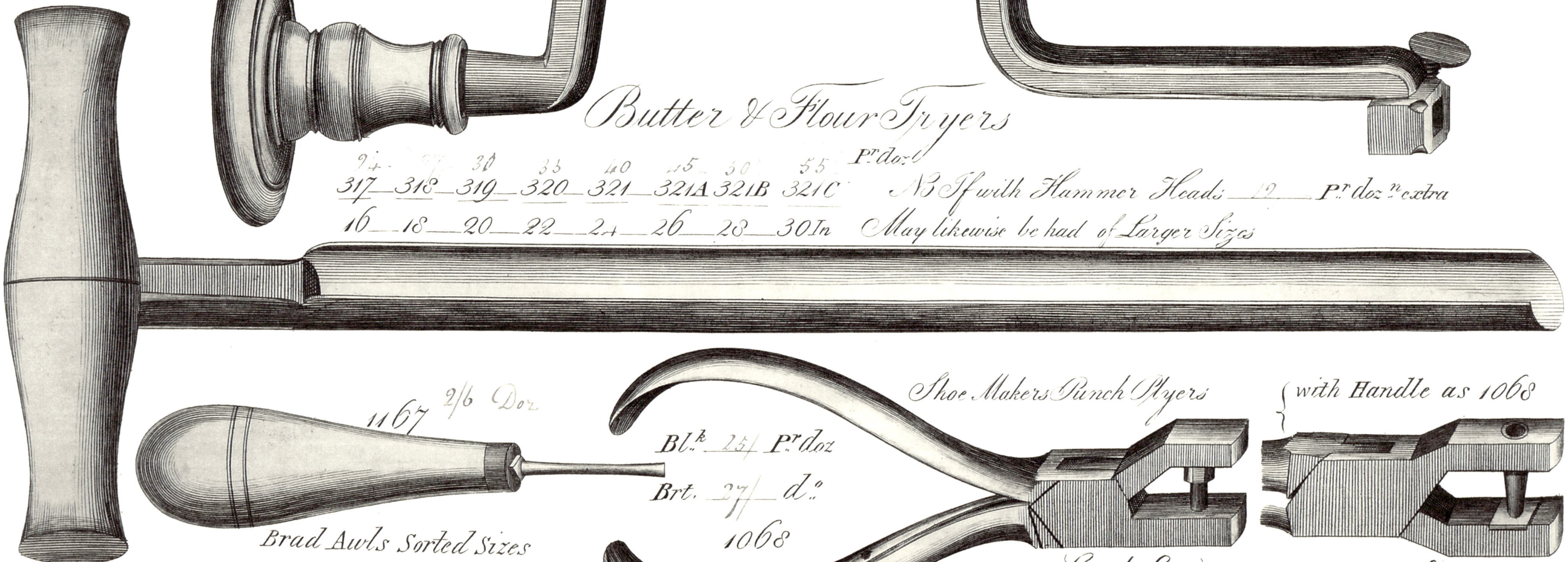

24	27	30	35	40	45	50	55	Pr doz
317	318	319	320	321	321A	321B	321C	NB If with Hammer Heads 12 Pr doz n extra
16	18	20	22	24	26	28	30 In	May likewise be had of Larger Sizes

1167 2/6 Doz

Brad Awls Sorted Sizes

Shoe Makers Punch Plyers

Bl.k 25/ Pr doz

Brt. 27/ do

1068

Lambs Ears / Larger sizes for Marking 42/ Pr dz

with Handle as 1068

1069 Blk. 25/ Brt 27/

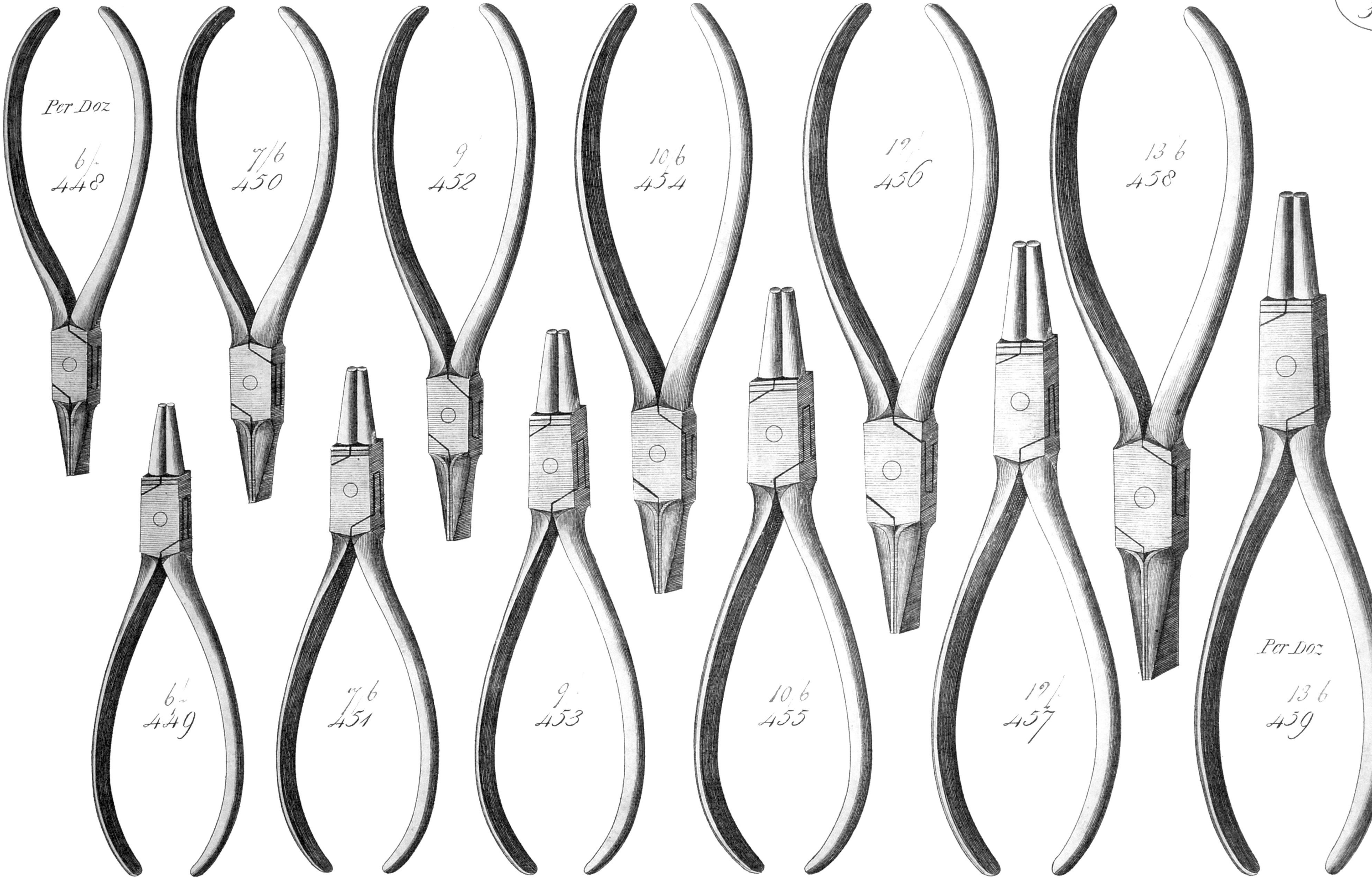
Per Doz
6/
448
7/6
450
9/
452
10/6
454
12/
456
13/6
458
6/
449
7/6
451
9/
453
10/6
455
12/
457
Per Doz
13/6
459

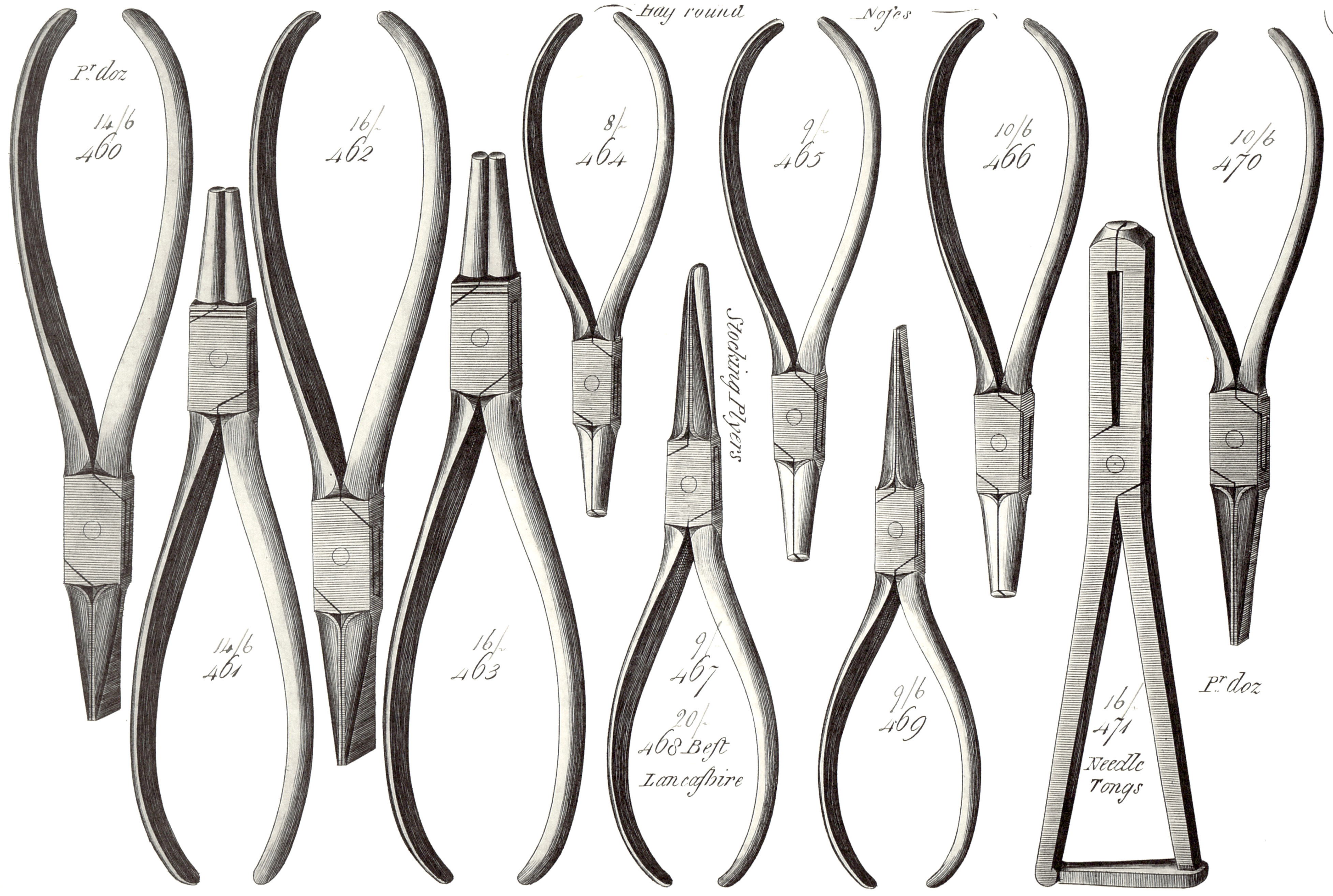
round Noses
Pr. doz
14/6
460
14/6
461
16/-
462
16/-
463
8/-
464
9/-
465
10/6
466
Stocking Plyers
9/-
467
20/-
468 Best
Lancashire
9/6
469
10/6
470
Pr. doz
16/-
471
Needle
Tongs

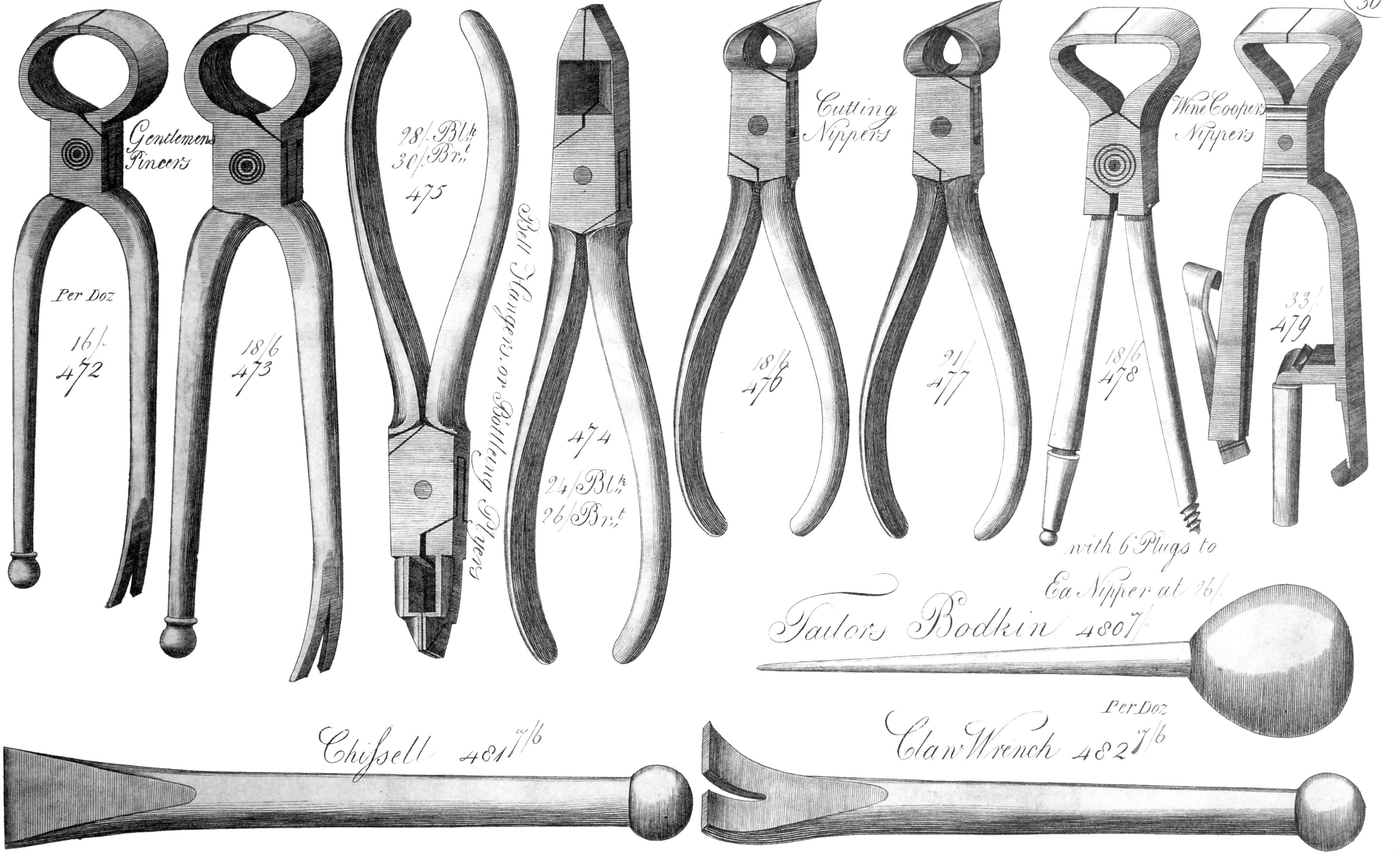
Gentlemens Pincers
Per Doz
16/- 472
18/6 473
28/- Blk 30/- Brt 475
Bell Hangers or Bottling Plyers
474
24/- Blk 26/- Brt
Cutting Nippers
18/6 476
21/- 477
Wine Coopers Nippers
18/6 478
33/- 479
with 6 Plugs to Ea Nipper at 26/-
Tailors Bodkin 480 7/-
Per Doz
Chissell 481 7/6
Claw Wrench 482 7/6

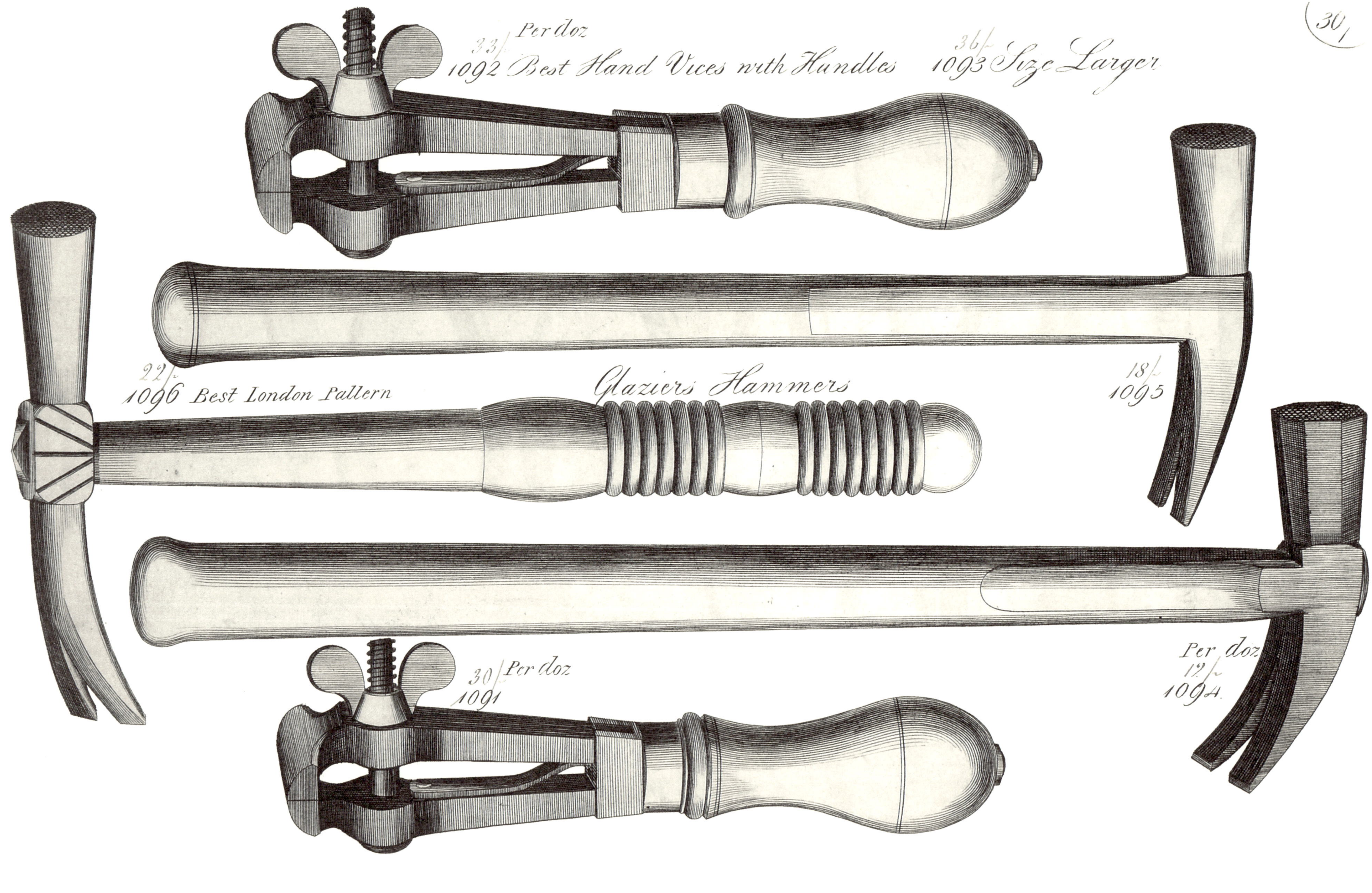
Per doz
33/-
1092 Best Hand Vices with Handles
36/-
1093 Size Larger
22/-
1096 Best London Pattern
Glaziers Hammers
18/-
1095
30/- Per doz
1091
Per doz
12/-
1094.

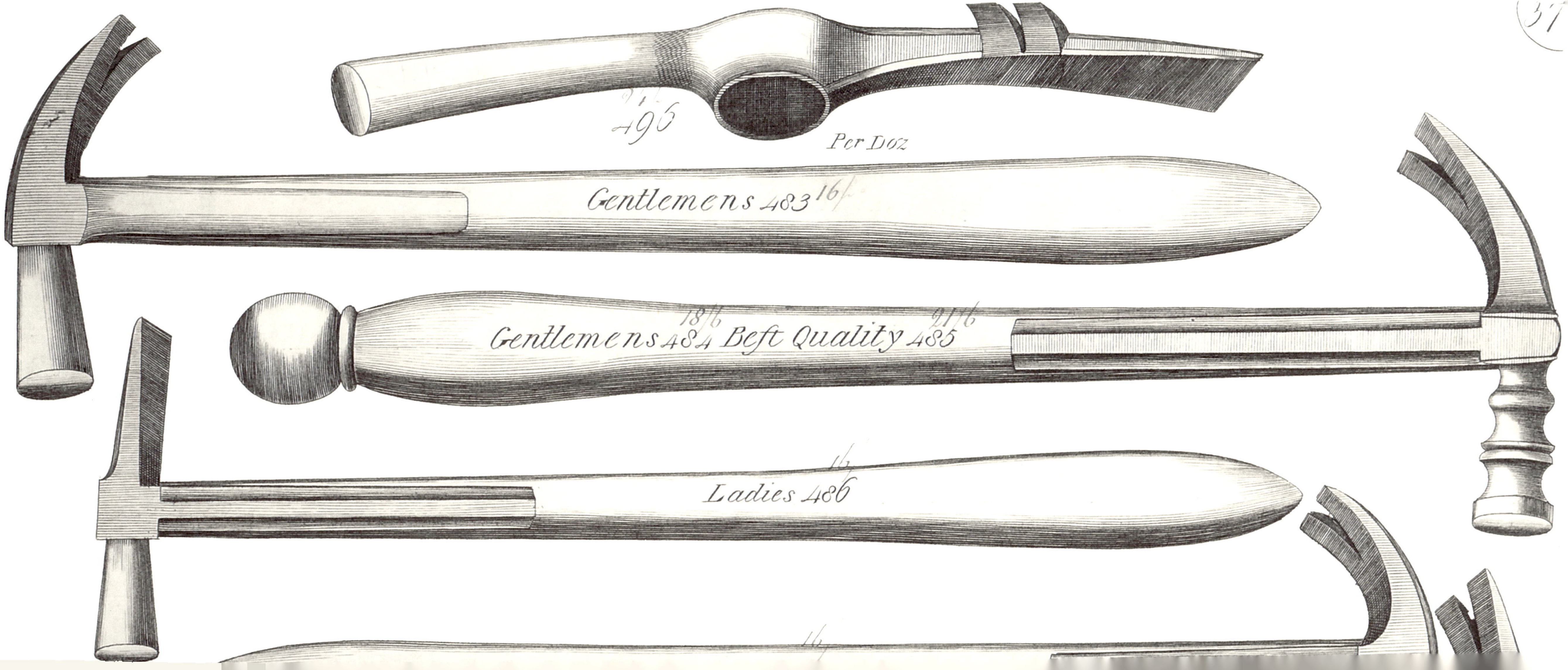
496
Per Doz
Gentlemens 483
Gentlemens 484 Beſt Quality 485
Ladies 486

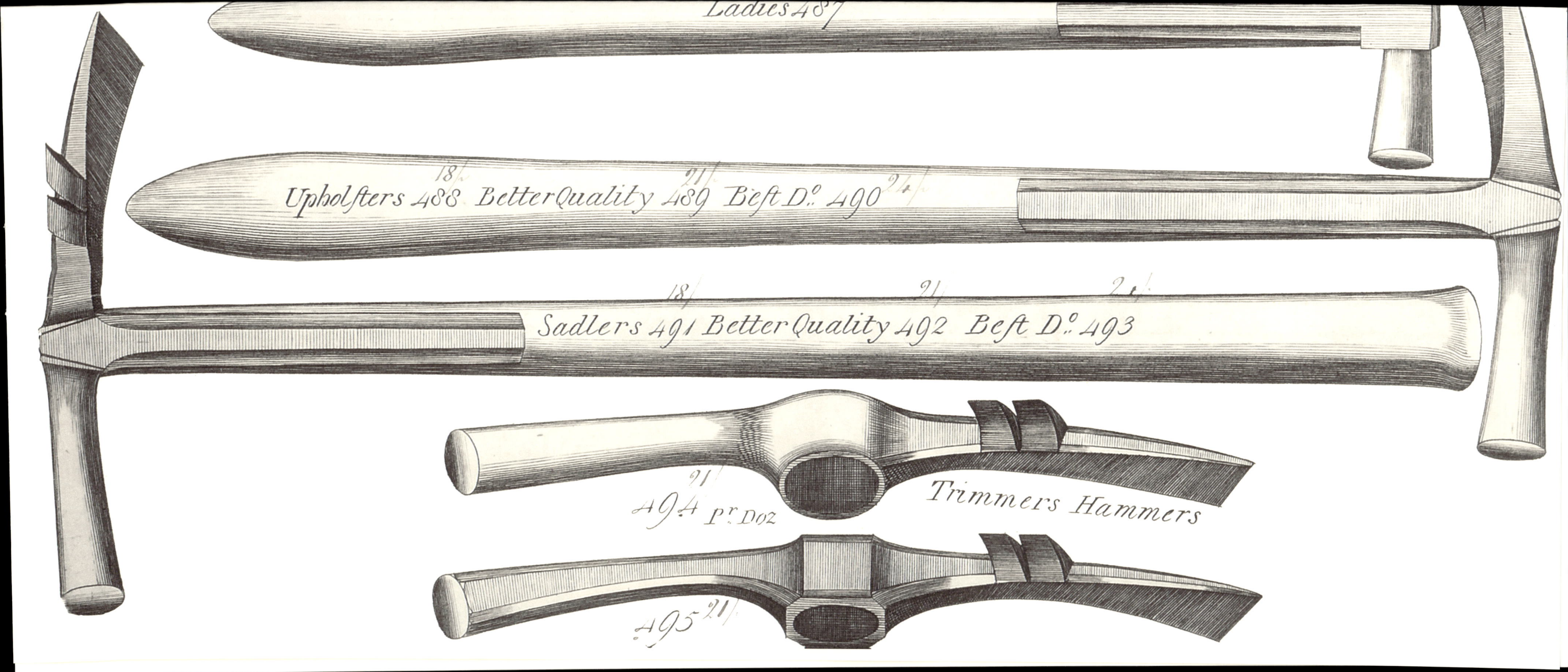

Ladies 487
Upholsters 488 18/- Better Quality 489 21/- Best D.o 490 24/-
Sadlers 491 18/- Better Quality 492 21/- Best D.o 493 24/-
Trimmers Hammers
494 21/- P.r Doz
495 21/-

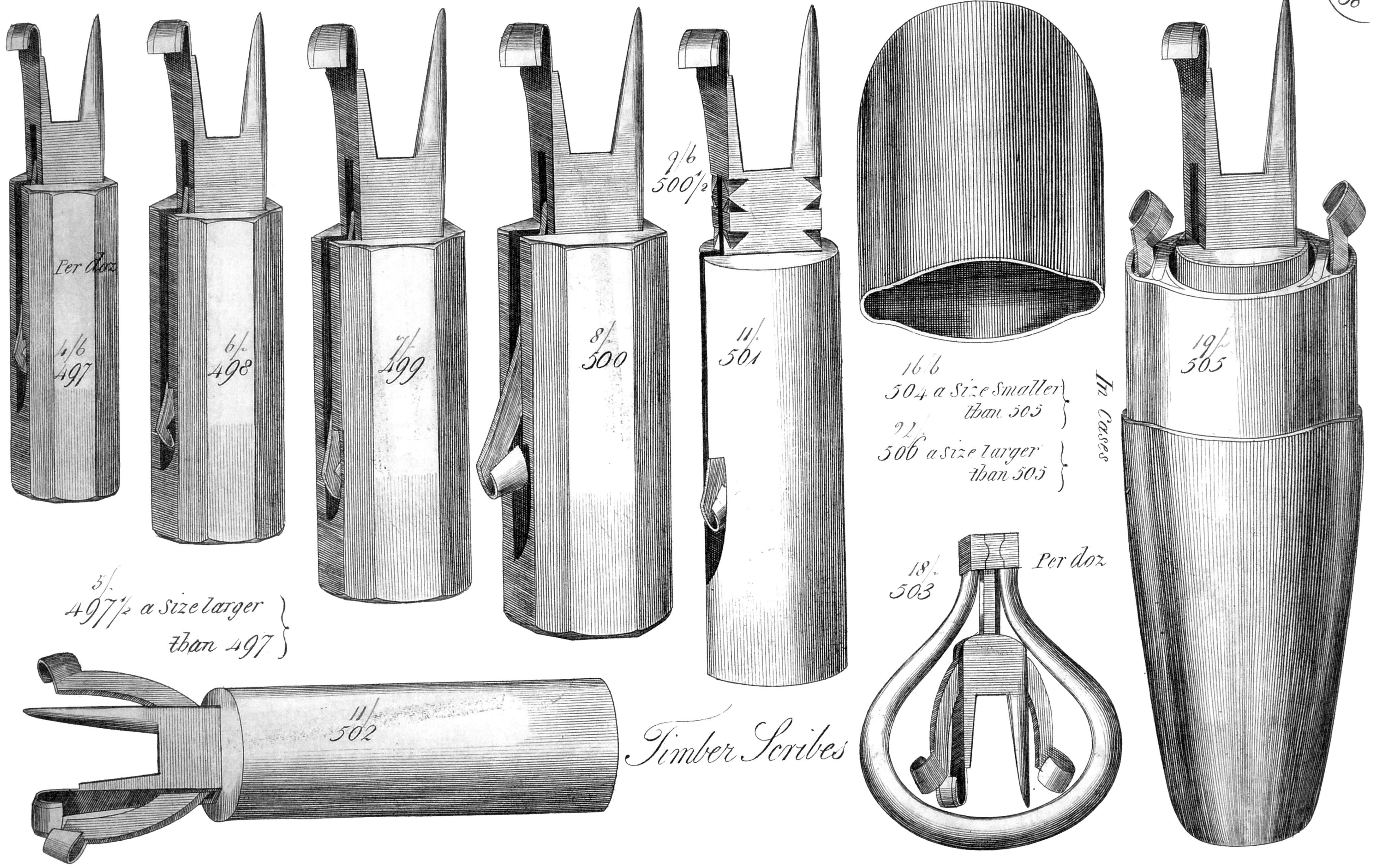
Per doz
4/6
497
6/
498
7/
499
8/
500
9/6
500½
11/
501
16/6
504 a Size Smaller than 505
9/
506 a size larger than 505
In Cases
19/
505
5/
497½ a Size larger than 497
11/
502
Timber Scribes
18/
503
Per doz

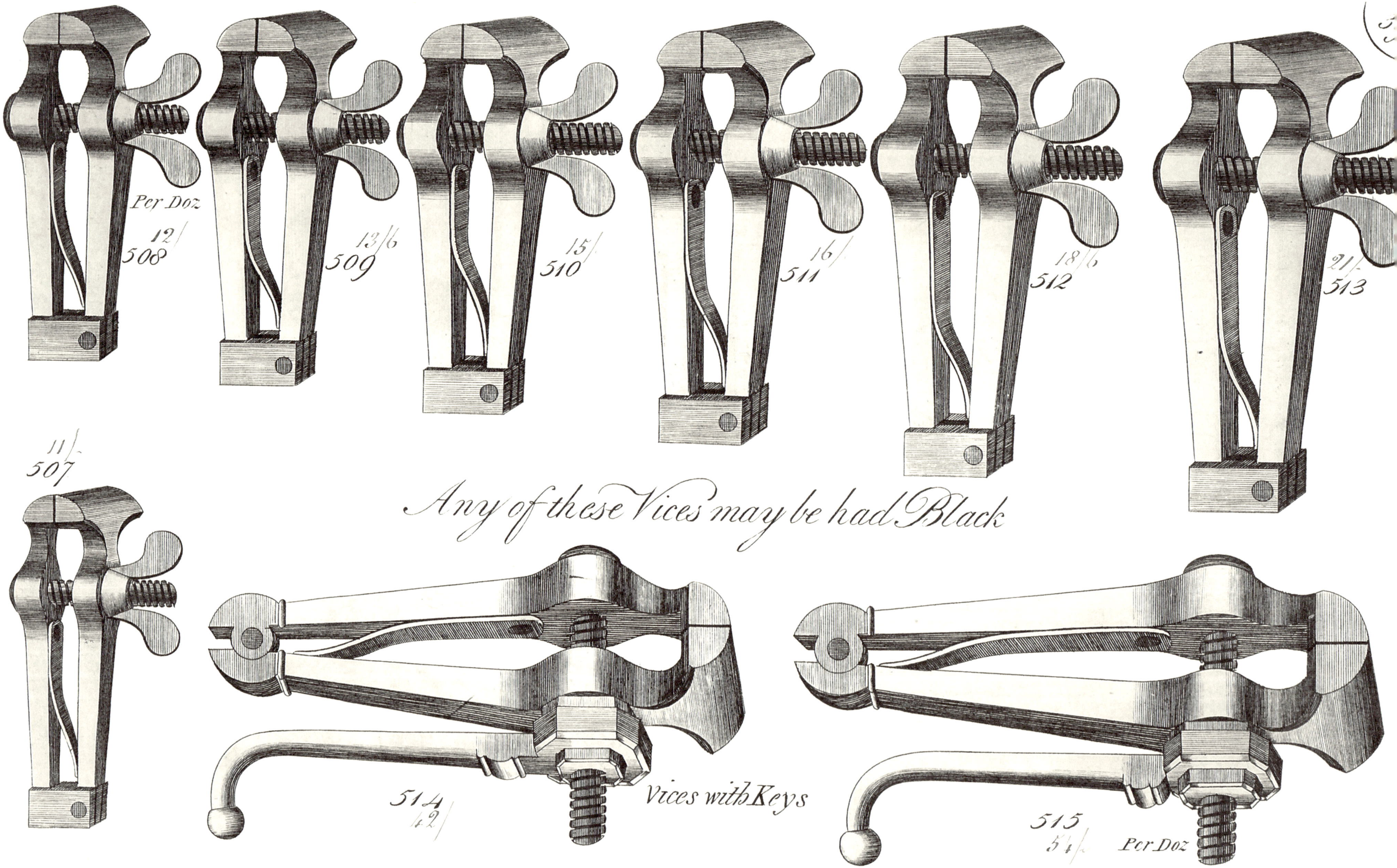

Per Doz
12/ 508
13/6 509
15/ 510
16/ 511
18/6 512
21/ 513
11/ 507
Any of these Vices may be had Black
514 42/
Vices with Keys
515 54/
Per Doz

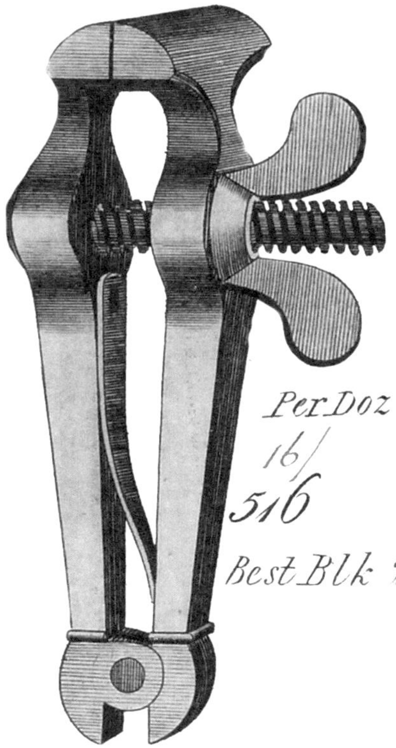

Per Doz
16/
516
Best Blk 20/

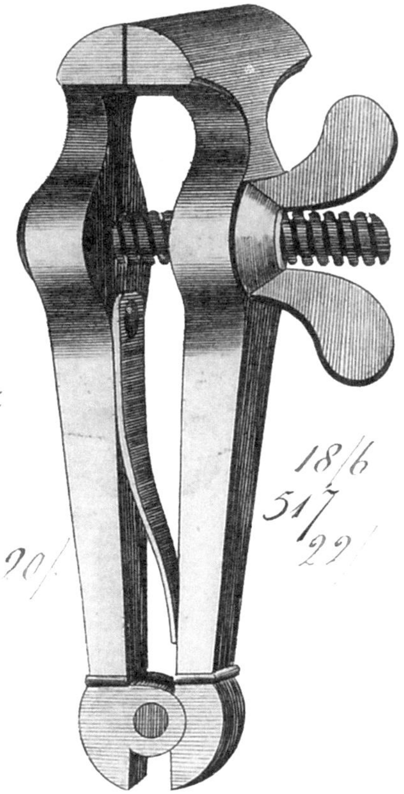

18/6
517
22/

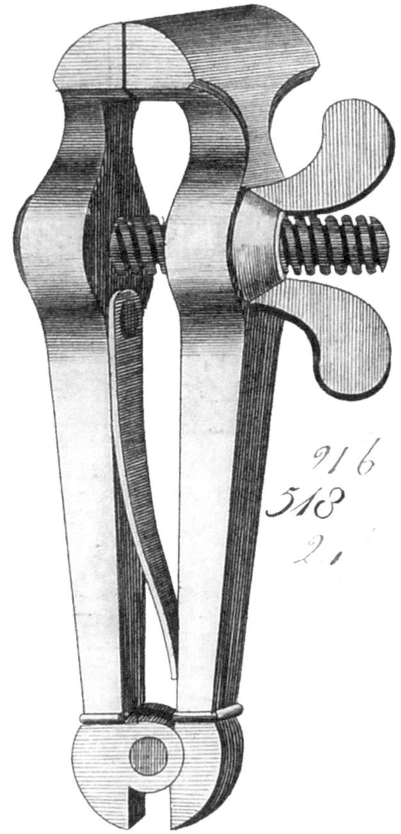

21/6
518
24/

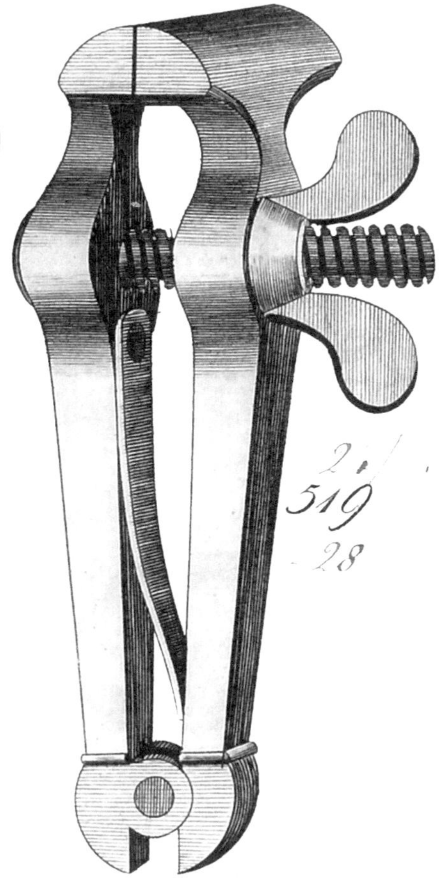

24/
519
28

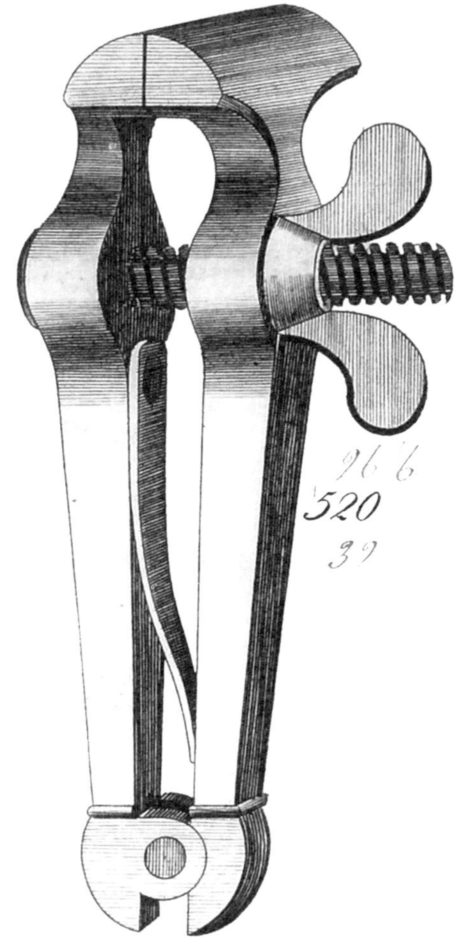

26/6
520
32

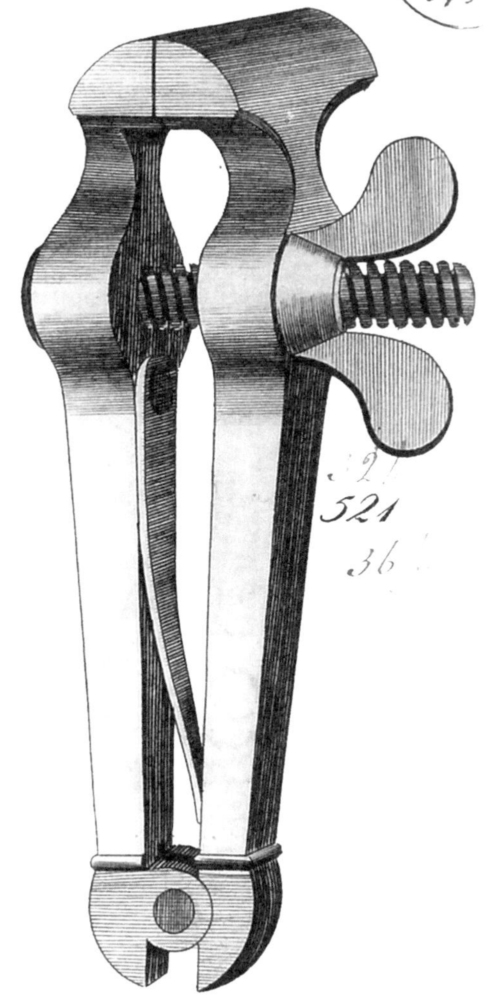

32/
521
36/

May be had Black of a Superior Quality nearly equal to Lancashire

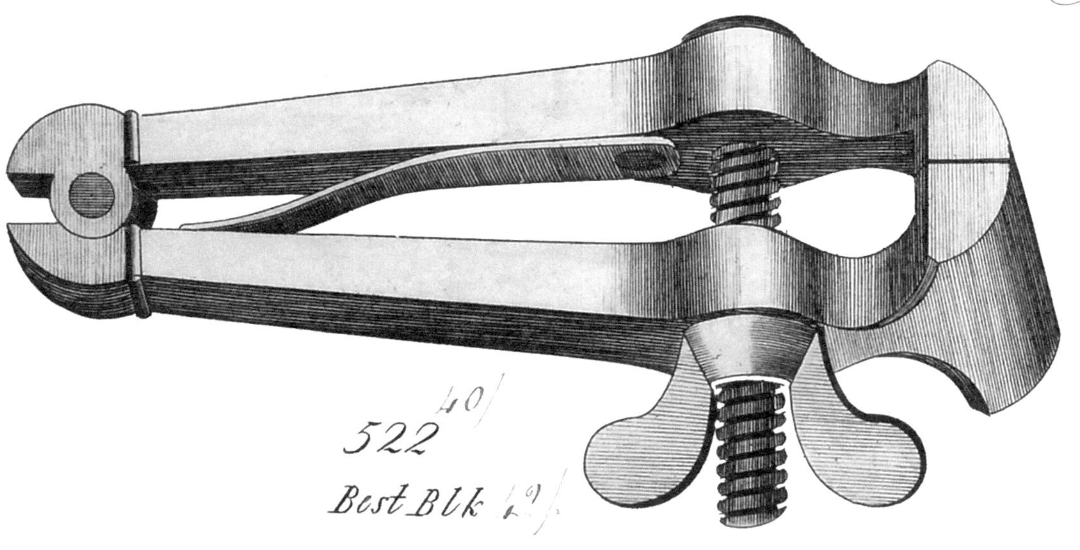

40/
522
Best Blk 42/

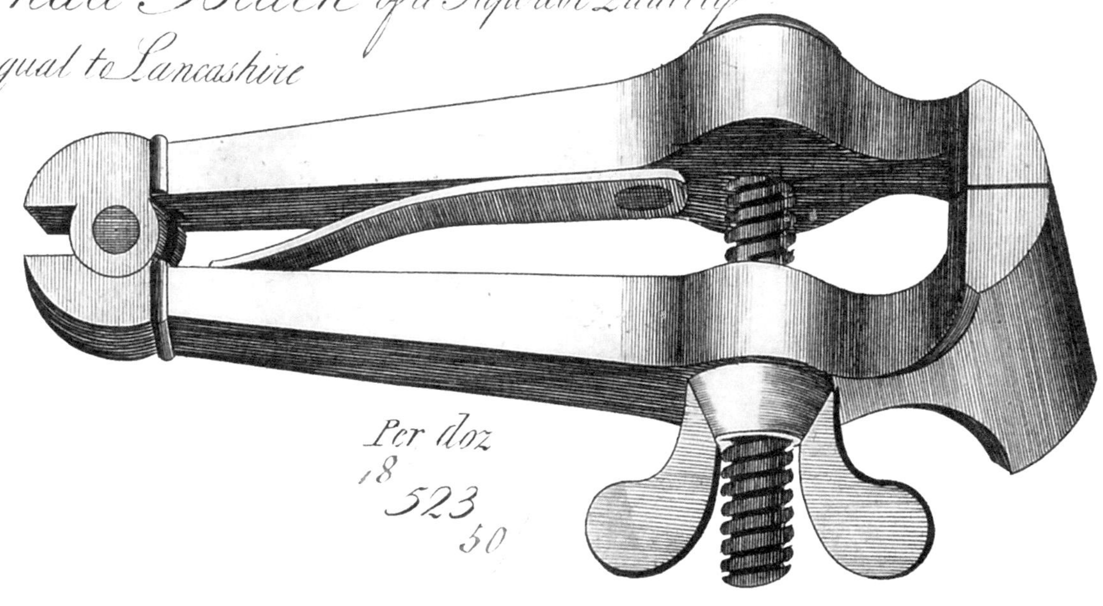

Per doz
18
523
30

Table Bick Irons

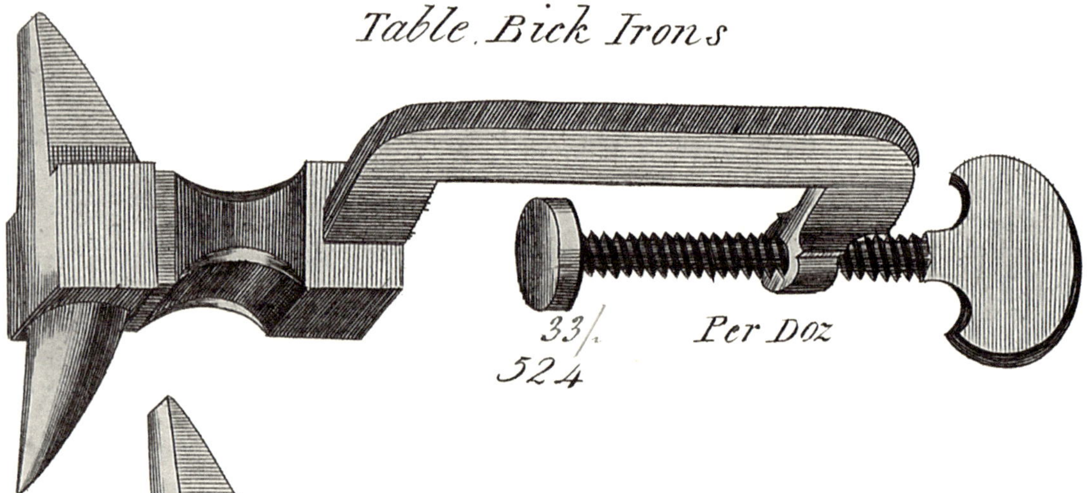

33/. Per Doz

524

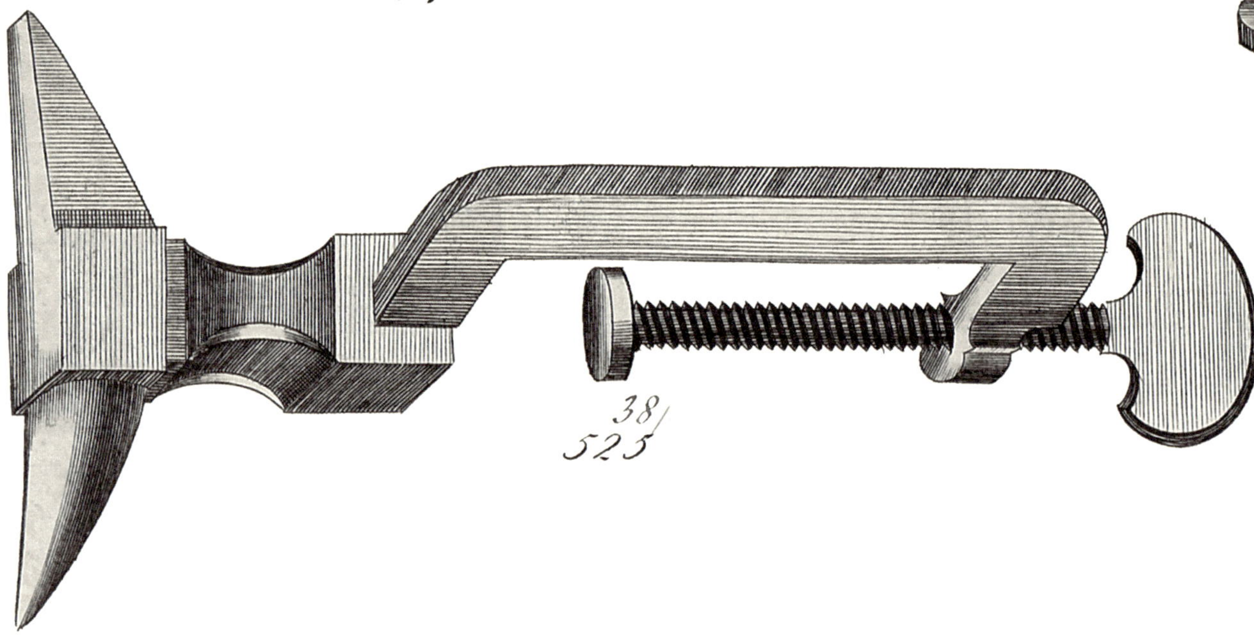

38/

525

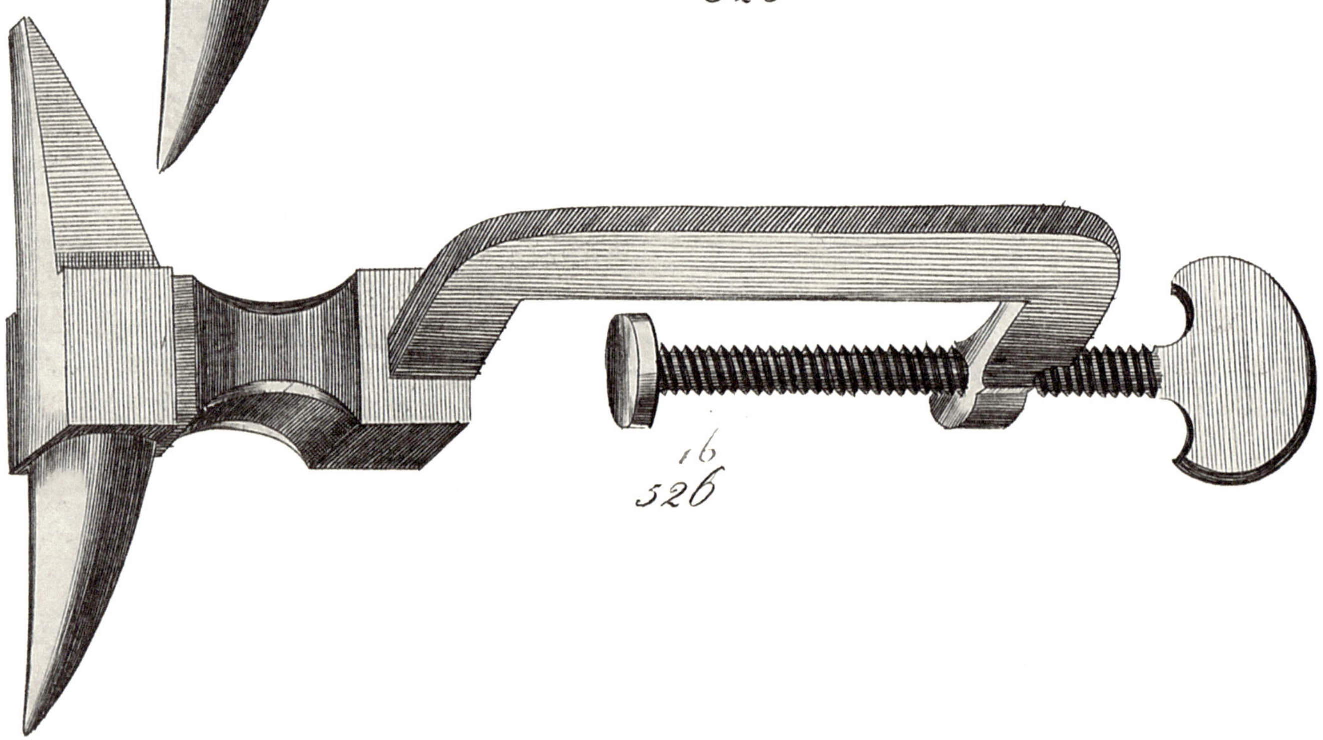

16

526

Table or Bench Vices

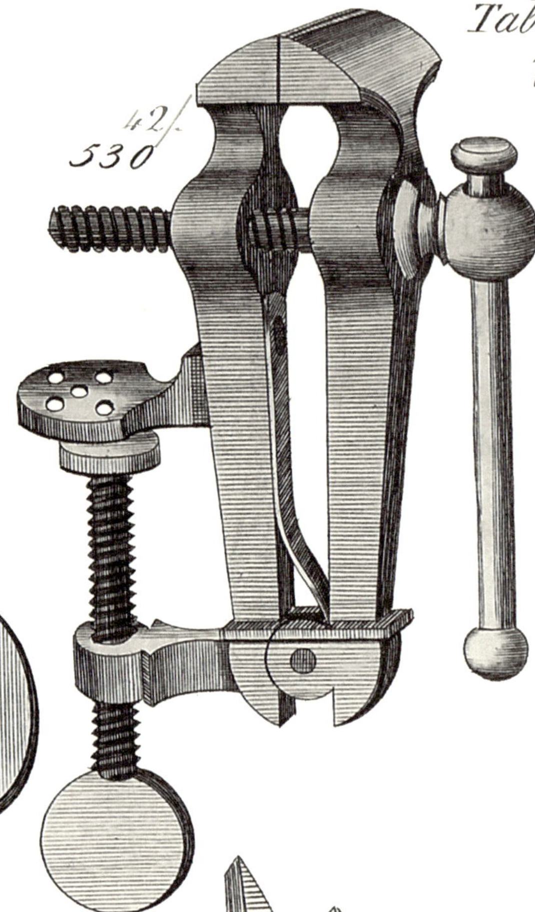

42/.

530

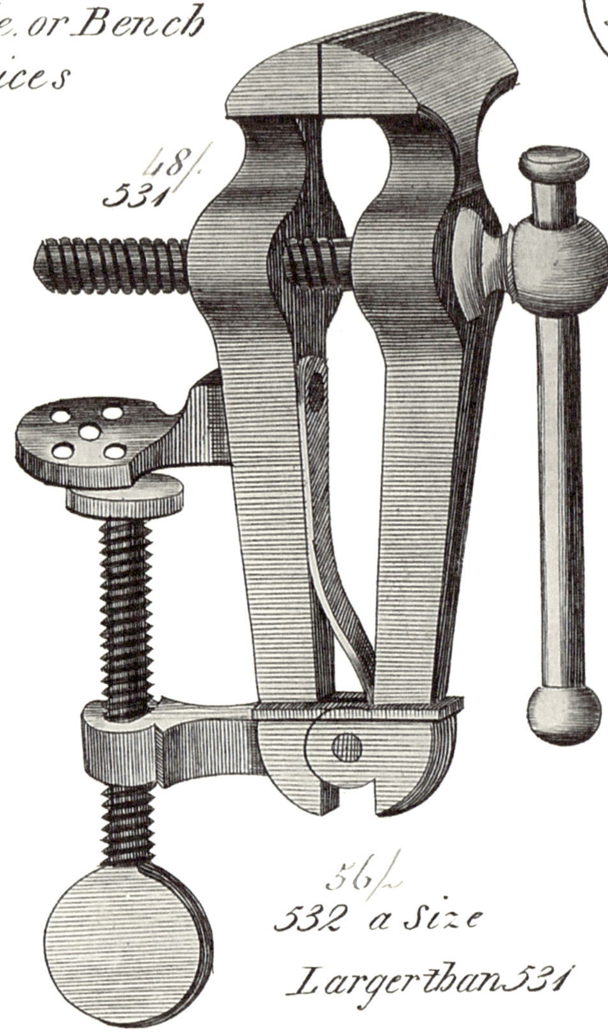

48/.

531

56/.

532 a Size Larger than 531

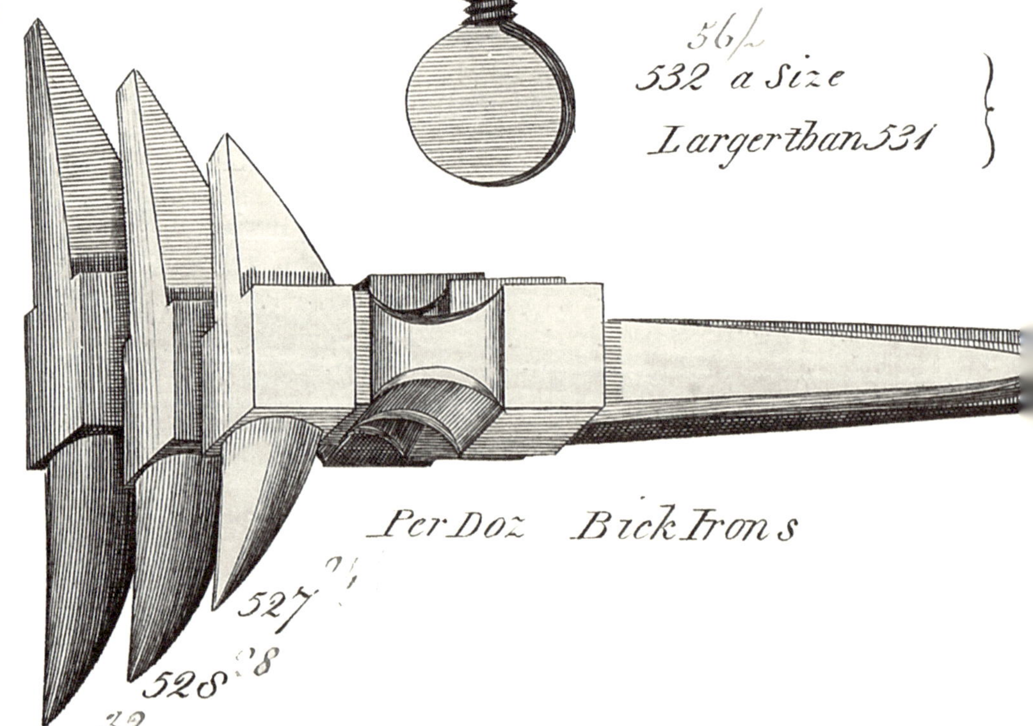

Per Doz Bick Irons

527 24

528 28

529 32

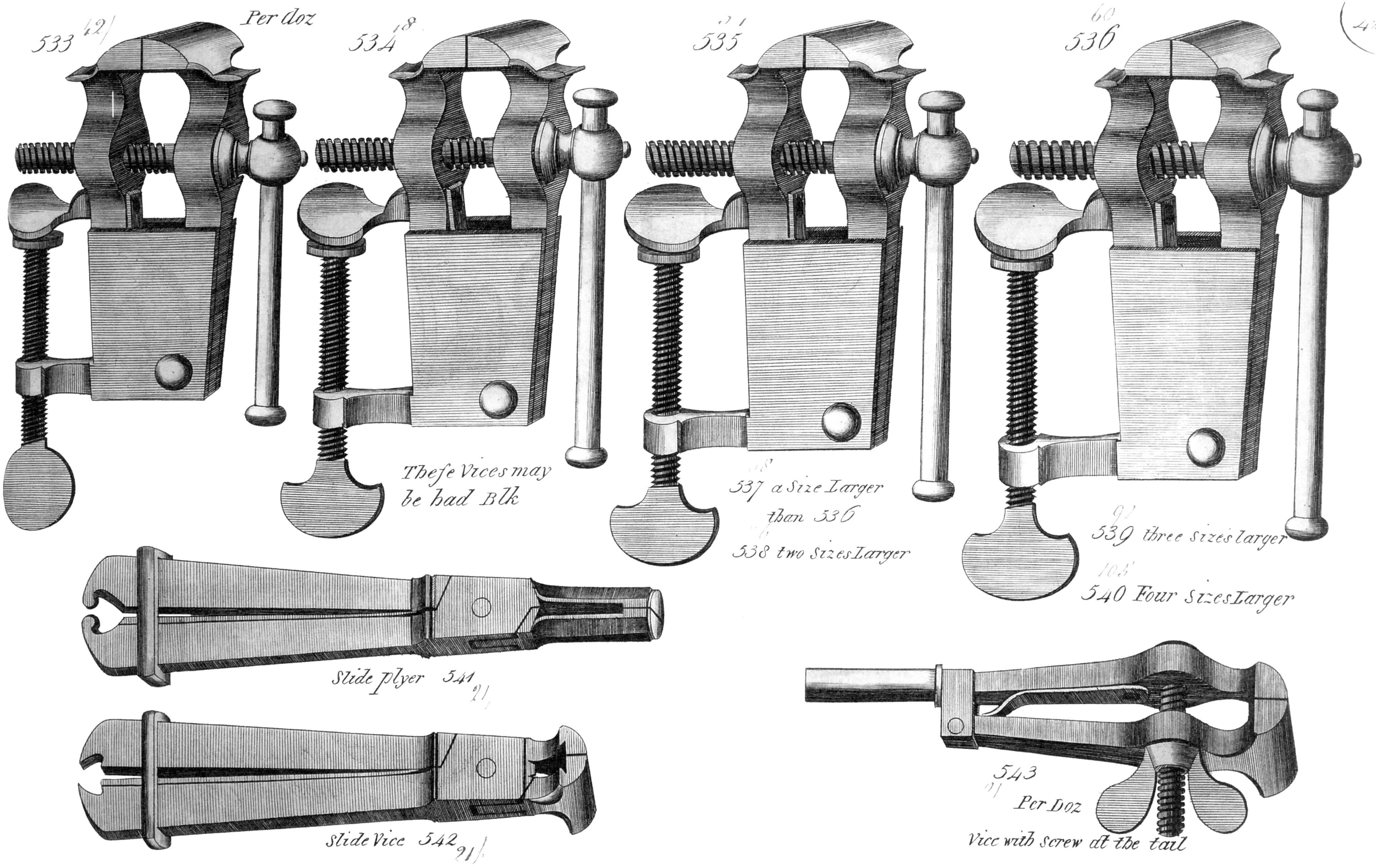
Per doz
533
534
535
536
These Vices may be had Blk
537 a Size Larger than 536
538 two Sizes Larger
539 three Sizes Larger
540 Four Sizes Larger
Slide plyer 541
Slide Vice 542
543
Per Doz
Vice with Screw at the tail

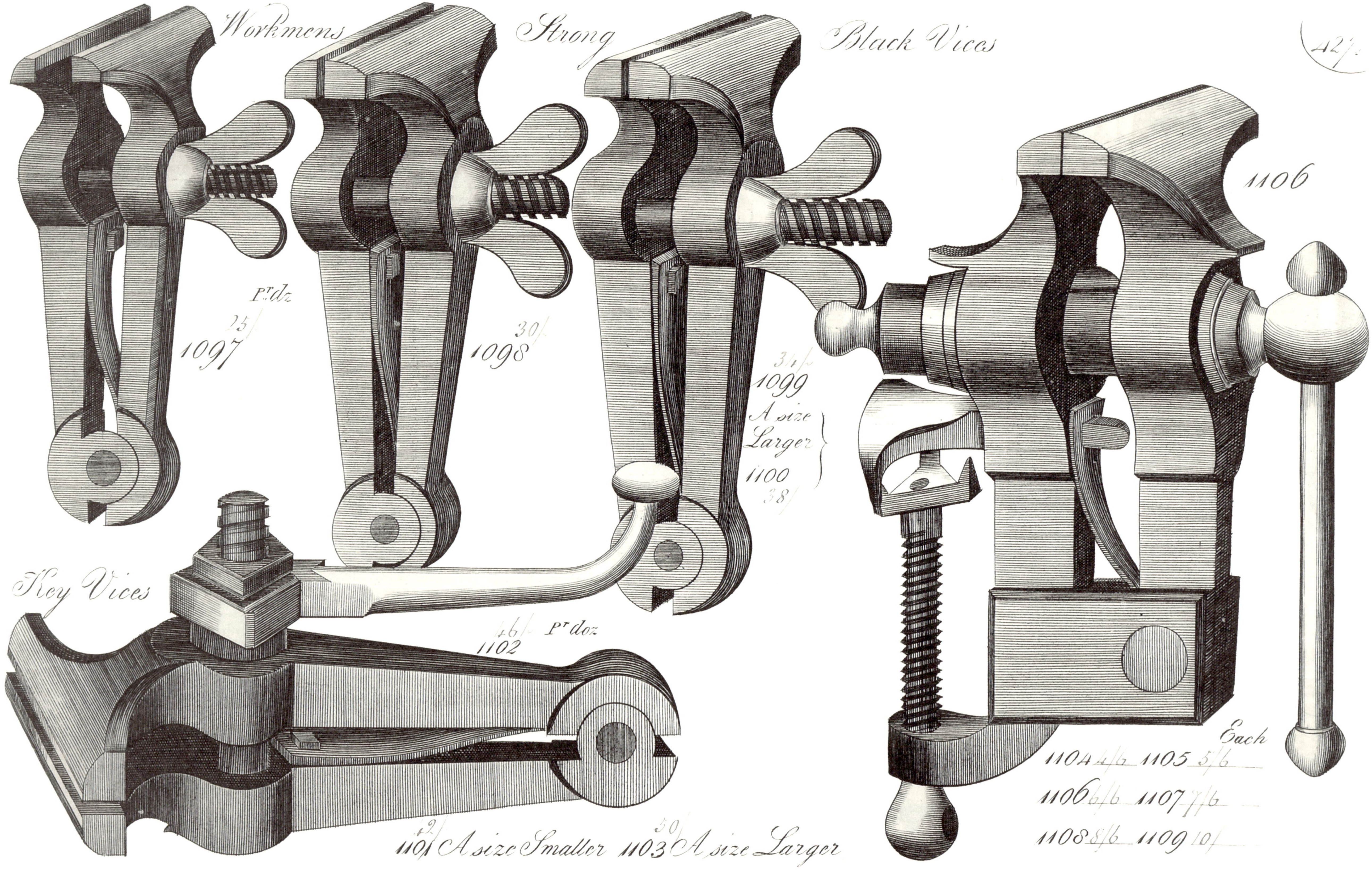
Workmens Strong Black Vices
Pr dz
25/ 1097
30/ 1098
34/ 1099
A size Larger
1100 38/
1106
Key Vices
46/ Pr doz
1102
42/ 1101 A size Smaller
50/ 1103 A size Larger
Each
1104 4/6 1105 5/6
1106 6/6 1107 7/6
1108 8/6 1109 10/

These Steel Boxes open with a Spring

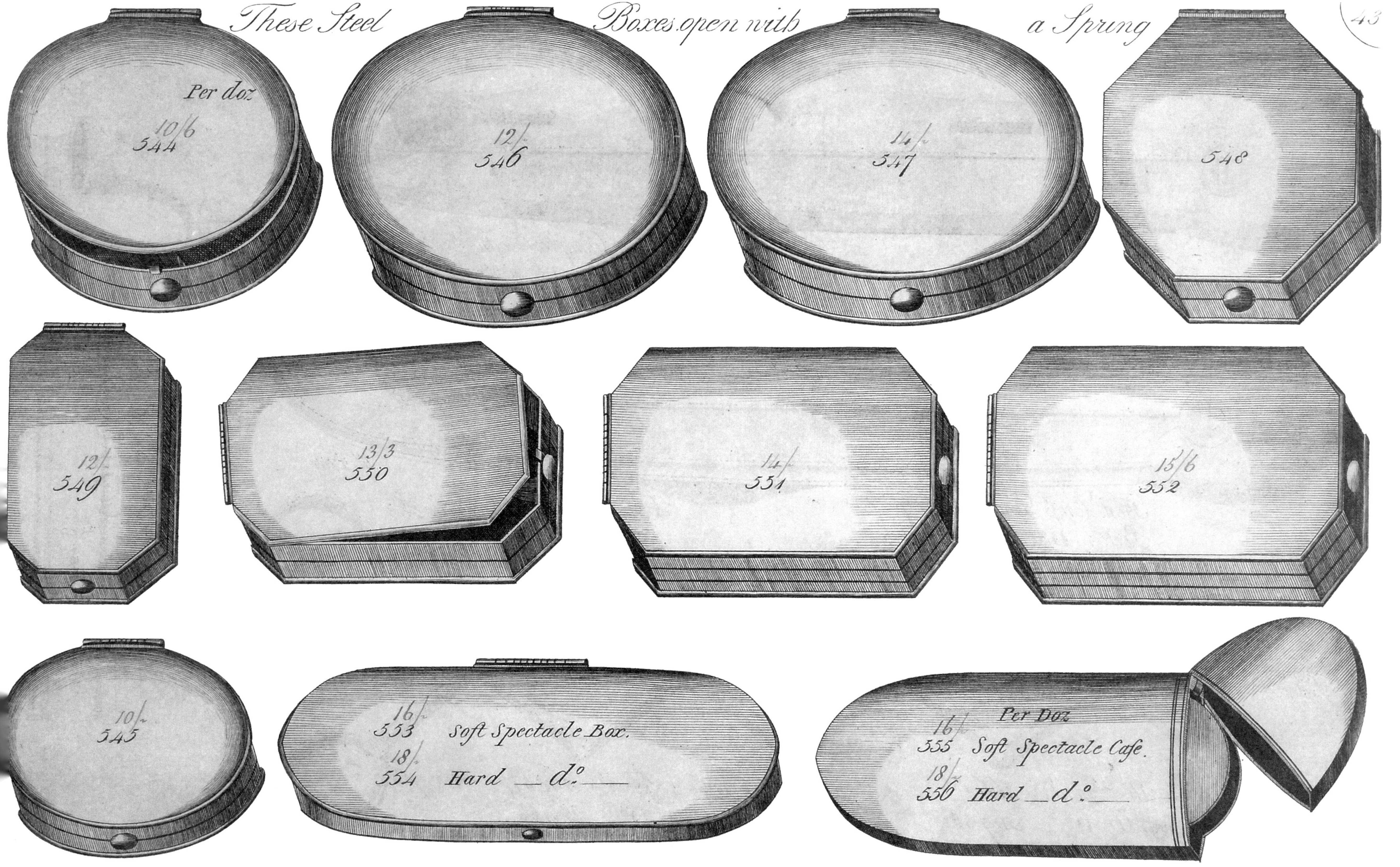

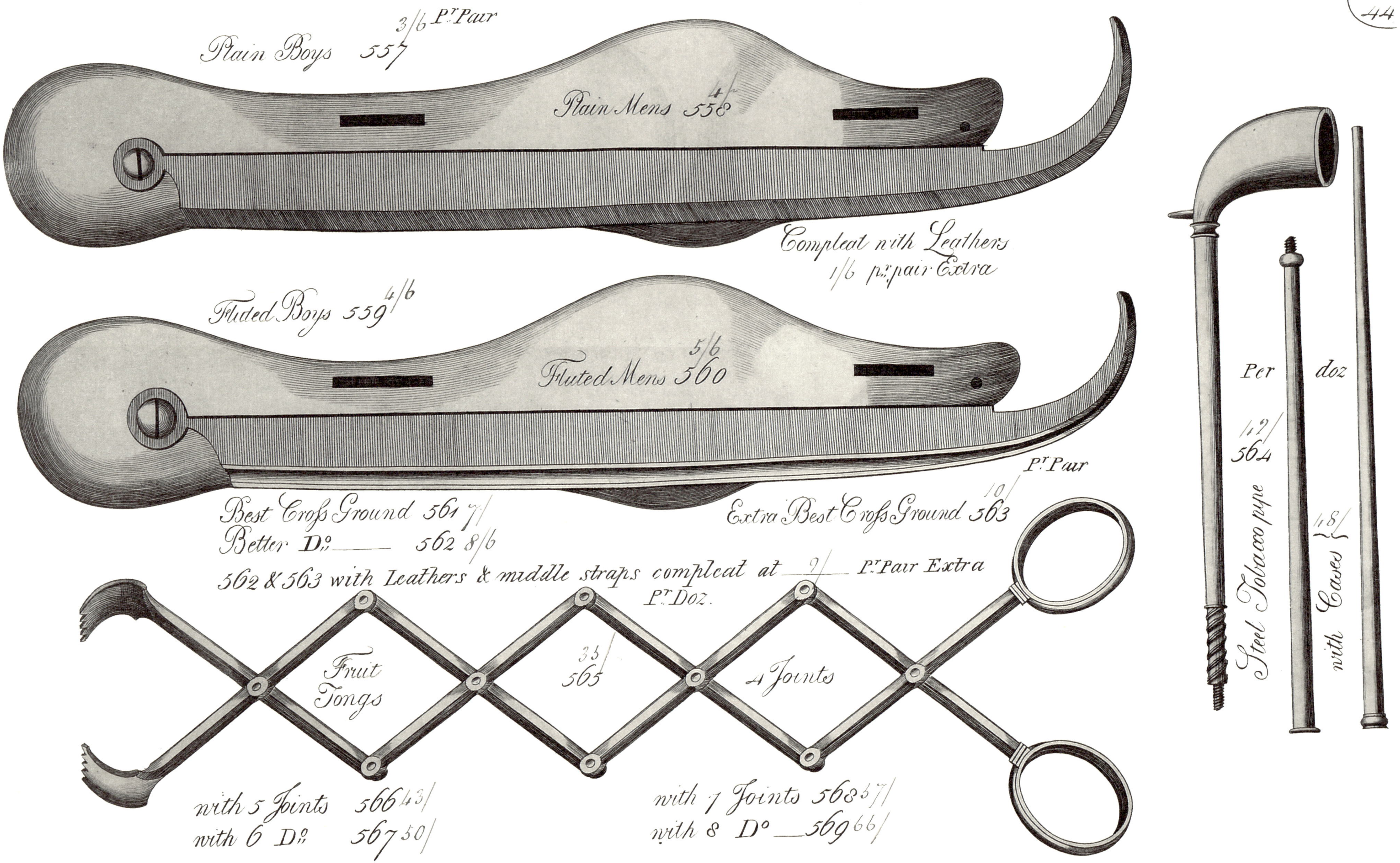
Plain Boys 557 3/6 Pr. Pair
Plain Mens 558 4/
Compleat with Leathers
1/6 pr. pair Extra
Fluted Boys 559 4/6
Fluted Mens 560 5/6
Best Cross Ground 561 7/
Better Do. 562 8/6
Extra Best Cross Ground 563 10/ Pr. Pair
562 & 563 with Leathers & middle straps compleat at 9/ Pr. Pair Extra
Pr. Doz.
Fruit Tongs 565 33/ 4 Joints
with 5 Joints 566 43/
with 6 Do. 567 50/
with 7 Joints 568 57/
with 8 Do 569 66/
Per doz
564 12/
Steel Tobacco pype
with Cases 18/

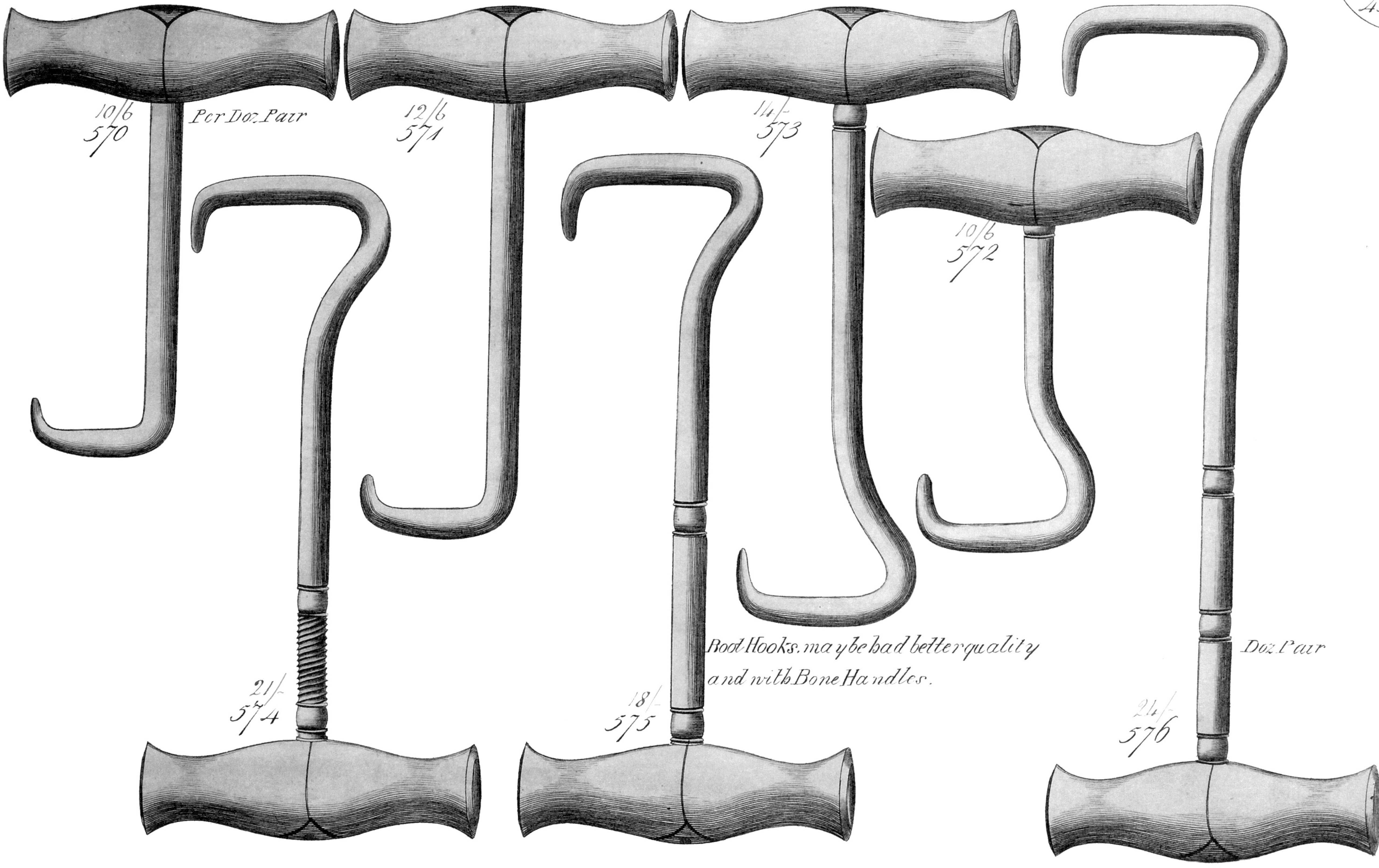
10/6
570
Per Doz. Pair
12/6
571
14/-
573
10/6
572
21/-
574
18/-
575
Boot Hooks, may be had better quality
and with Bone Handles.
24/-
576
Doz. Pair

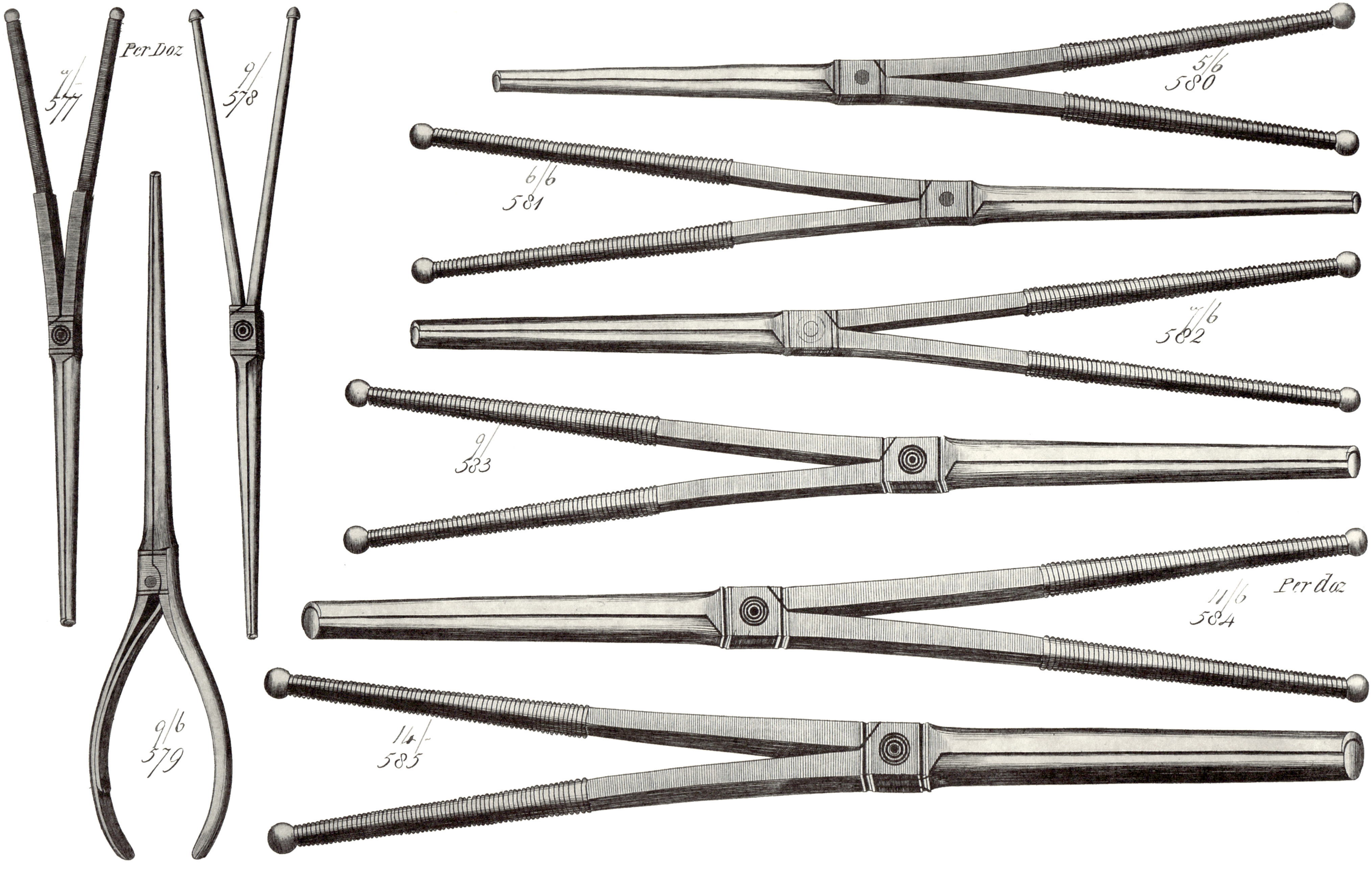

Per Doz
7/-
577
9/
578
9/6
579
5/6
580
6/6
581
7/6
582
9/
583
Per doz
11/6
584
14/-
585

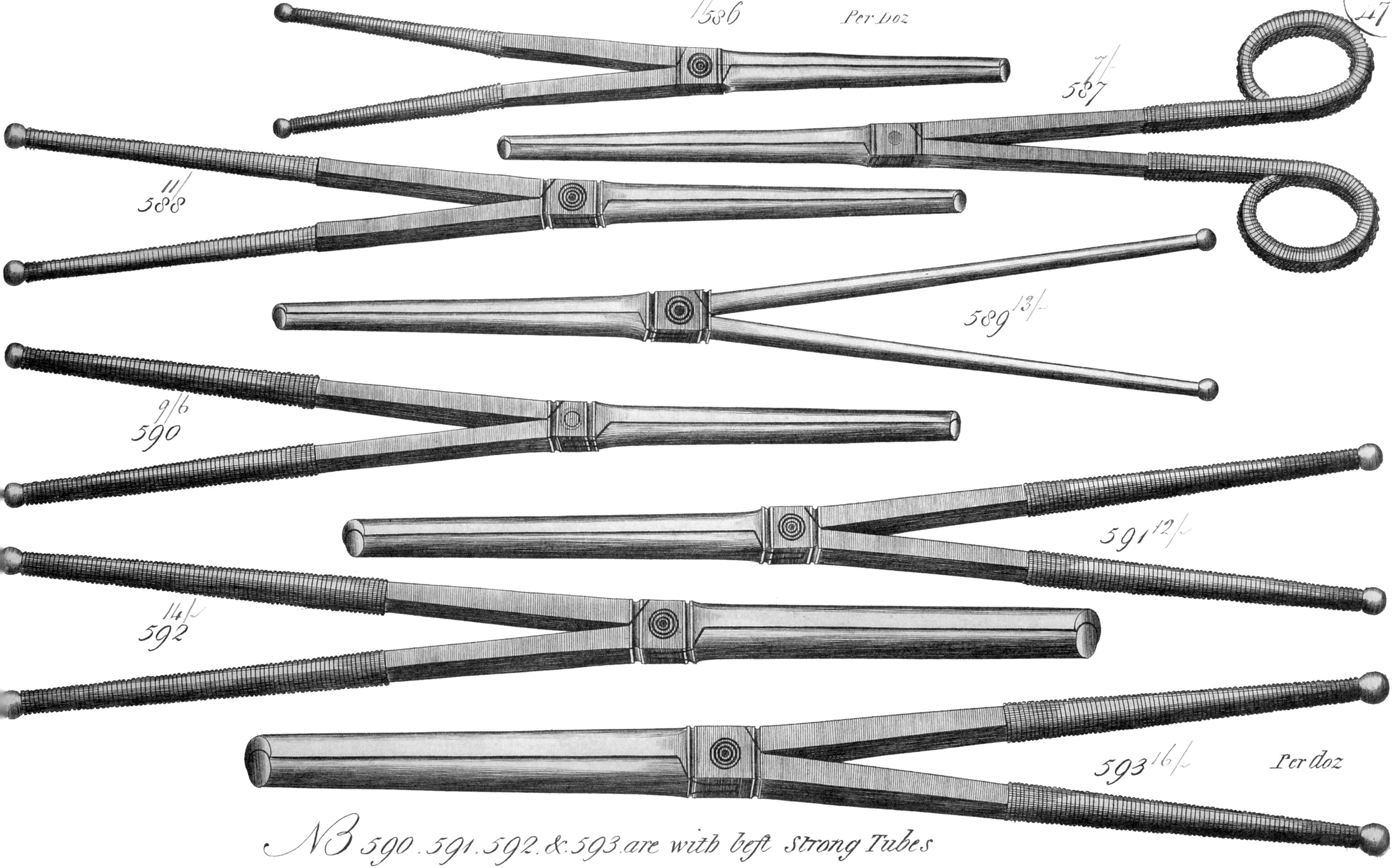

NB 590. 591. 592. & 593. are with best Strong Tubes

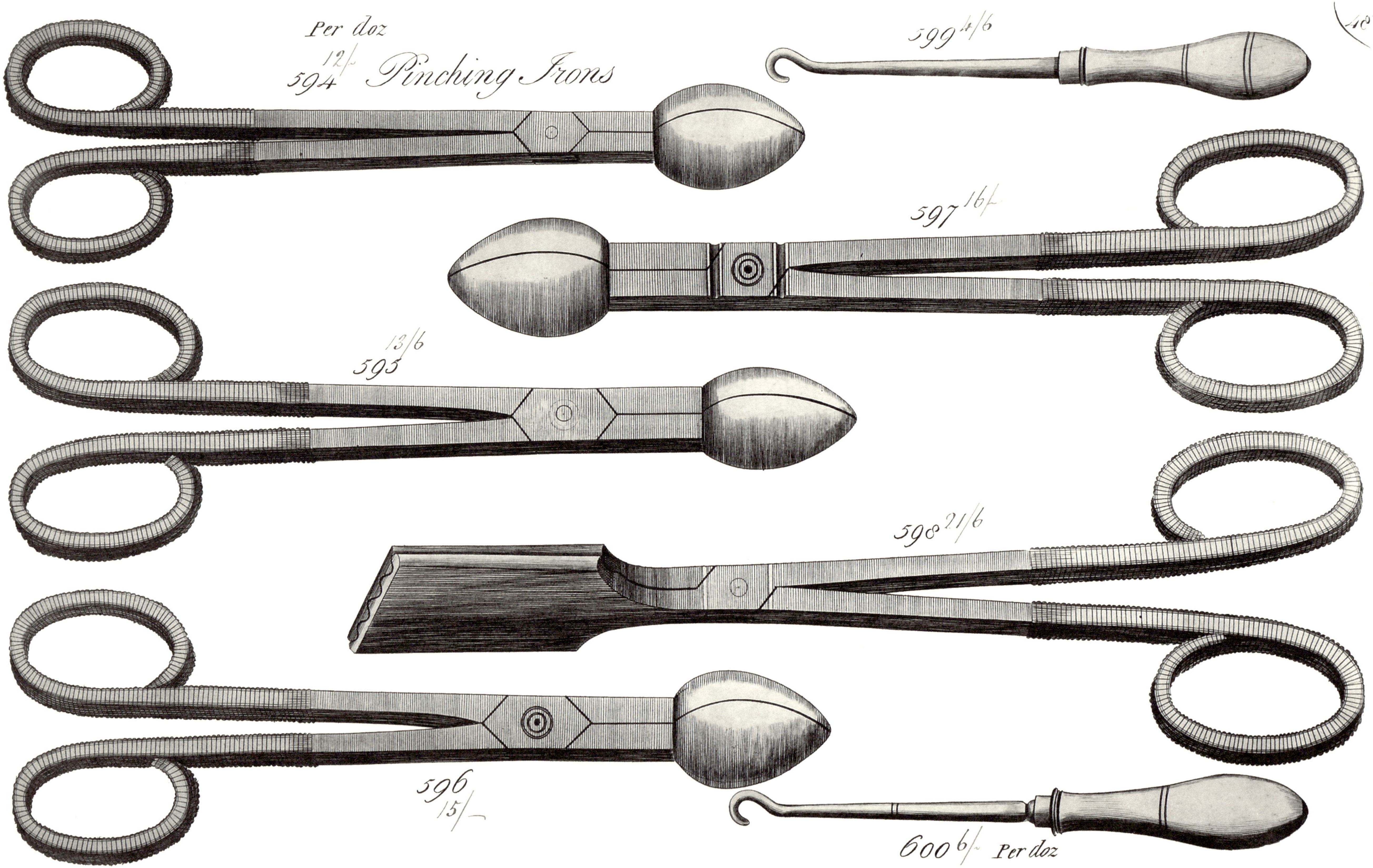
Per doz
594 12/- Pinching Irons
599 4/6
597 16/-
595 13/6
598 21/6
596 15/-
600 6/- Per doz

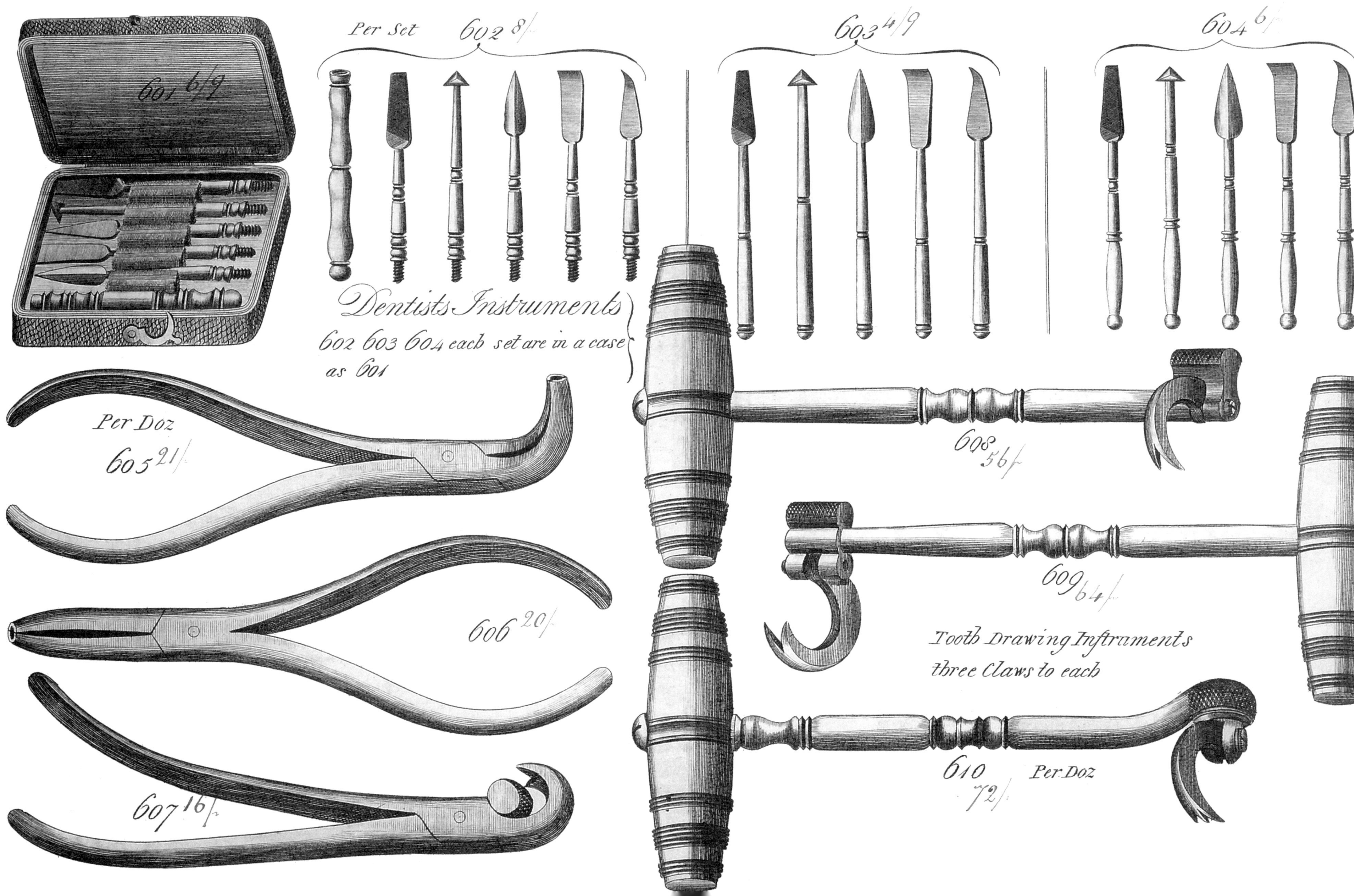
601 6/9
Per Set 602 8/-
603 4/9
604 6/-
Dentists Instruments
602 603 604 each set are in a case as 601
Per Doz
605 21/-
606 20/-
607 16/-
608 56/-
609 64/-
Tooth Drawing Inftruments three Claws to each
610 72/- Per Doz

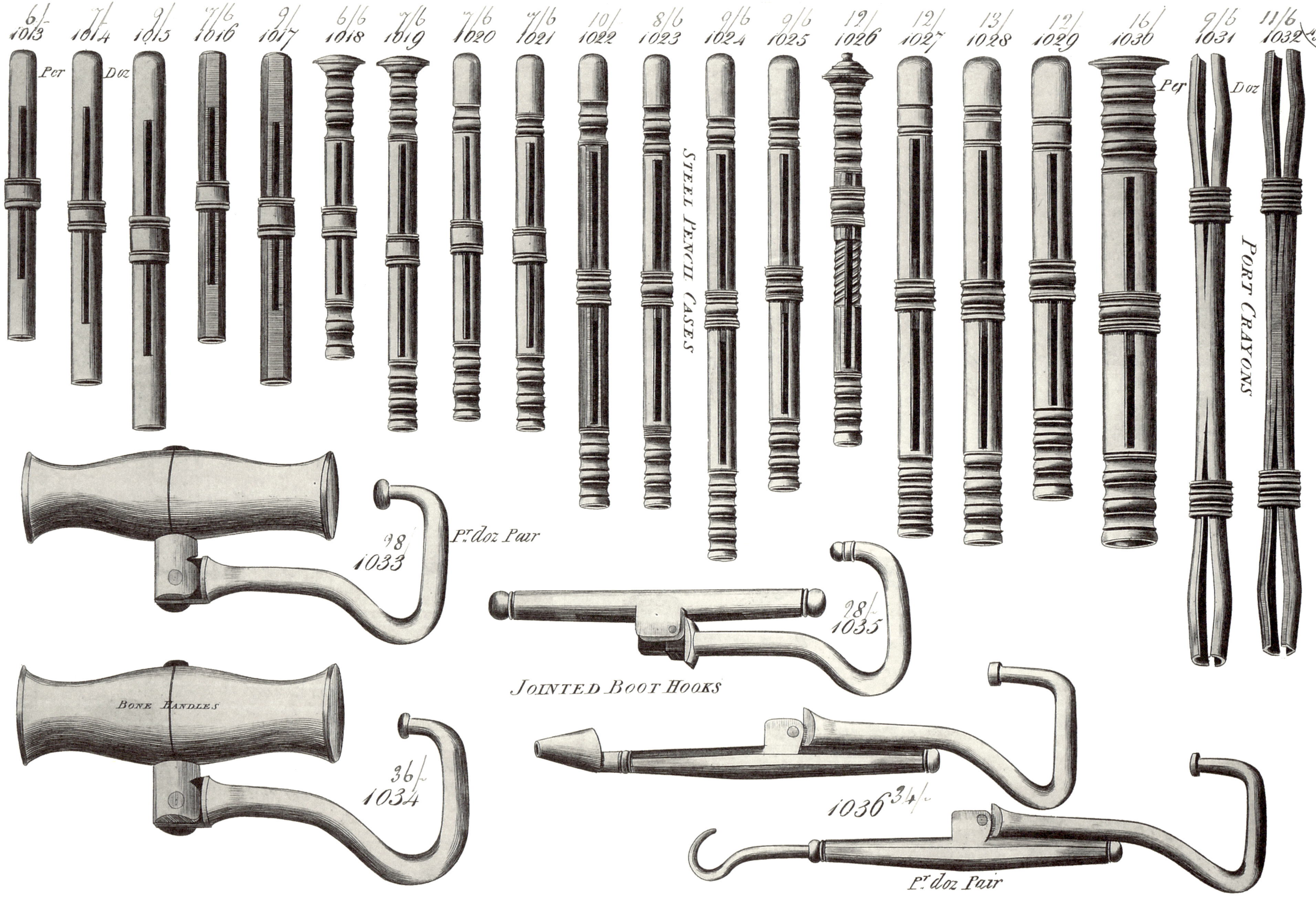

6/- 1013
7/- 1014
9/- 1015
7/6 1016
9/- 1017
6/6 1018
7/6 1019
7/6 1020
7/6 1021
10/- 1022
8/6 1023
9/6 1024
9/6 1025
19/- 1026
12/- 1027
13/- 1028
12/- 1029
16/- 1030
9/6 1031
11/6 1032
Per Doz
Per Doz
STEEL PENCIL CASES
PORT CRAYONS
98/- 1033
Pr. doz Pair
98/- 1035
JOINTED BOOT HOOKS
BONE HANDLES
36/- 1034
1036 34/-
Pr. doz Pair

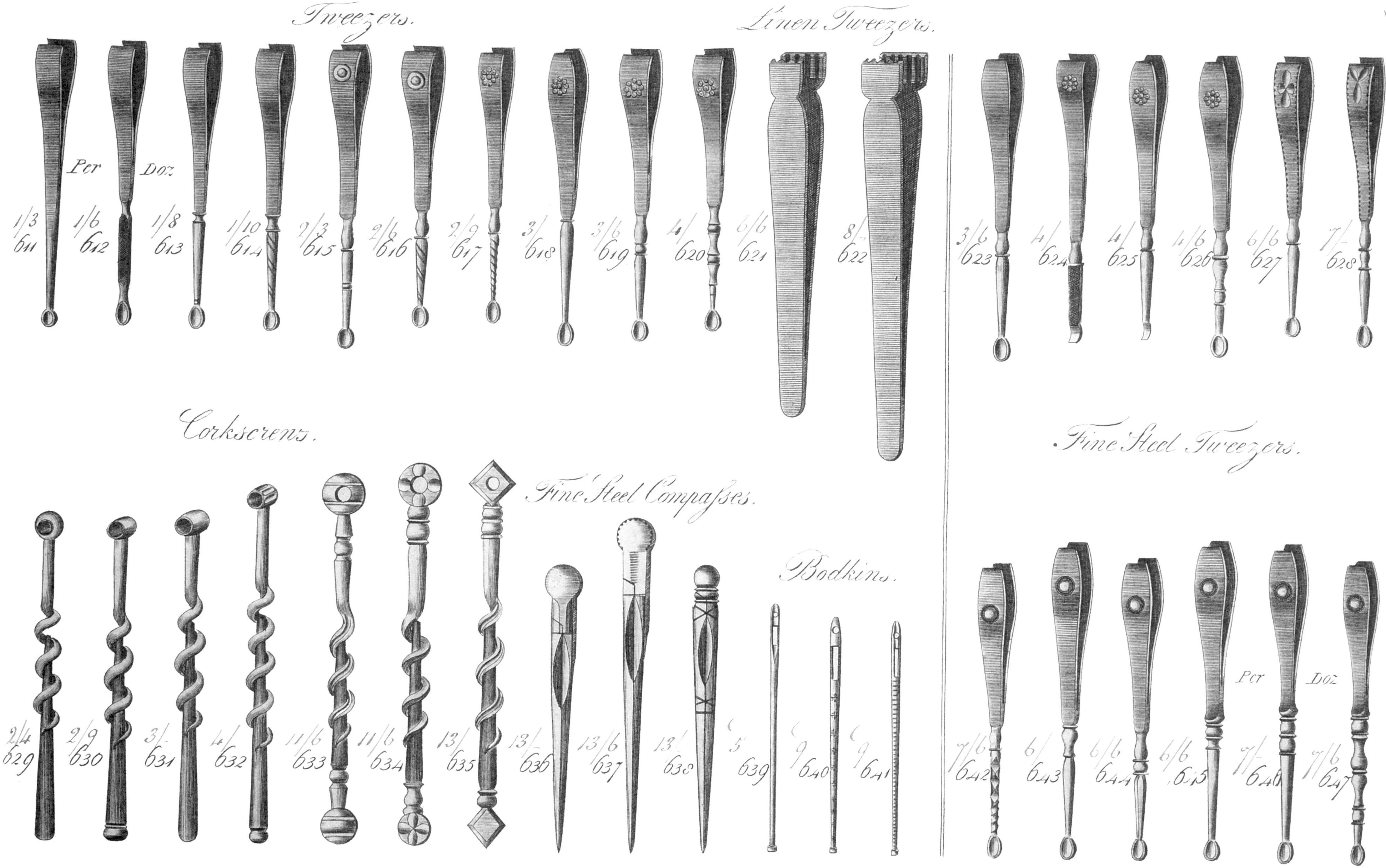
Tweezers.
Per Doz
1/3 611
1/6 612
1/8 613
1/10 614
2/3 615
2/6 616
2/9 617
3/ 618
3/6 619
4/ 620
Linen Tweezers.
6/6 621
8/ 622
3/6 623
4/ 624
4/ 625
4/6 626
6/6 627
7/ 628
Corkscrews.
2/4 629
2/9 630
3/ 631
4/ 632
11/6 633
11/6 634
13/ 635
Fine Steel Compasses.
13/ 636
13/6 637
13/ 638
Bodkins.
5 639
9 640
9 641
Fine Steel Tweezers.
Per Doz
7/6 642
6/ 643
6/6 644
6/6 645
7/ 646
7/6 647

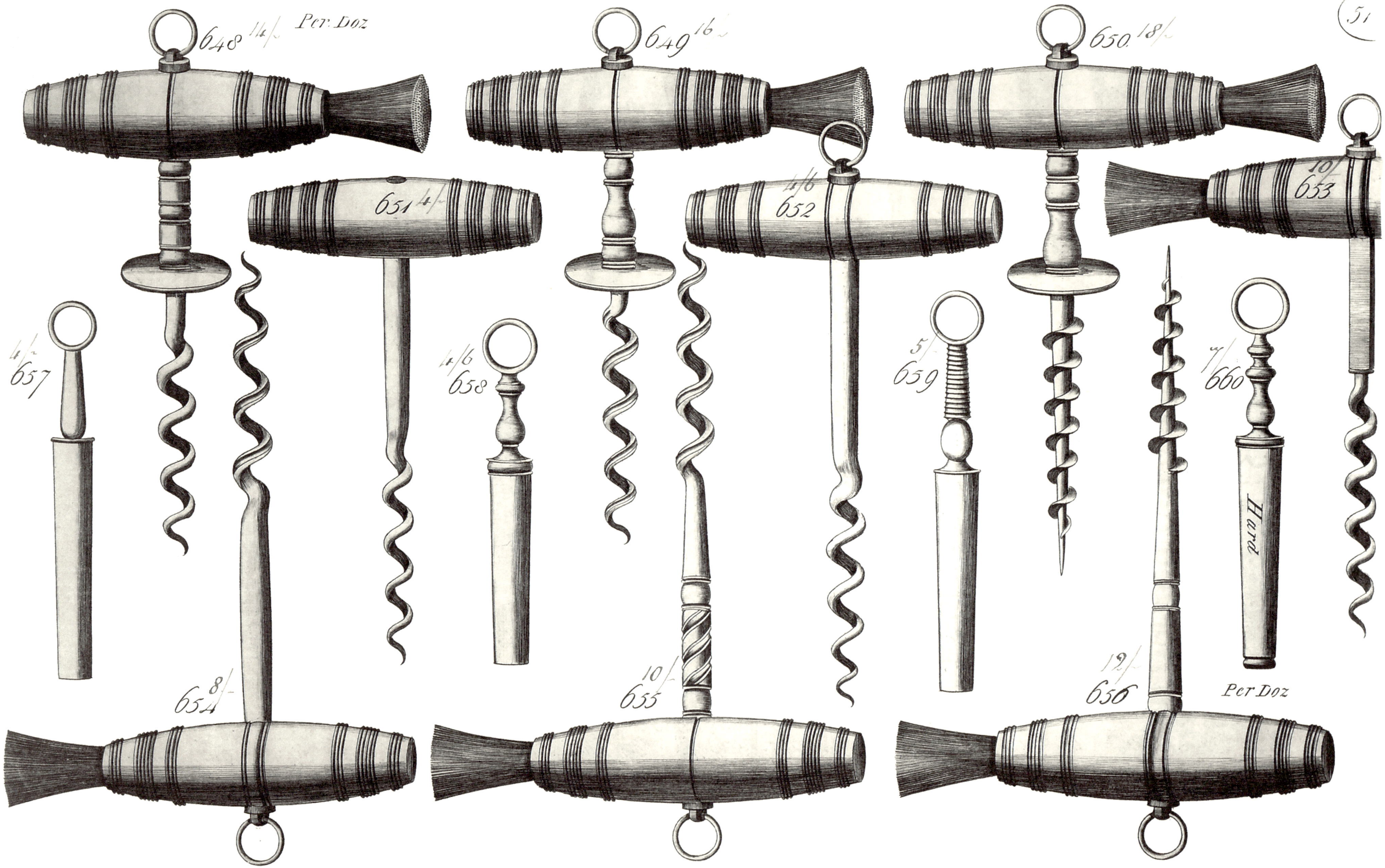
648 14/- Per Doz
649 16/-
650 18/-
651 4/-
652 4/6
653 10/-
657 4/-
658 4/6
659 5/-
660 7/-
Hard
654 8/-
655 10/-
656 12/-
Per Doz

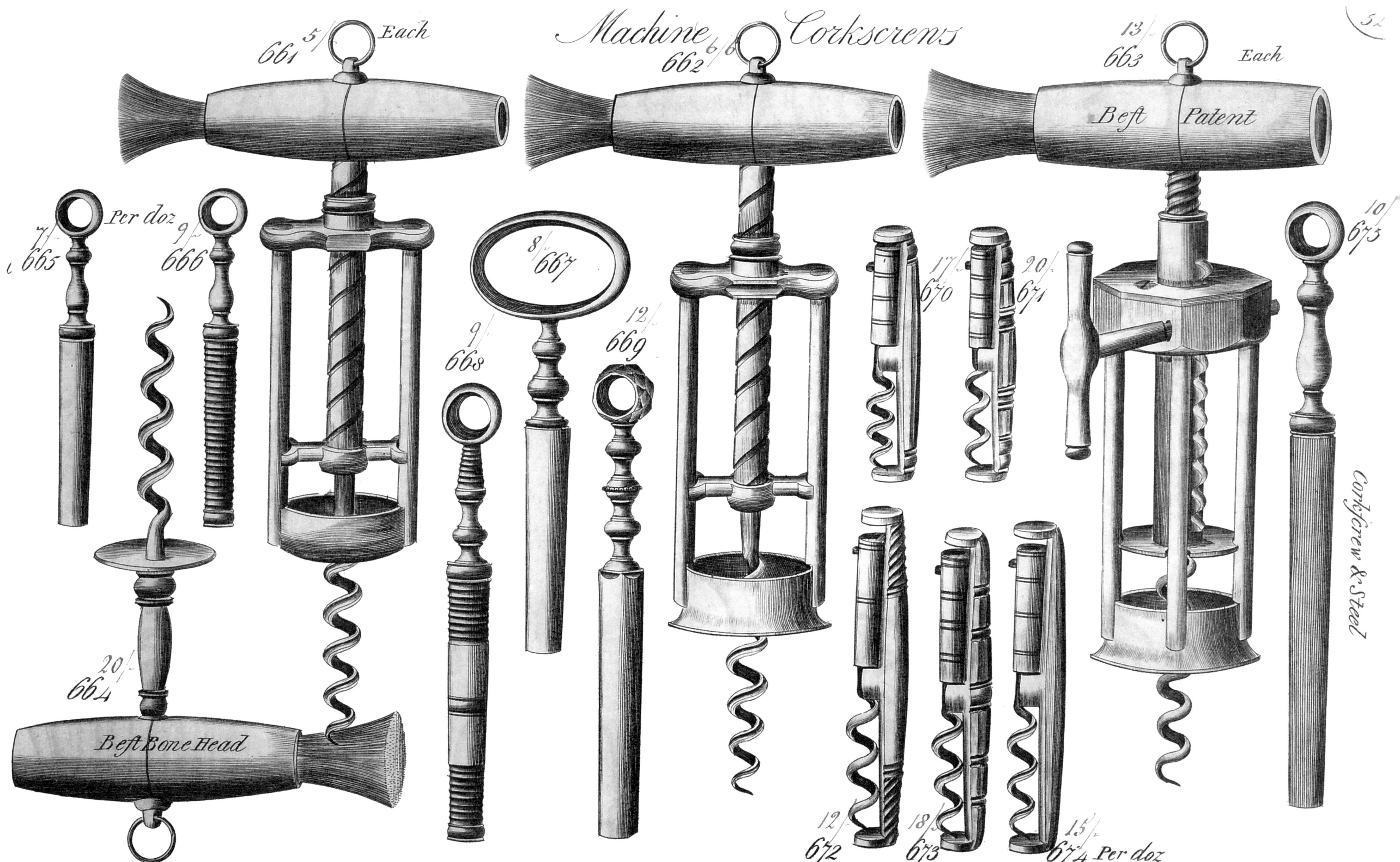
Machine Corkscrews
661 5/ Each
662 6/6
663 13/ Each
Best Patent
7/ Per doz
665
9/
666
8/
667
9/
668
12/
669
17/
670
20/
671
10/
675
Corkscrew & Steel
20/
664
Best Bone Head
12/
672
18/
673
15/
674 Per doz

2/6
676
Per doz
5/-
677
6/6
677½
Hard.
Boot Hook
Pr. Single
Doz
6/-
678
Horse Picker
6/-
679
8/6
680
5/-
681
7/-
682
8/-
683
Vial Corkscrews.
9/6
684
13/-
685
9/-
686
17/-
687
7/-
688
Extra Best.
10/6
689
8/-
690
9/-
691
7/-
692
9/6
693
10/6
694
14/-
695
12/6
696
24/-
697
Pr. doz
56/-
698

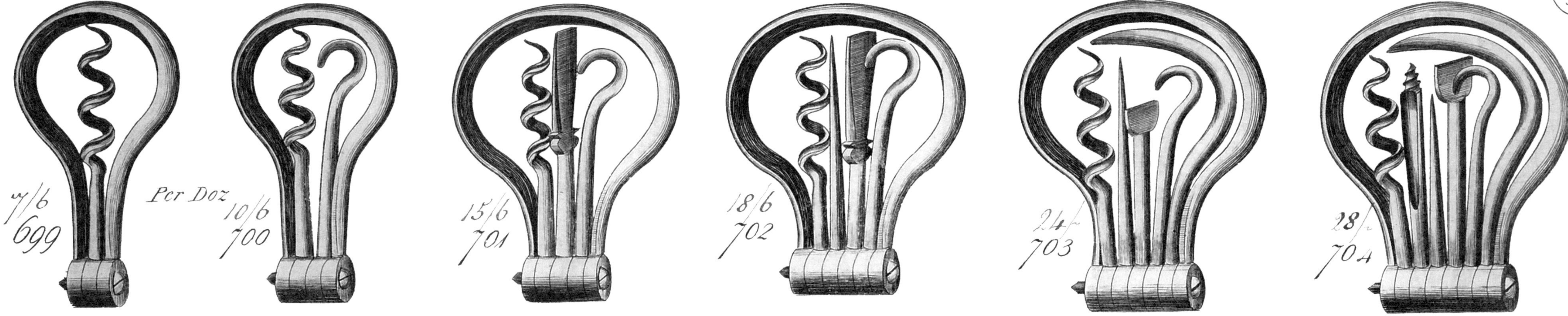

7/6 699

Per Doz 10/6 700

15/6 701

18/6 702

24/- 703

28/- 704

Best Round Joint Corkscrews &c. &c.

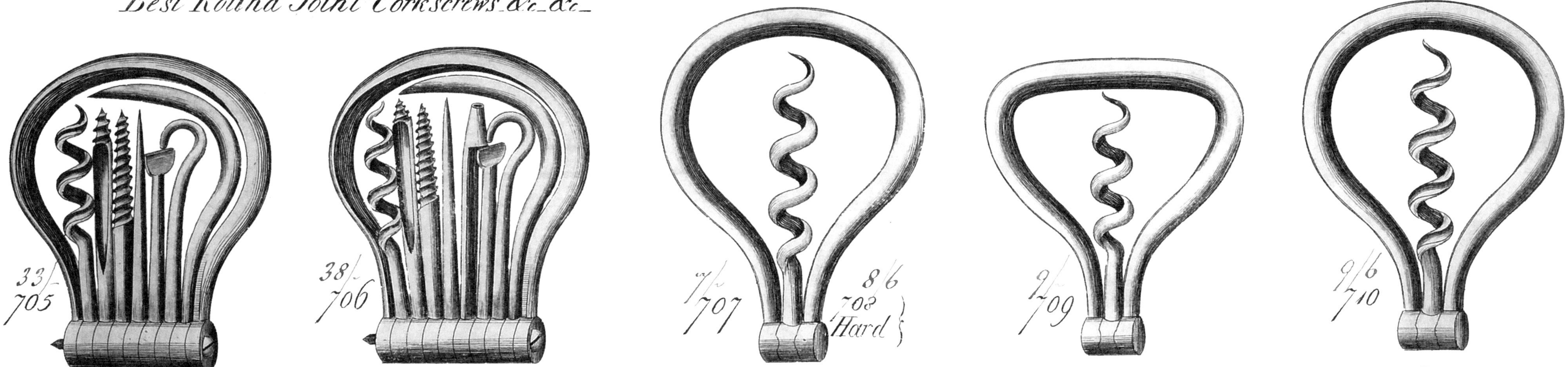

33/- 705

38/- 706

7/- 707

8/6 708 Hard

9/- 709

9/6 710

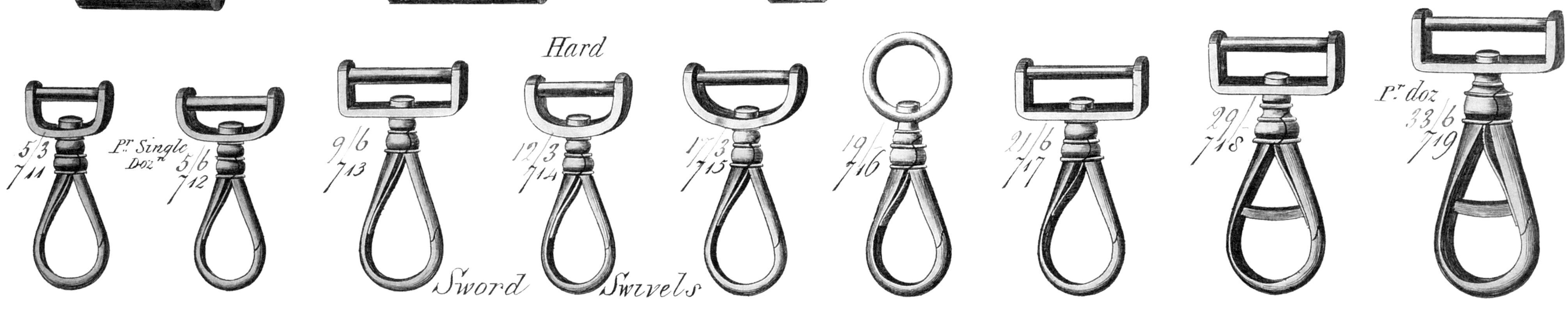

5/3 711

Pr. Single Dozn 5/6 712

9/6 713

Hard 12/3 714

17/3 715

19/- 716

21/6 717

29/- 718

Pr. doz 33/6 719

Sword Swivels

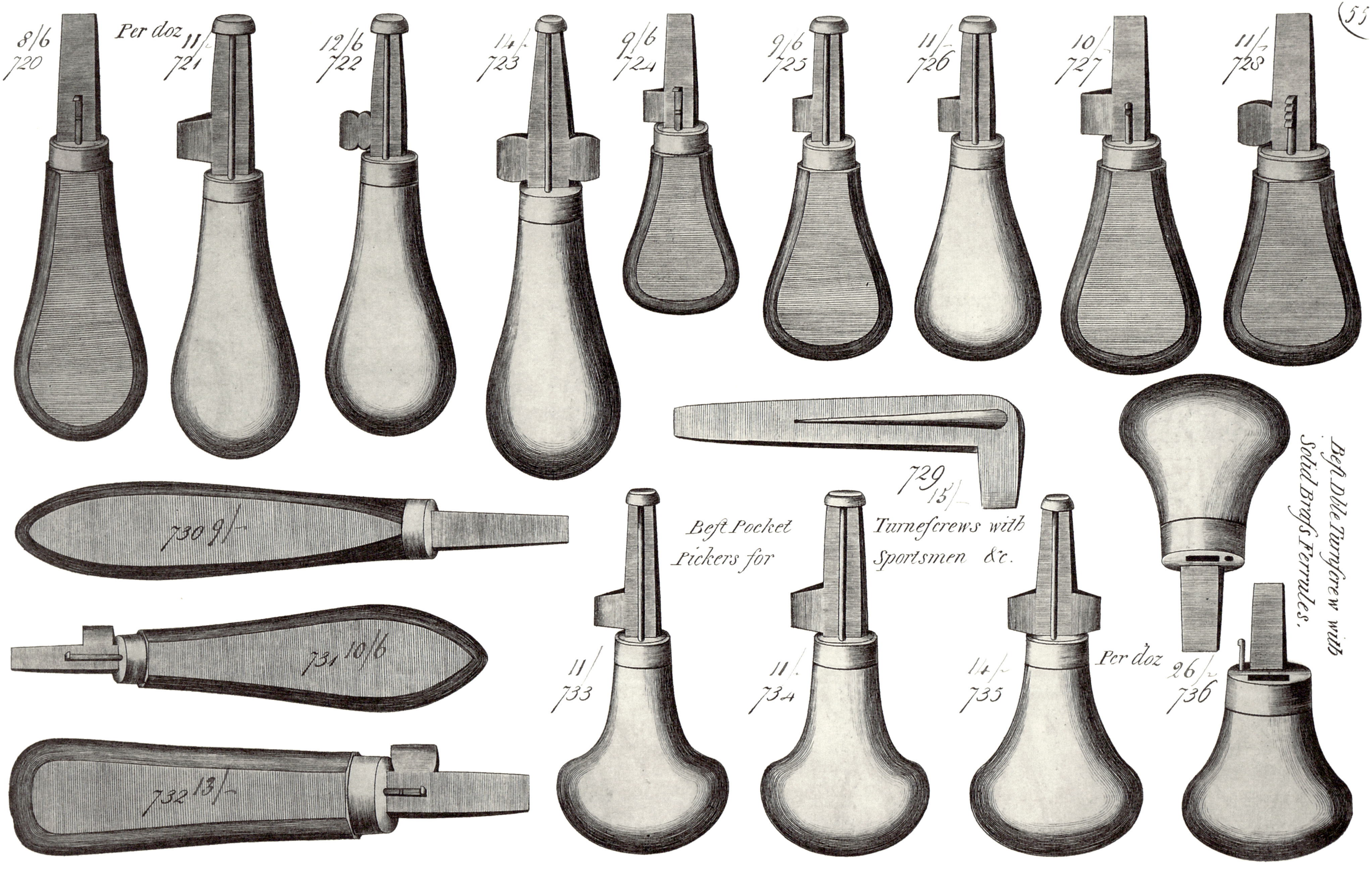
8/6
720
Per doz
11/-
721
12/6
722
14/-
723
9/6
724
9/6
725
11/-
726
10/-
727
11/-
728
729
15/-
Beſt Dble Turnſcrew with
Solid Braſs Ferrules.
730 9/-
731 10/6
732 13/-
Beſt Pocket Turneſcrews with
Pickers for Sportsmen &c.
11/
733
11/-
734
14/-
735
Per doz
26/-
736

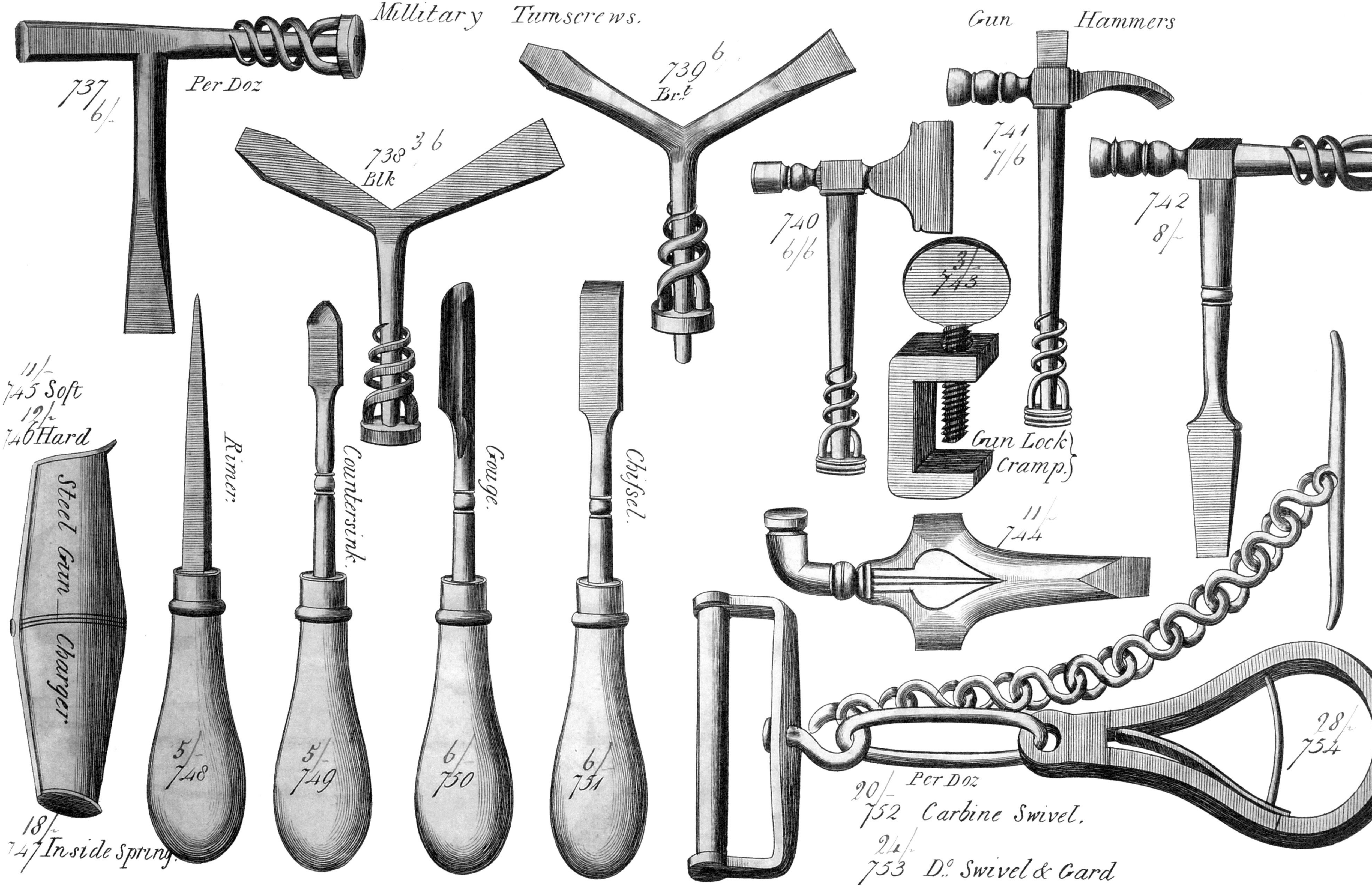
Millitary Turnscrews.
Gun Hammers
737 6/- Per Doz
738 3/6 Blk
739 6/- Brt
740 6/6
741 7/6
742 8/-
743 3/-
Gun Lock Cramp.
744 11/-
745 Soft 11/-
746 Hard 12/-
Steel Gun Charger
747 Inside Spring 18/-
Rimer
748 5/-
Countersink.
749 5/-
Gouge.
750 6/-
Chisel.
751 6/-
754 28/-
752 Carbine Swivel. 20/- Per Doz
753 Do. Swivel & Gard 24/-

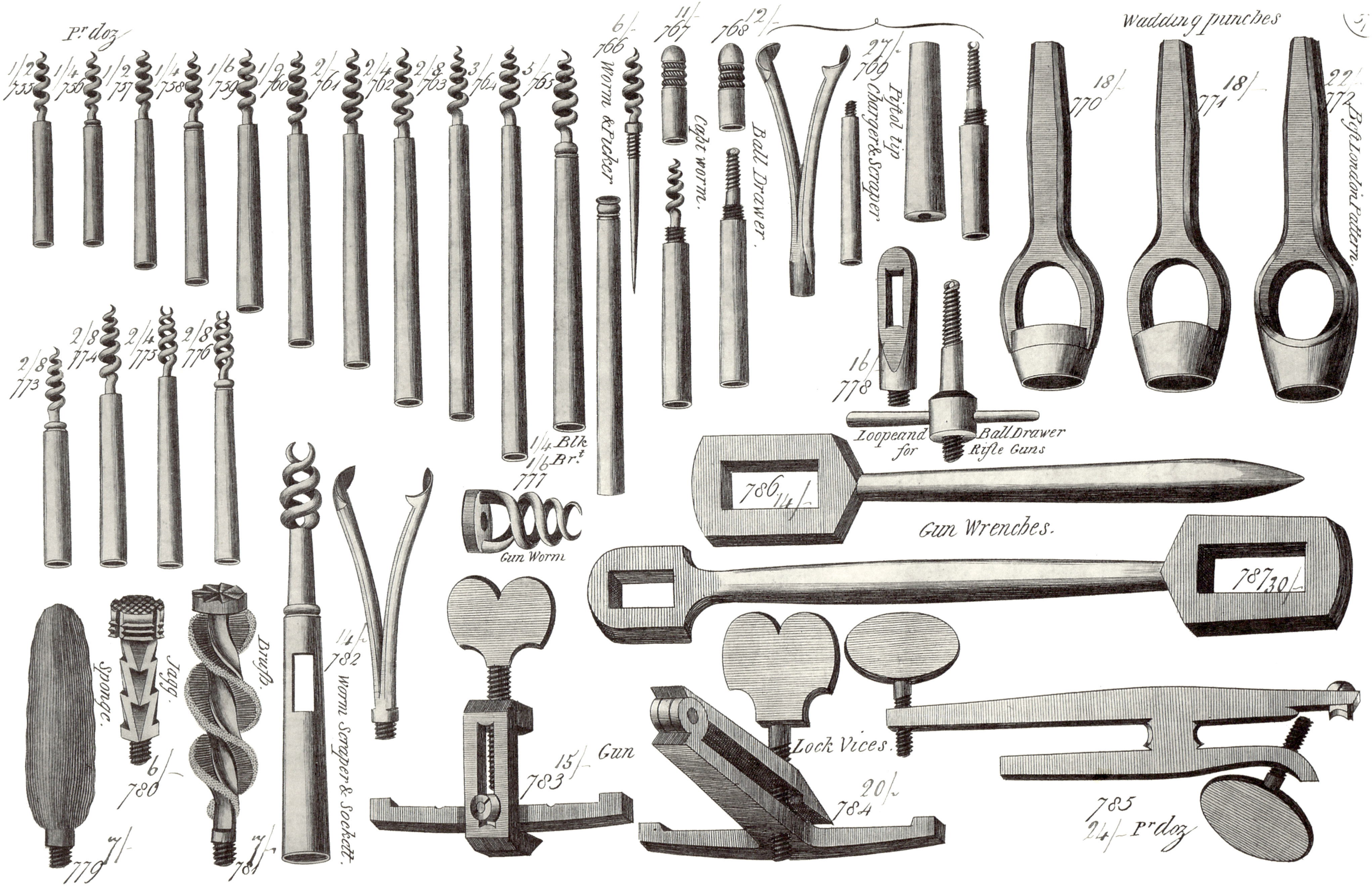
Pr doz
1/2 755
1/4 756
1/2 757
1/4 758
1/6 759
1/9 760
2/ 761
2/4 762
2/8 763
3/ 764
3/ 765
6/ 766 Worm & Picker
11/ 767
768 12/
Cast worm.
Ball Drawer.
27/ 769 Pistol tip Charger & Scraper
Wadding punches
18/ 770
18/ 771
22/ 772 Best London Pattern.
2/8 773
2/8 774
2/4 775
2/8 776
1/4 Blk 1/6 Brt 777
Gun Worm
16/ 778
Loop and for Ball Drawer Rifle Guns
786 14/
Gun Wrenches.
787 30/
Sponge.
Jagg.
Brush.
7/ 779
6/ 780
7/ 781
14/ 782 Worm Scraper & Sockett.
15/ 783 Gun
Lock Vices.
20/ 784
785 24/ Pr doz

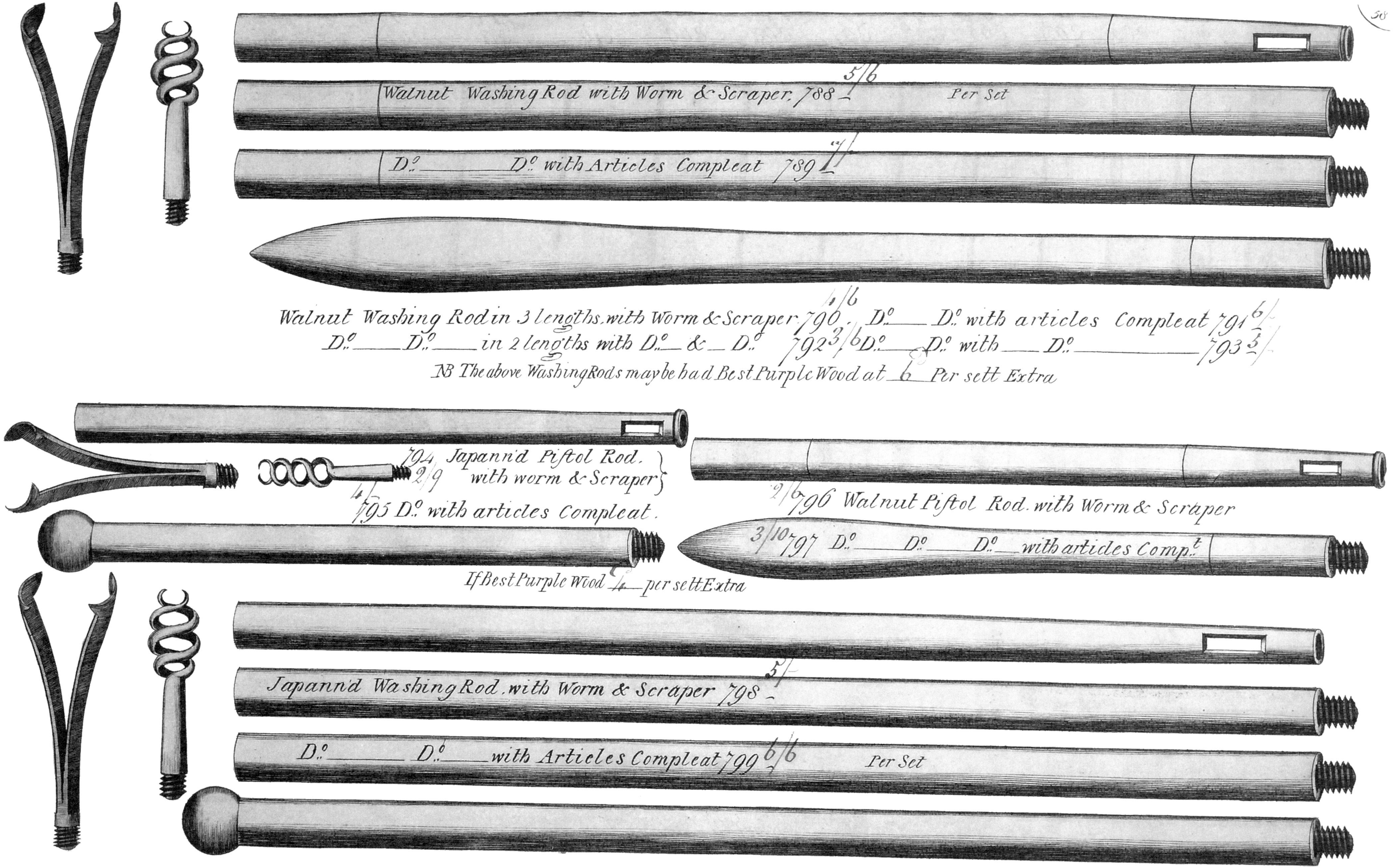
Walnut Washing Rod with Worm & Scraper 788 5/6 Per Set
Do. Do. with Articles Compleat 789 7/-
Walnut Washing Rod in 3 lengths with Worm & Scraper 790 4/6 Do. Do. with articles Compleat 791 6/-
Do. Do. in 2 lengths with Do. & Do. 792 3/6 Do. Do. with Do. 793 5/-
NB The above Washing Rods may be had Best Purple Wood at 6 Per sett Extra
794 2/9 Japann'd Pistol Rod. with worm & Scraper
4/- 795 Do. with articles Compleat.
2/6 796 Walnut Pistol Rod. with Worm & Scraper
3/10 797 Do. Do. Do. with articles Compt.
If Best Purple Wood 4 per sett Extra
Japann'd Washing Rod. with Worm & Scraper 798 5/-
Do. Do. with Articles Compleat 799 6/6 Per Set

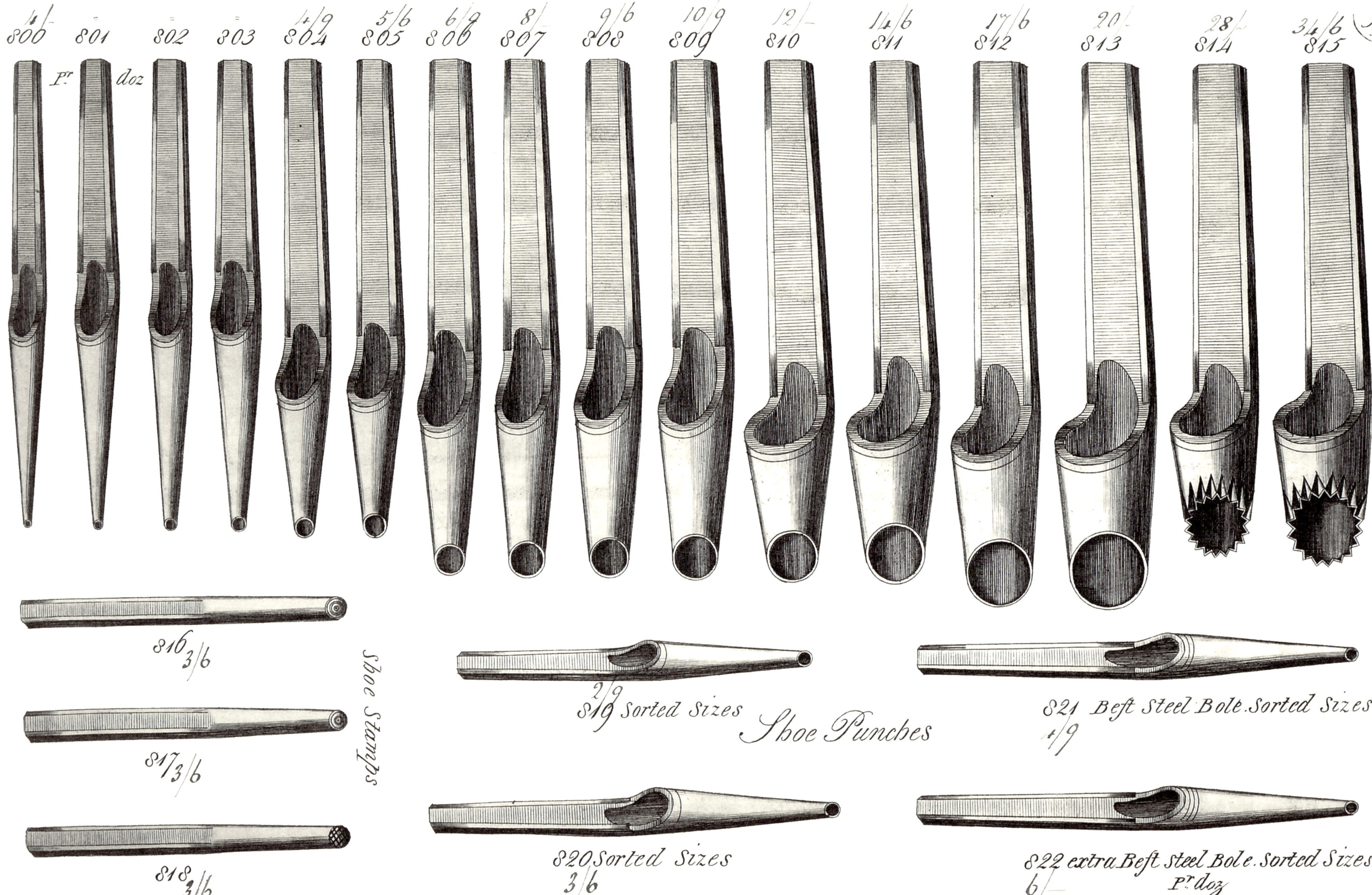
4/- 800
801
802
803
4/9 804
5/6 805
6/9 806
8/- 807
9/6 808
10/9 809
12/- 810
14/6 811
17/6 812
20/- 813
28/- 814
34/6 815
Pr doz
816 3/6
817 3/6
818 3/6
Shoe Stamps
819 2/9 Sorted Sizes
Shoe Punches
821 4/9 Beſt Steel Bole. Sorted Sizes
820 Sorted Sizes 3/6
822 extra Beſt steel Bole. Sorted Sizes 6/- Pr doz

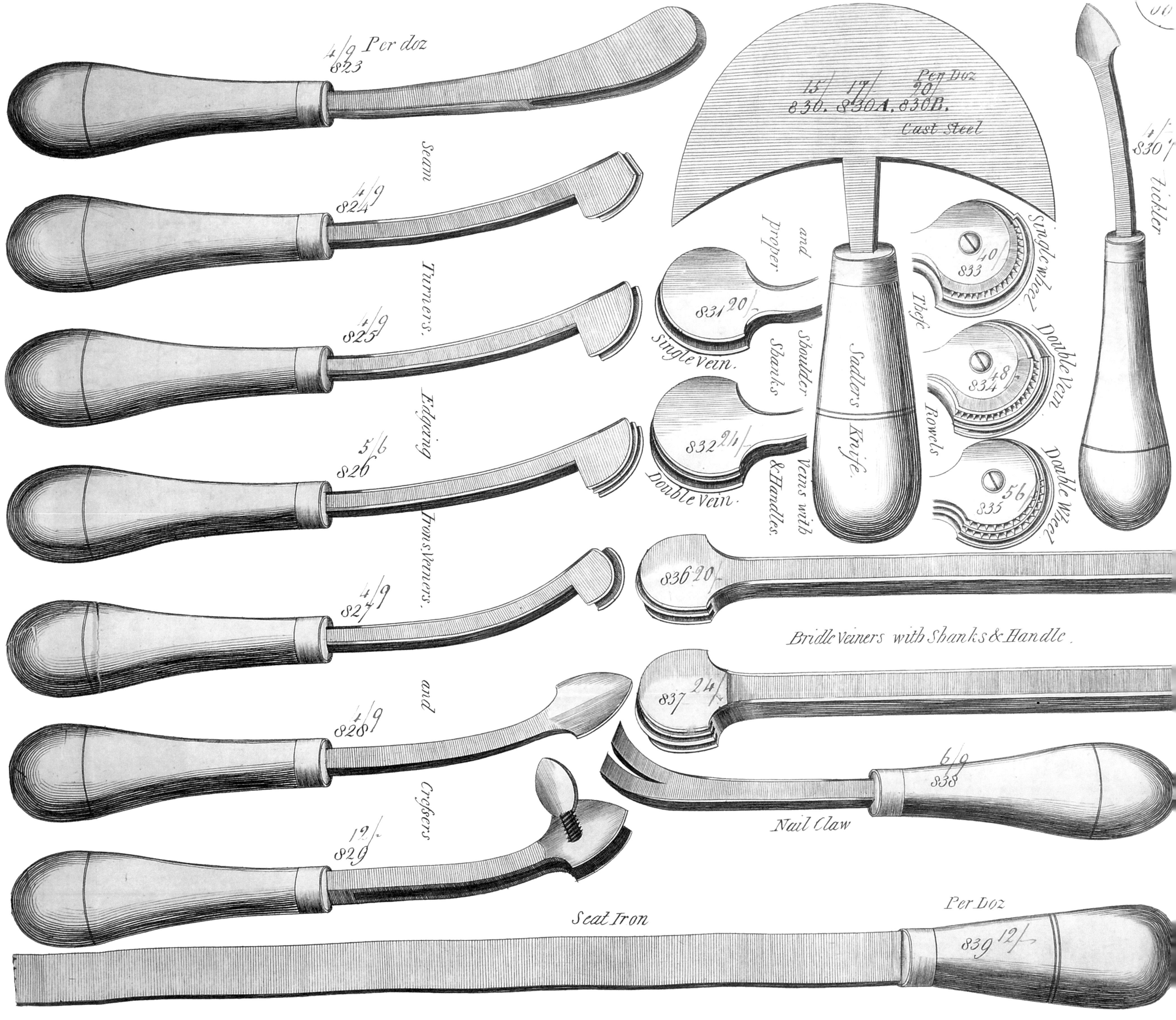

4/9 Per doz
823
824 4/9
825 4/9
826 5/6
827 4/9
828 4/9
829 12/-
Seam Turners. Edging Irons Veiners. and Creasers
15/ 17/ Per Doz 20/
830. 830A. 830B.
Cast Steel
Sadlers Knife.
831 20/-
Single Vein.
832 24/-
Double Vein.
Shoulder Shanks
and proper Veins with & Handles.
833 40/-
Single Wheel
834 48/-
Double Vein
835 56/-
Double Wheel
These Rowels
830 4/
Tickler
836 20/-
Bridle Veiners with Shanks & Handle.
837 24/-
838 6/9
Nail Claw
Per Doz
839 12/-
Seat Iron

Cantle Strainer

Ea

843 5/6

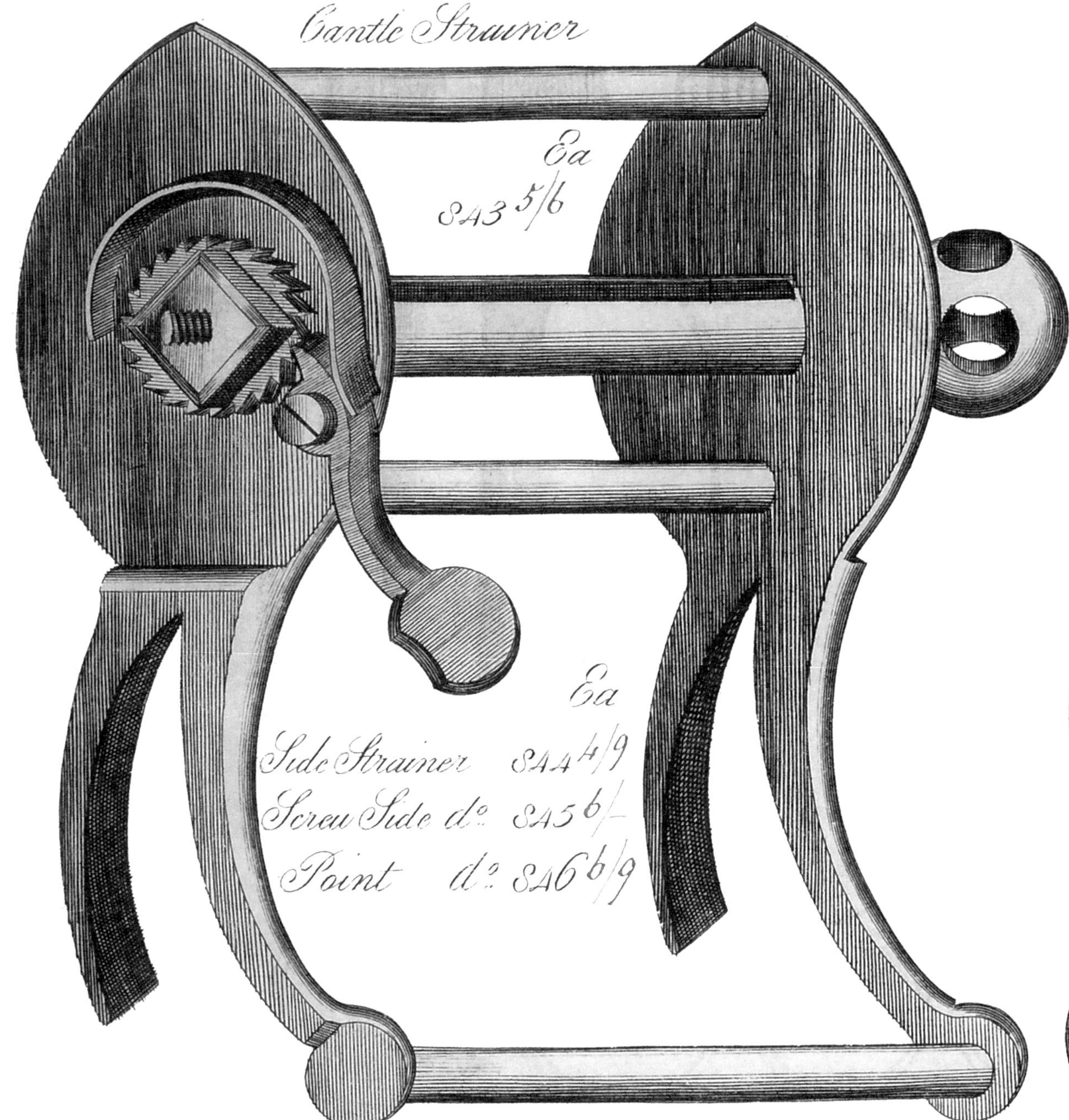

Ea

Side Strainer 844 4/9

Screw Side d° 845 6/-

Point d° 846 6/9

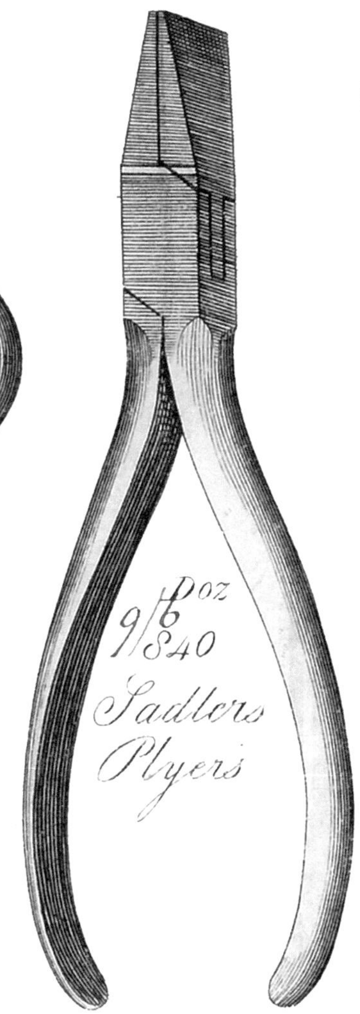

Doz

9/6

840

Sadlers Plyers

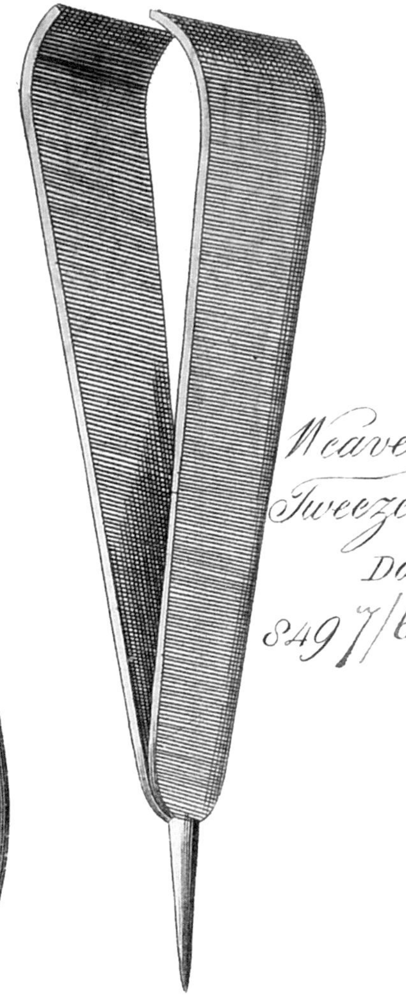

Weavers Tweezers

Doz

849 7/6

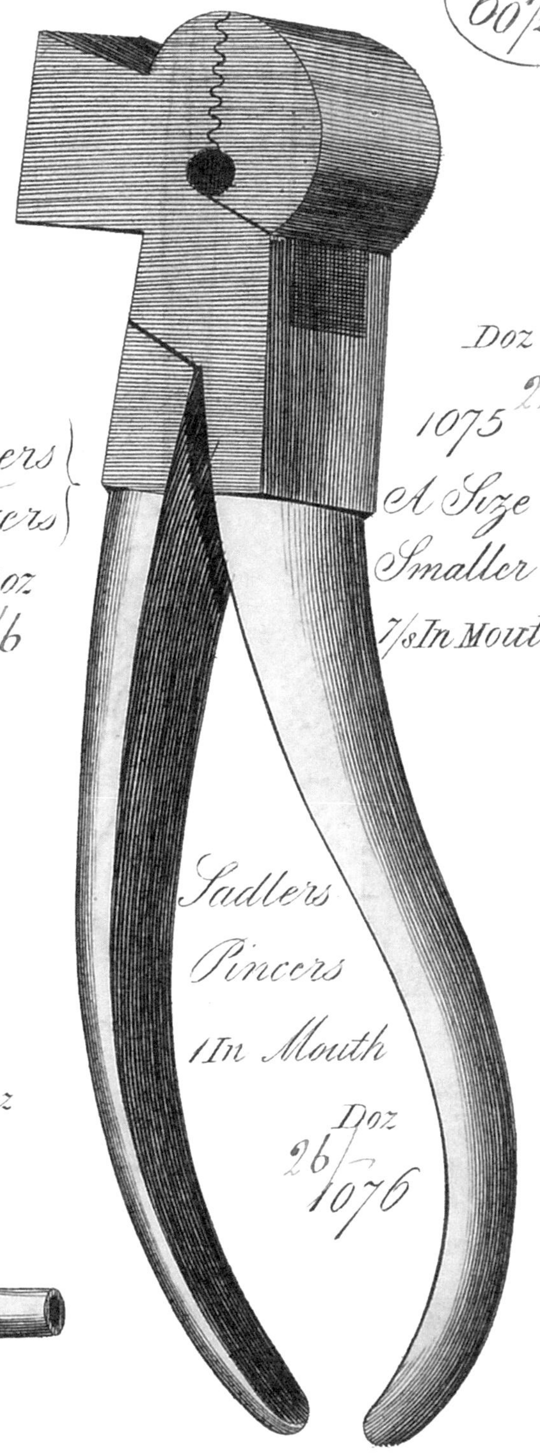

Doz

1075 24/-

A Size Smaller

7/8 In Mouth

Sadlers Pincers

1 In Mouth

Doz

26/

1076

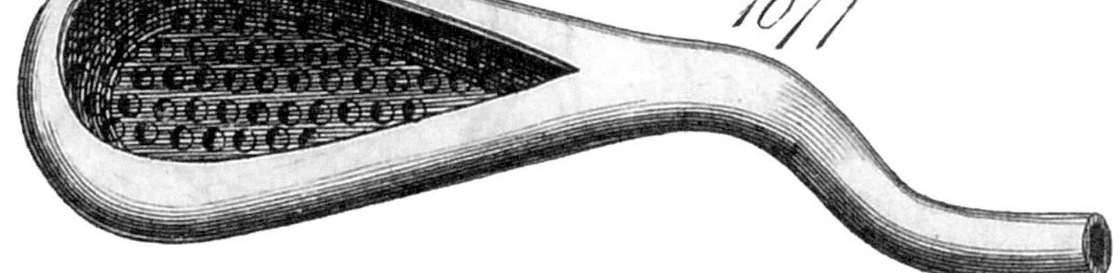

Sadlers Palms

13/6 Doz

1077

847 21/6 A Sett of Sadlers Strainers two Cantles & two plain sides

848 28/ A Compleat Set of d° two Cantles one plain side one Screw side & one Point

Sadlers Tools in Sets Compleat from 80/- to 112/- Per Set

61
Brace Makers & Sadlers Pricking Irons at 1/6 Per Doz Teeth
Brace Makers Pricker
Saddle Flap Pricker
Round Tooth Prickers
Saddle Strap Pricker
Harness Pricker
Bridle Pricker
Oval Bridle Pricker
Screw Racer 1125 12/-
Single Racer 1124 3/-
Head Knife 1163 8/-
4/5 1126 split 4/2 1127
Per Doz
Best Plain Key Rings
Best Dyed Key Rings
9 1128 1/2 1133
10 1129 1/6 1134
1/- 1130 1/11 1135
1/3 1131 2/3 1136
Pr doz 1/6 1132 Joint 2/7 1137 Split
1/6 1138 1/11 1143
1/11 1139 2/3 1144
2/3 1140 2/9 1145
2/7 1141 3/3 1146
3/4 1142 Joint 4/3 1147 Split
Pr doz 9 1152 Comn Split 1/11 1157 Split all round
8 1151 1/6 1156
6 1/2 1150 1/3 1155
5 1/2 1149 1/- 1154
4 1/2 1148 9 1153
Best Hoop Rings 1162 12/-
10/6 1161
9/- 1160
8/3 1159
Doz 6/6 1158

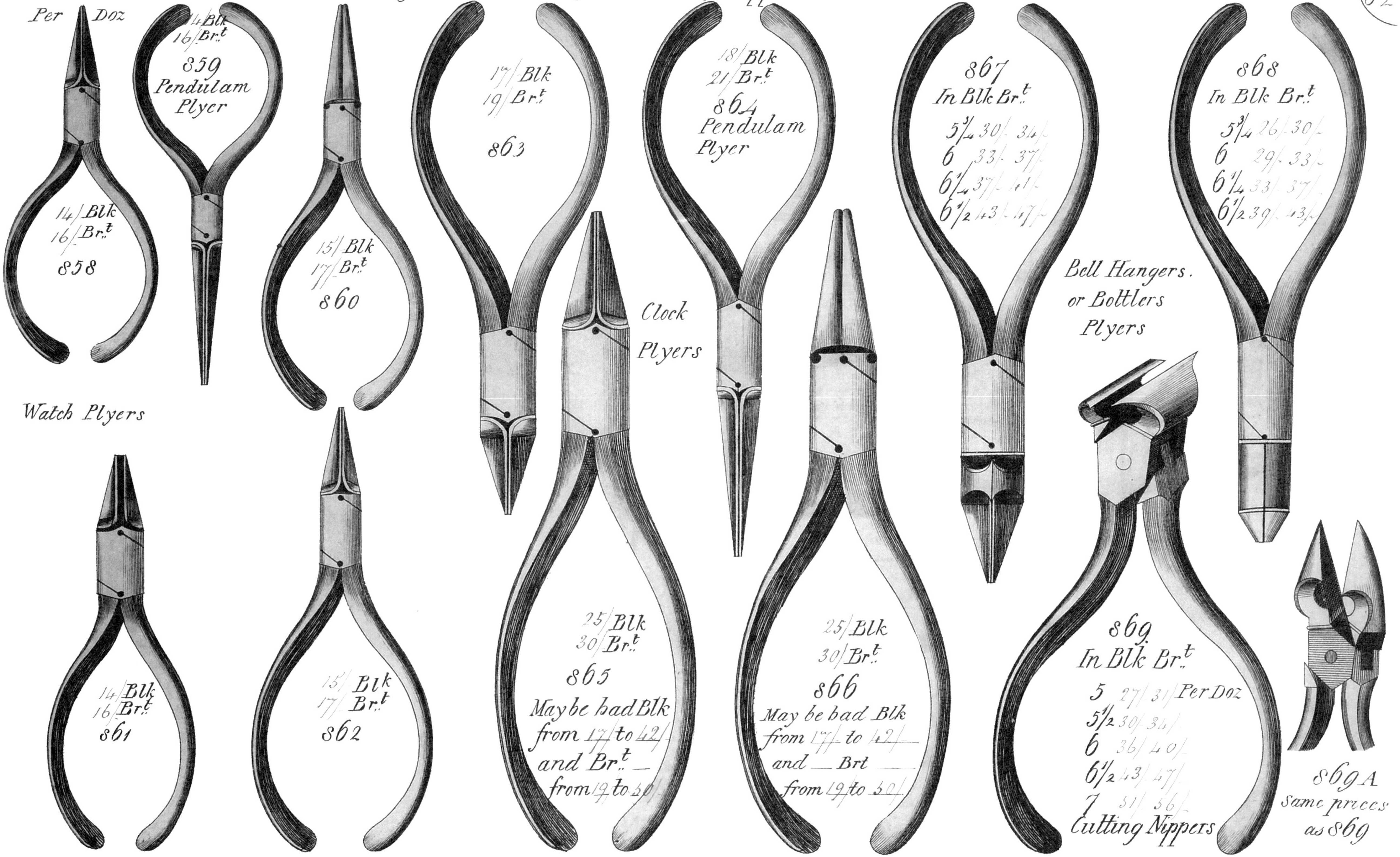
Per Doz
14/ Blk
16/ Br.t
859
Pendulam Plyer
14/ Blk
16/ Br.t
858
Watch Plyers
15/ Blk
17/ Br.t
860
17/ Blk
19/ Br.t
863
18/ Blk
21/ Br.t
864
Pendulam Plyer
867
In Blk Br.t
5¾ 30/- 34/-
6 33/- 37/-
6¼ 37/- 41/-
6½ 43/- 47/-
868
In Blk Br.t
5¾ 26/- 30/-
6 29/- 33/-
6¼ 33/- 37/-
6½ 39/- 43/-
Bell Hangers. or Bottlers Plyers
Clock Plyers
14/ Blk
16/ Br.t
861
15/ Blk
17/ Br.t
862
25/ Blk
30/ Br.t
865
May be had Blk from 17/ to 42/ and Br.t from 19/ to 50/
25/ Blk
30/ Br.t
866
May be had Blk from 17/ to 42/ and Brt from 19/ to 50/
869
In Blk Br.t
5 27/ 31/ Per Doz
5½ 30/ 34/
6 36/ 40/
6½ 43/ 47/
7 51/ 56/
Cutting Nippers
869A
Same prices as 869

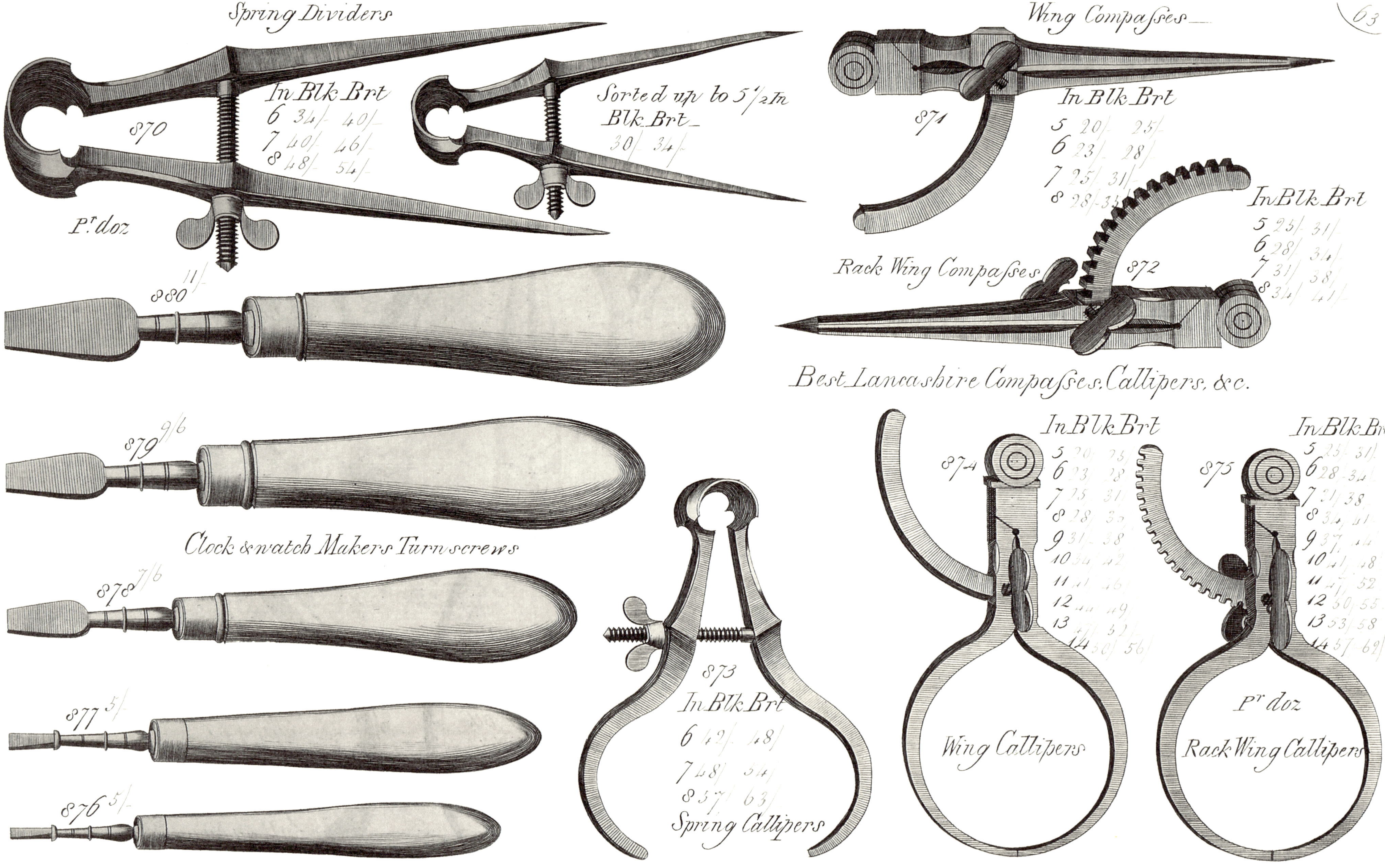
Spring Dividers
870
In Blk Brt
6 34/- 40/-
7 40/- 46/-
8 48/- 54/-
Pr doz
Sorted up to 5½ In
Blk Brt
30/- 34/-
Wing Compasses
871
In Blk Brt
5 20/- 25/-
6 23/- 28/-
7 25/- 31/-
8 28/- 35/-
Rack Wing Compasses
872
In Blk Brt
5 25/- 31/-
6 28/- 34/-
7 31/- 38/-
8 34/- 41/-
Best Lancashire Compasses, Callipers, &c.
880 11/-
879 9/6
Clock & watch Makers Turnscrews
878 7/6
877 5/-
876 5/-
873
In Blk Brt
6 42/- 48/-
7 48/- 54/-
8 57/- 63/-
Spring Callipers
874
In Blk Brt
5 20/ 25/
6 23/ 28/
7 25/ 31/
8 28/ 35/
9 31/- 38/
10 34/ 42/
11 41/ 46/
12 44/ 49/
13 47/ 52/
14 50/ 56/
Wing Callipers
875
In Blk Brt
5 25/- 31/
6 28/- 34/
7 31/ 38/
8 34/ 41/
9 37/ 44/
10 41/ 48/
11 47/ 52/
12 50/ 55/
13 53/ 58/
14 57/ 62/
Pr doz
Rack Wing Callipers

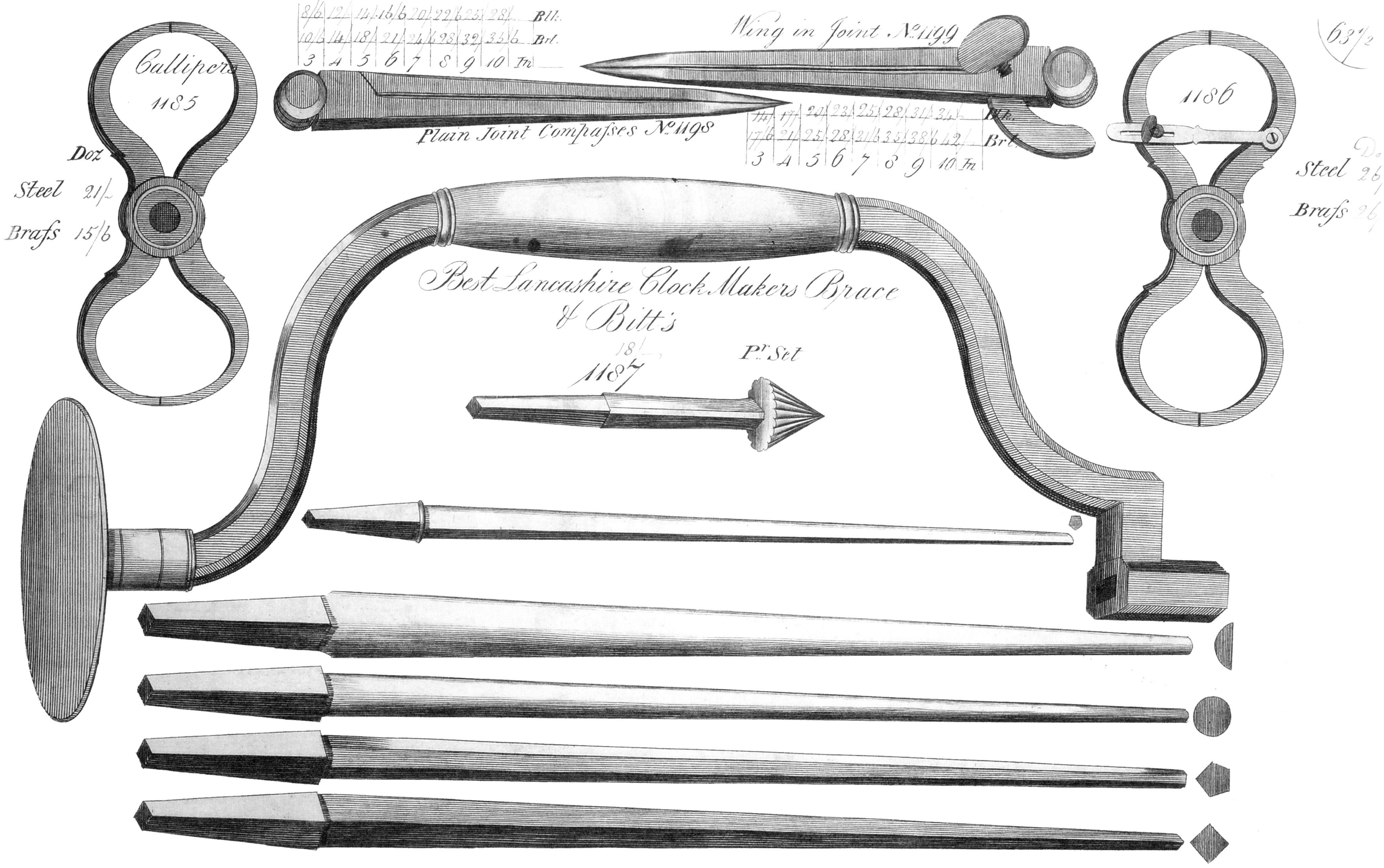

Plain Joint Compasses No. 1198

8/6	12/-	14/-	16/6	20/-	22/6	25/-	28/-	Blk.
10/6	14/-	18/-	21/-	24/6	28/-	32/-	35/6	Brl.
3	4	5	6	7	8	9	10	In

Wing in Joint No. 1199

14/-	17/-	20/-	23/-	25/-	28/-	31/-	34/-	Blk.
17/6	21/-	25/-	28/-	31/6	35/-	38/6	42/-	Brl.
3	4	5	6	7	8	9	10	In

Best Lancashire Vices. &c.

881 — 8/6 Blk each, 10/6 Brt

May be had Blk or Brt from 10/6 to 30/ & upwards

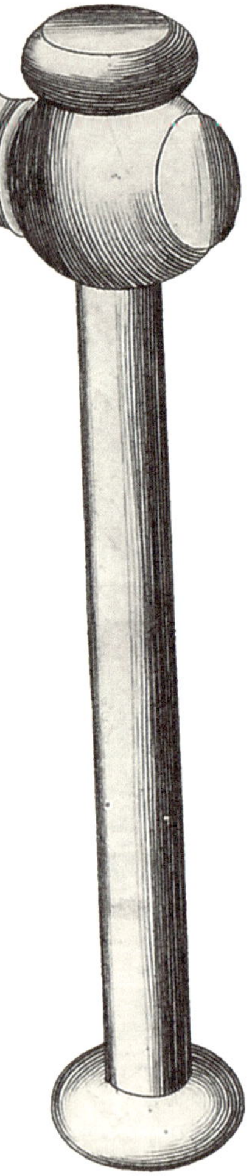

882 — Blk 12/, Brt 15/

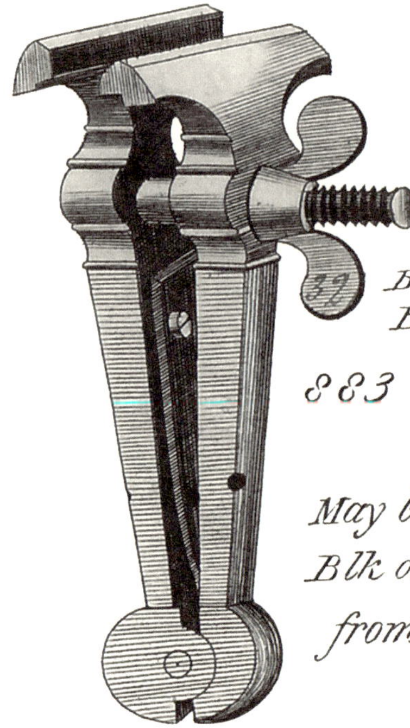

883 — 32 Blk doz, Brt 35/

May be had Blk or Brt from 32/ to 36/

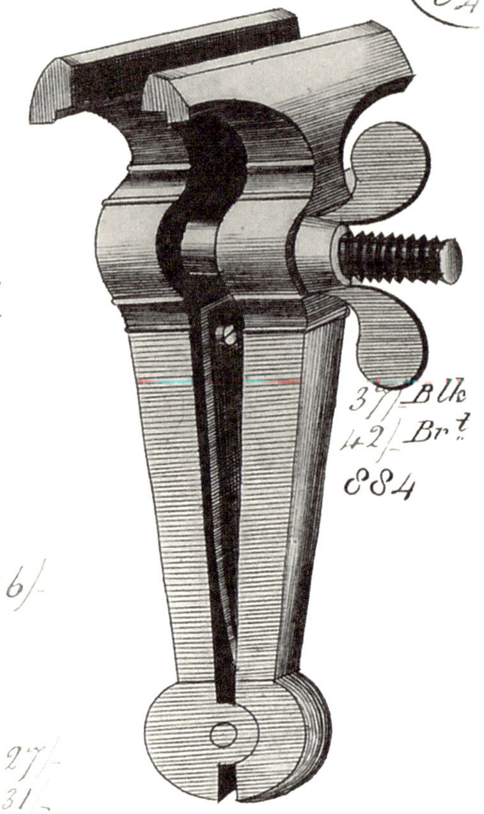

884 — 37/ Blk, 42/ Brt

Sliding Tongs.

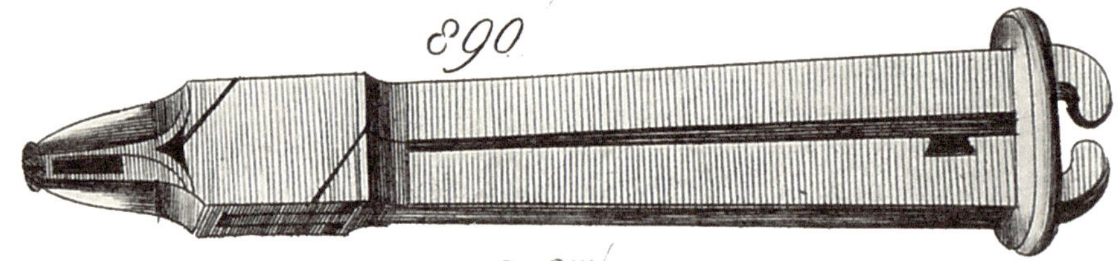

890 — Blk 27/, Brt 31/

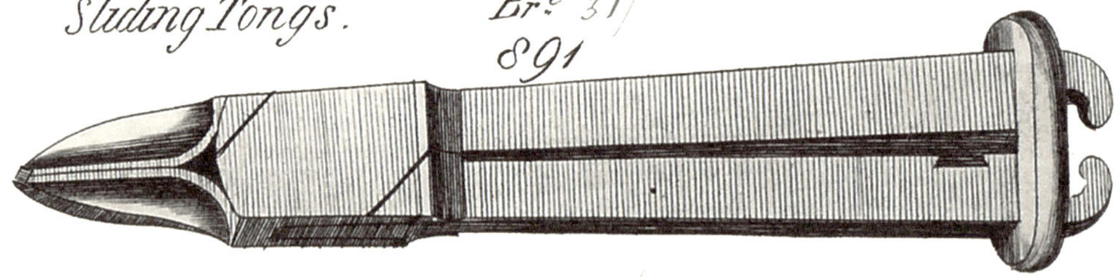

891 — Blk 27/, Brt 31/

892 — Blk 31/, Brt 38/

Clock & Watch Hammers.

886 — 12/ Per Doz

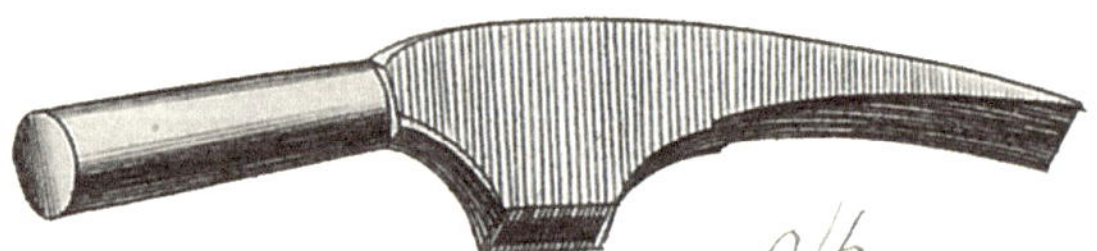

885 — 9/6

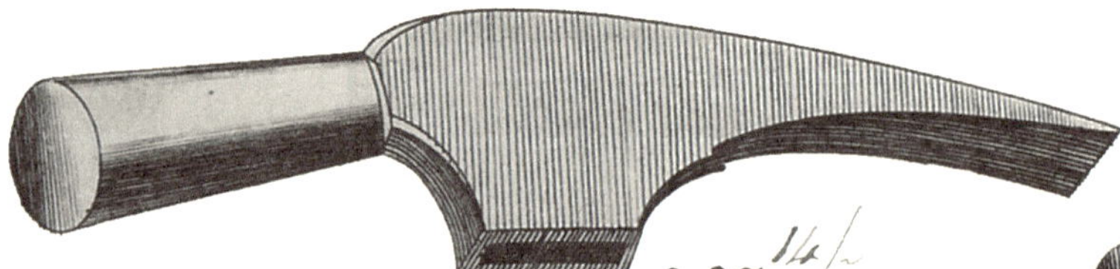

887 — 14/

888 — 16/6

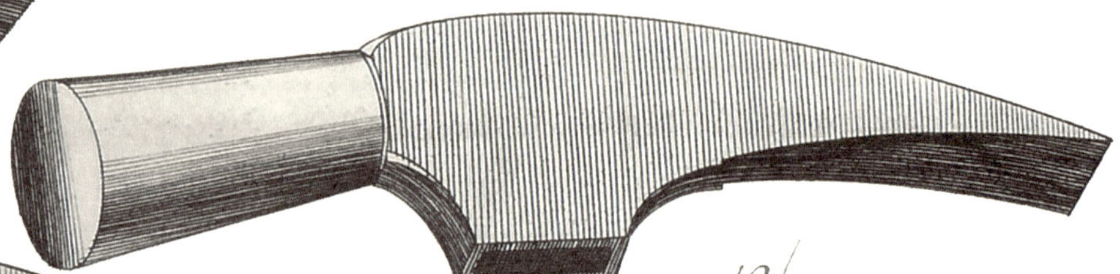

889 — 19/

Clock & Watch Hammers with round Faces at Same prices

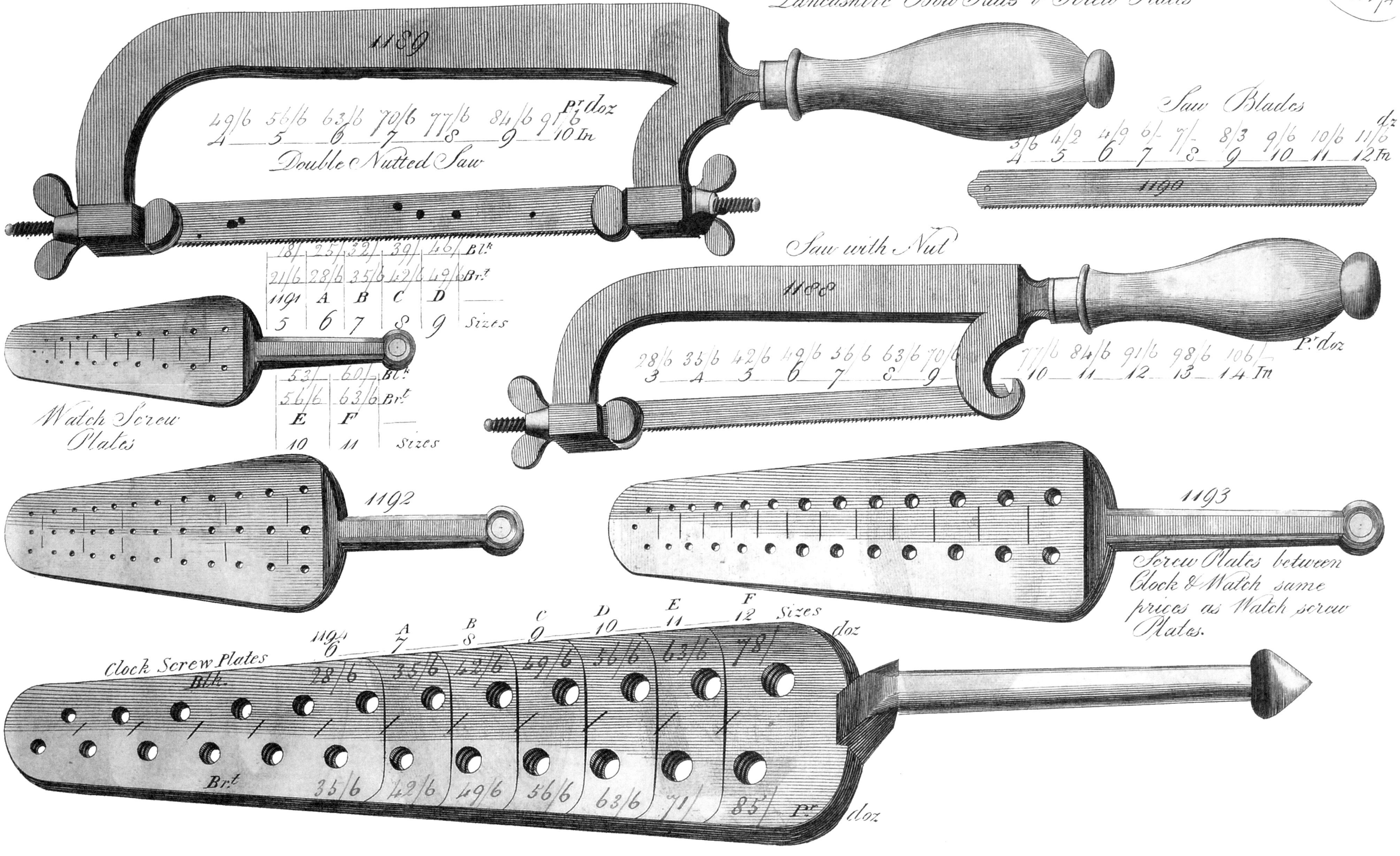
1189
Pr doz
49/6 56/6 63/6 70/6 77/6 84/6 91/6
4 5 6 7 8 9 10 In
Double Nutted Saw
Saw Blades
dz
3/6 4/2 4/9 6/- 7/- 8/3 9/6 10/6 11/6
4 5 6 7 8 9 10 11 12 In
1190
18/ 25/ 32/ 39/ 46/ Blk
21/6 28/6 35/6 42/6 49/6 Brt
1191 A B C D
5 6 7 8 9 Sizes
Saw with Nut
1188
Pr doz
28/6 35/6 42/6 49/6 56/6 63/6 70/6 77/6 84/6 91/6 98/6 106/-
3 4 5 6 7 8 9 10 11 12 13 14 In
53/ 60/ Blk
56/6 63/6 Brt
E F
10 11 Sizes
Watch Screw Plates
1192
1193
Screw Plates between Clock & Watch same prices as Watch screw Plates.
Clock Screw Plates
1194 A B C D E F Sizes
6 7 8 9 10 11 12
Blk
28/6 35/6 42/6 49/6 56/6 63/6 78/ doz
Brt
35/6 42/6 49/6 56/6 63/6 71/ 85/ Pr doz

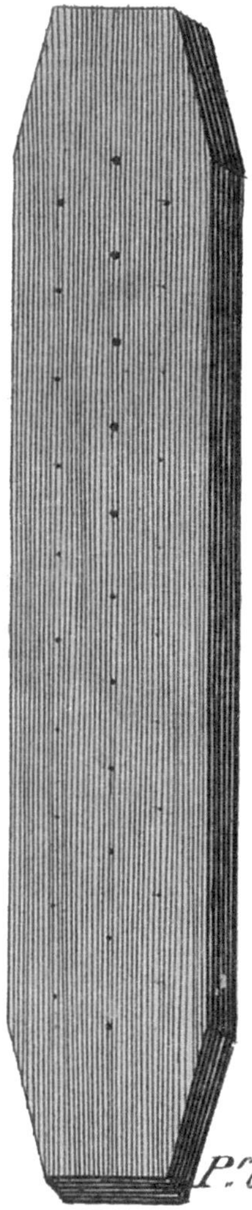

Pr doz.

32 / Blk.

36 / Brt

A 198

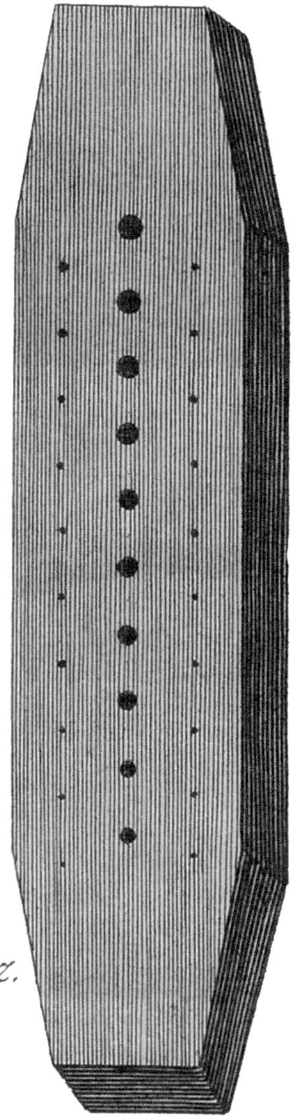

37 / Blk.

42/6 Brt

A 199

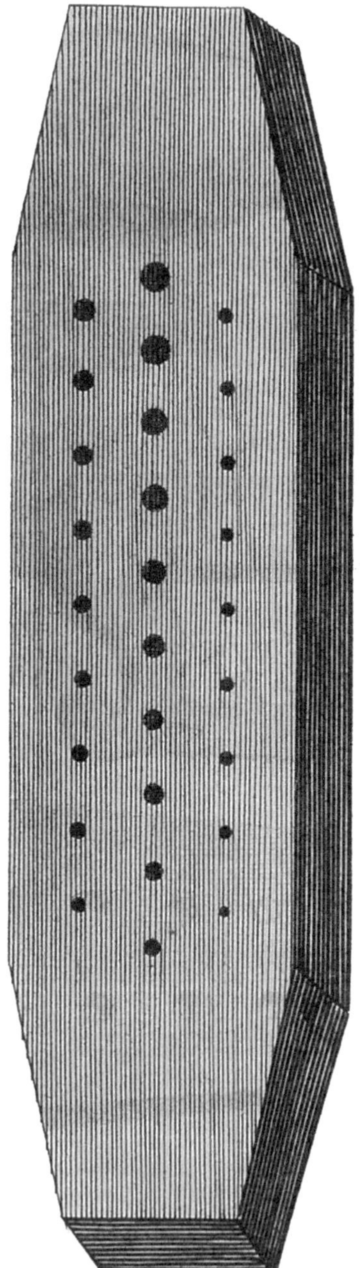

46 / Blk.

52 / Brt

A 200

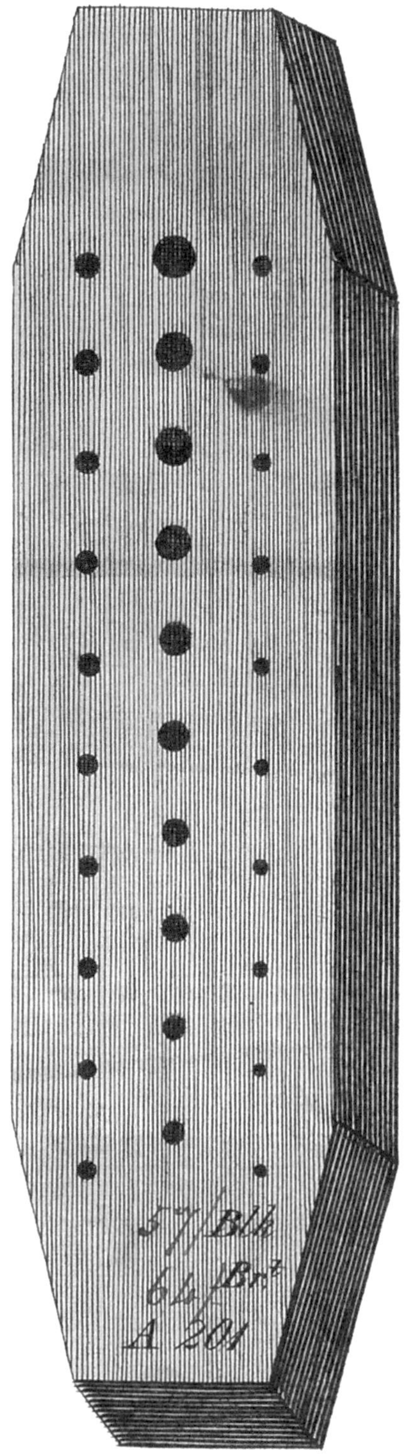

57 / Blk

64 / Brt

A 201

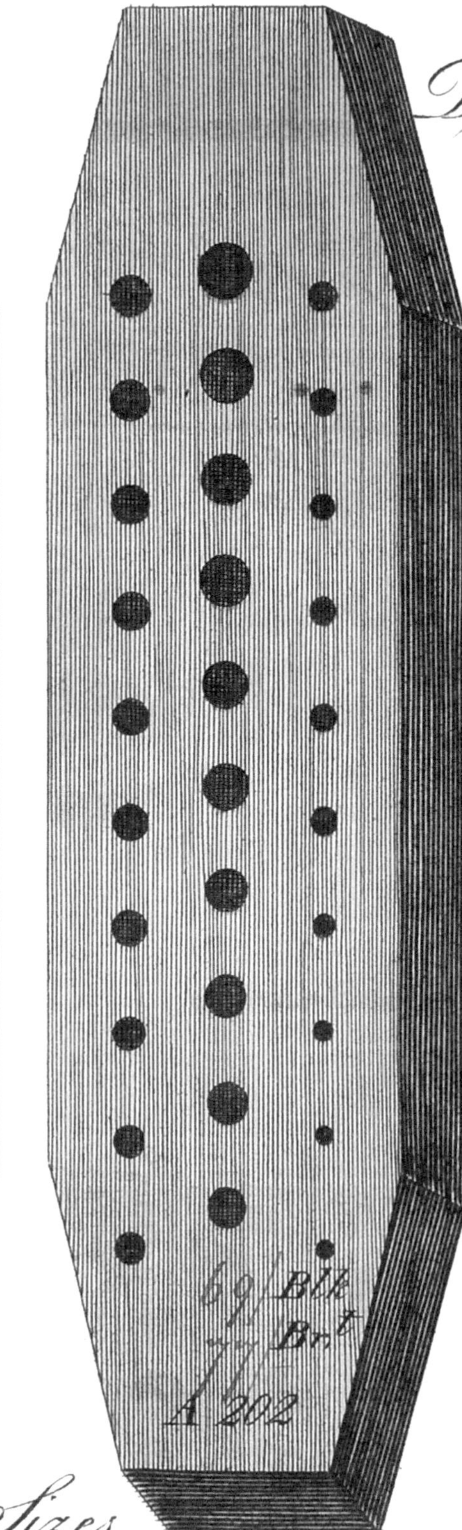

69 / Blk

77 / Brt

A 202

Lancashire wire Drawing Plates may be had Larger Sizes

Draw Bench Plyers

Doz

1195

Size Larger

1196

two Sizes Larger

1197

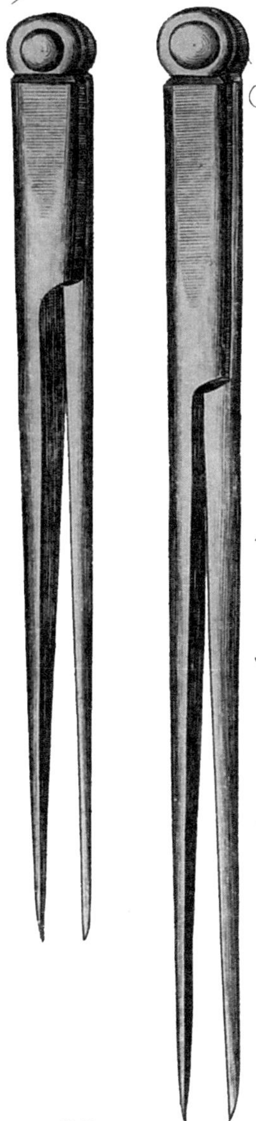

893 Round Head Compasses

Size	Price
5 Inch	2/3
5½	2/6
6	2/9
6½	3/
7	3/6
8	4/9
9	6/6
10	8/6
11	10/6
12 In	12/6

Round Head. Double Joint Compasses

Size	Price
9 Inch	8/6
10	10/6
12	14/6

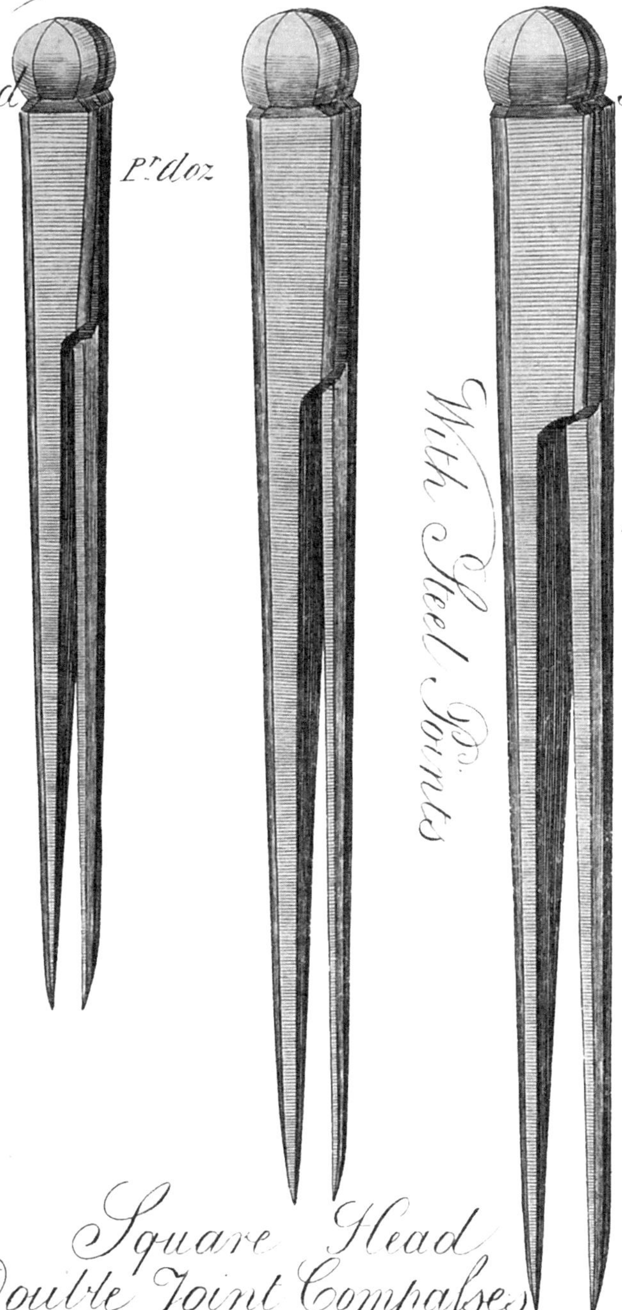

894 Square Head Compasses

Pr doz

With Steel Points

Size	Price
5 Inch	3/
5½	3/6
6	4/
6½	4/6
7	5/6
8	6/6
9	8/6
10	10/6
11	12/6
12 In	14/6

Square Head Double Joint Compasses

Size	Price	Size	Price
6 In	5/6	10 In	12/6
7	7/	11	14/6
8	8/	12	16/6
9	10/6		

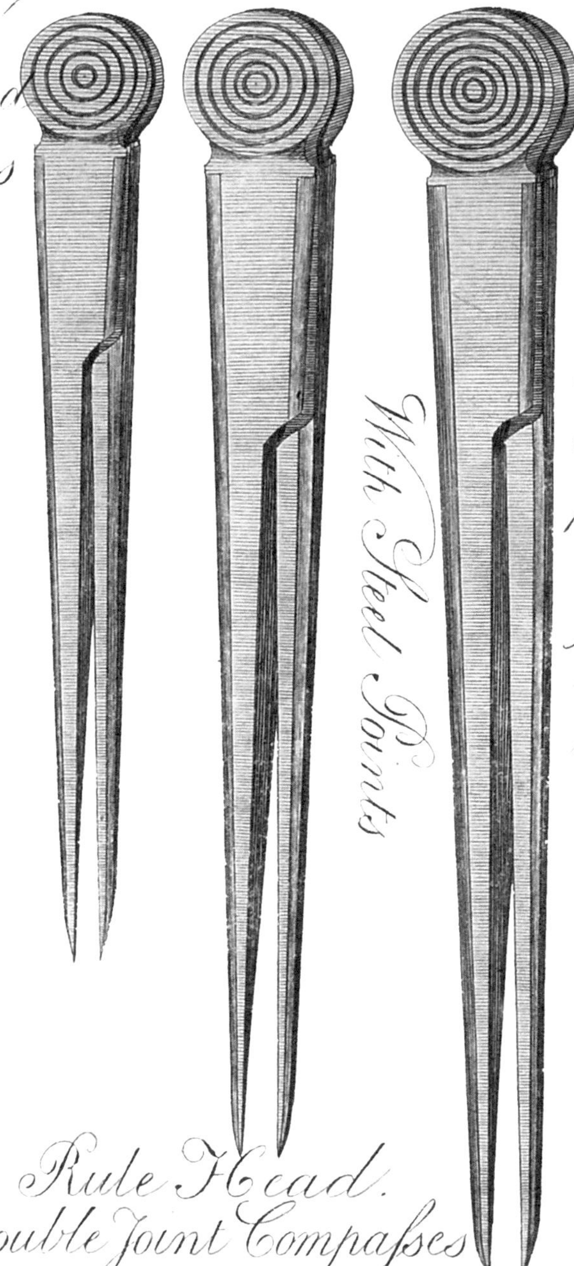

895 Rule Joint Compasses

With Steel Points

Size	Price
5 Inch	3/9
5½	4/3
6	4/9
6½	5/6
7	6/6
8	8/6
9	10/6
10	12/6
11	15/
12 In	17/6

Rule Head. Double Joint Compasses

Size	Price	Size	Price
6 In	6/3	10 In	14/6
7	8/	11	17/
8	10/	12	19/6
9	12/6		

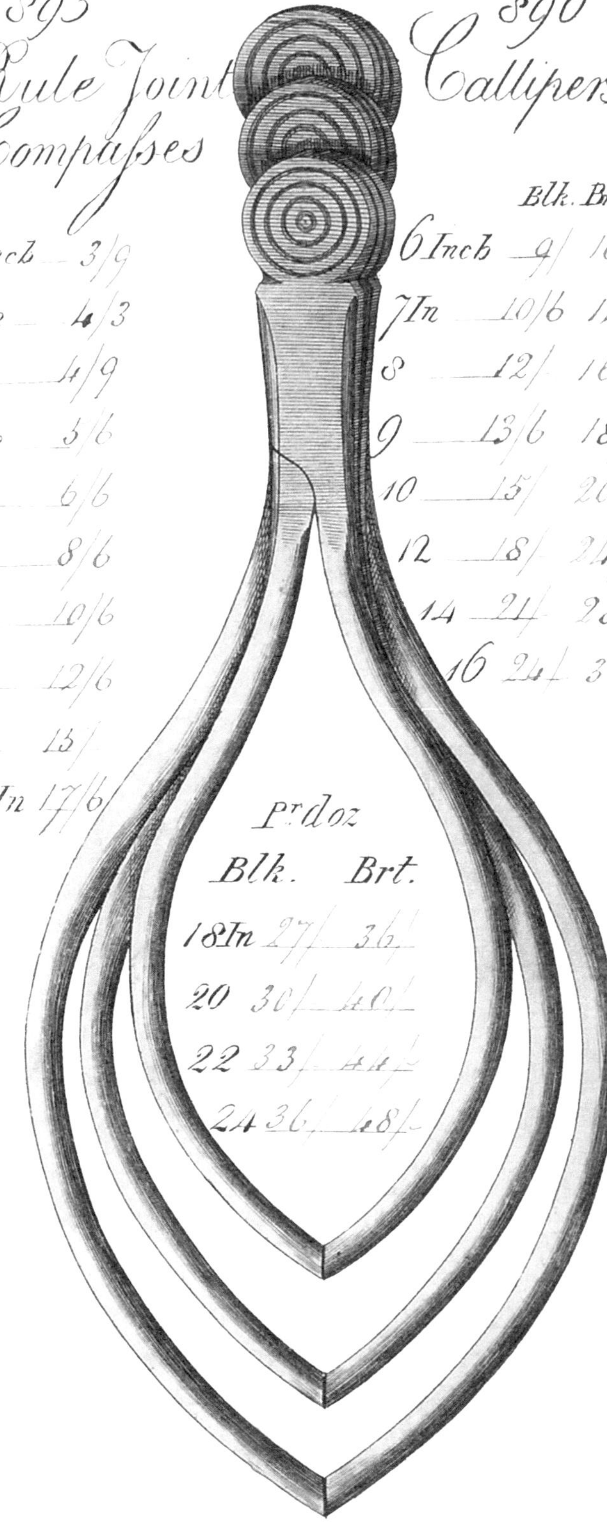

896 Callipers

	Blk.	Brt.
6 Inch	9/	10/
7 In	10/6	14/
8	12/	16/
9	13/6	18/
10	15/	20/
12	18/	24/
14	21/	28/
16	24/	32/

Pr doz

	Blk.	Brt.
18 In	27/	36/
20	30/	40/
22	33/	44/
24	36/	48/

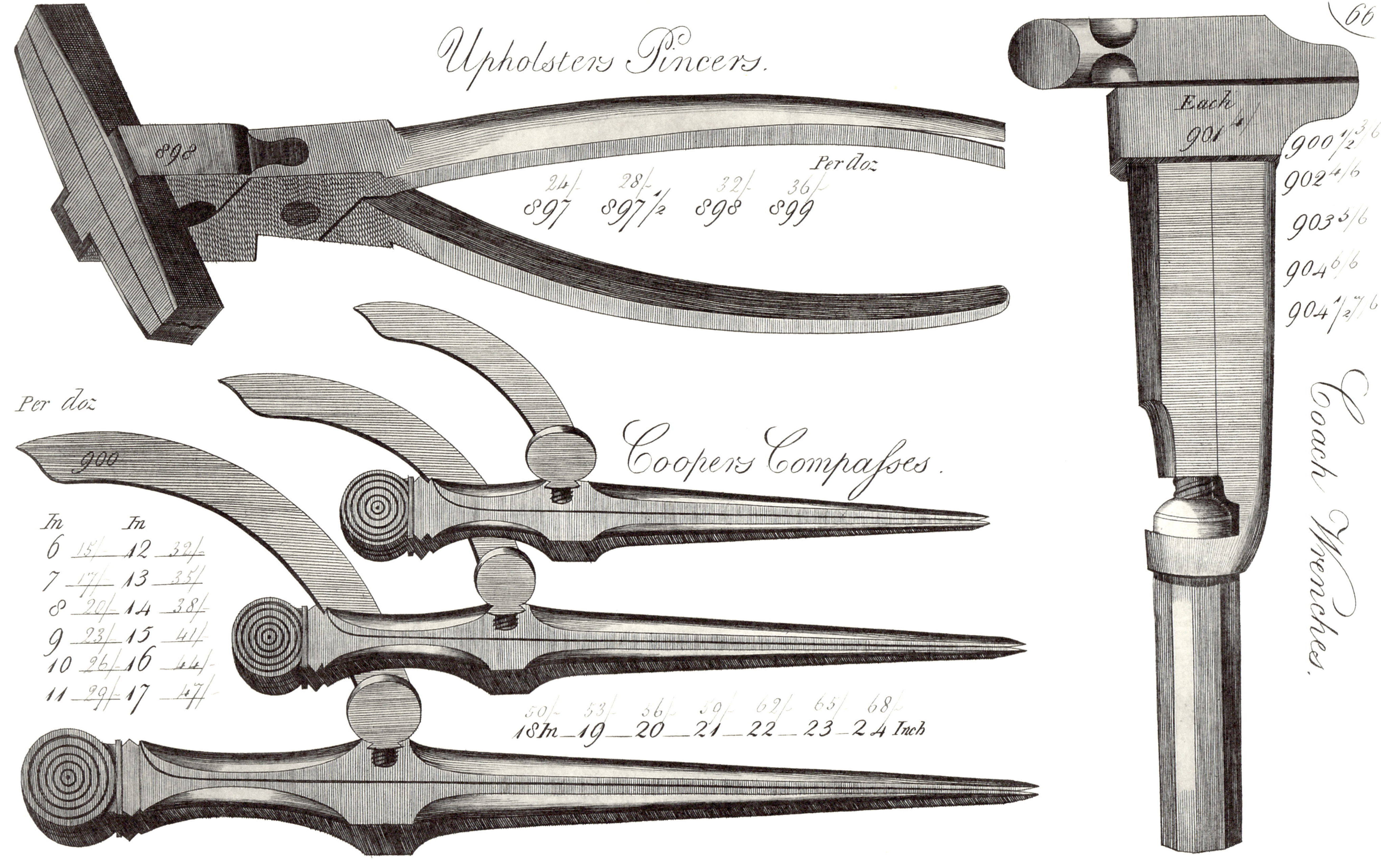
Upholsters Pincers.
898
Per doz
24/- 28/- 32/- 36/-
897 897½ 898 899
Each
901 4/-
900½ 3/6
902 4/6
903 5/6
904 6/6
904½ 7/6
Coach Wrenches.
Per doz
900
Coopers Compasses.
In In
6 15/- 12 32/-
7 17/- 13 35/-
8 20/- 14 38/-
9 23/- 15 41/-
10 26/- 16 44/-
11 29/- 17 47/-
50/- 53/- 56/- 59/- 62/- 65/- 68/-
18 In 19 20 21 22 23 24 Inch

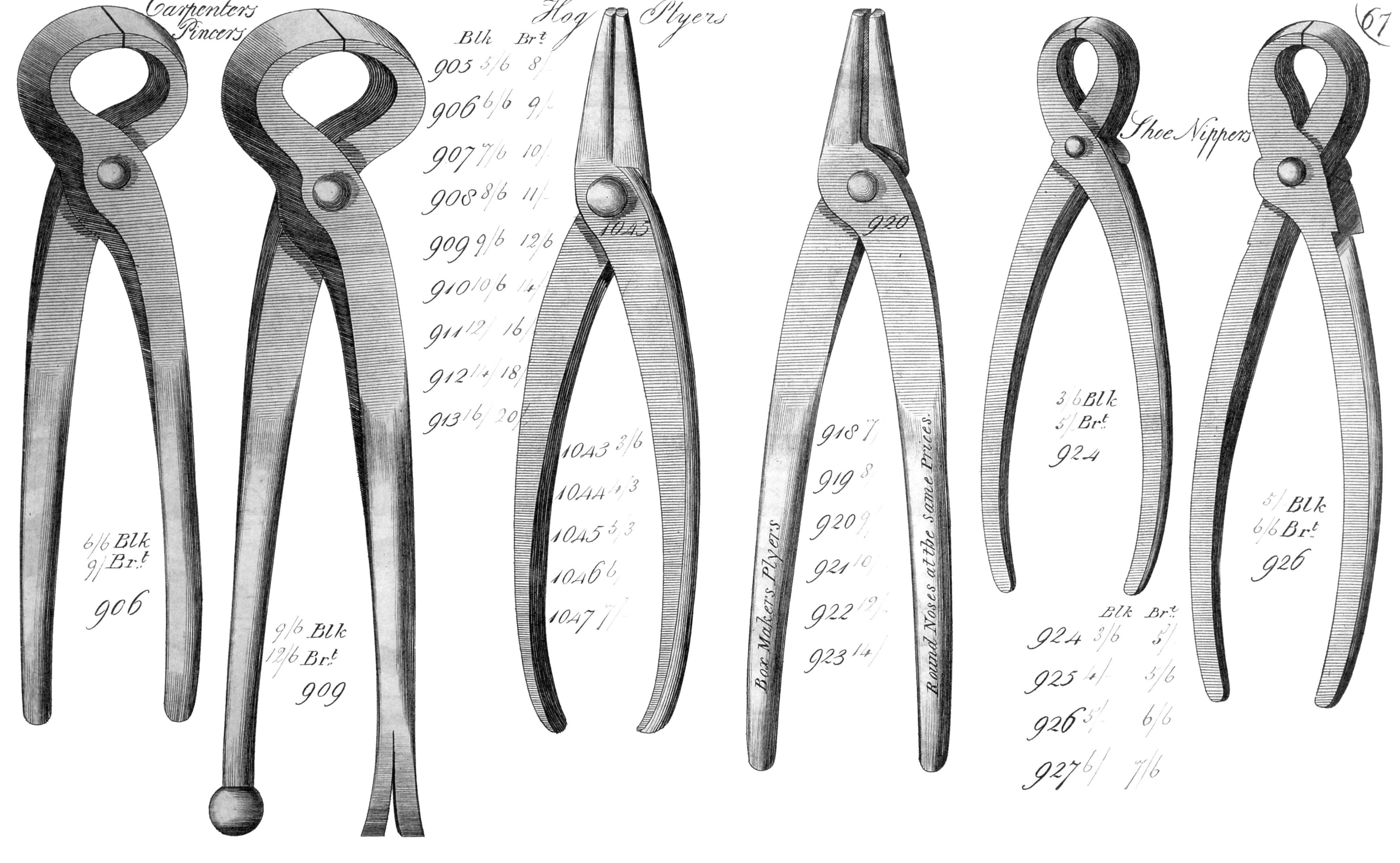
Carpenters Pincers
6/6 Blk
9/ Br.t
906
9/6 Blk
12/6 Br.t
909
Hog Plyers
Blk Br.t
905 5/6 8/
906 6/6 9/
907 7/6 10/
908 8/6 11/
909 9/6 12/6
910 10/6 14/
911 12/ 16/
912 14/ 18/
913 16/ 20/
1043
1043 3/6
1044 4/3
1045 5/3
1046 6/
1047 7/
920
Box Makers Plyers
918 7/
919 8/
920 9/
921 10/
922 12/
923 14/
Round Noses at the same Prices
Shoe Nippers
3/6 Blk
5/ Br.t
924
5/ Blk
6/6 Br.t
926
Blk Br.t
924 3/6 5/
925 4/ 5/6
926 5/ 6/6
927 6/ 7/6

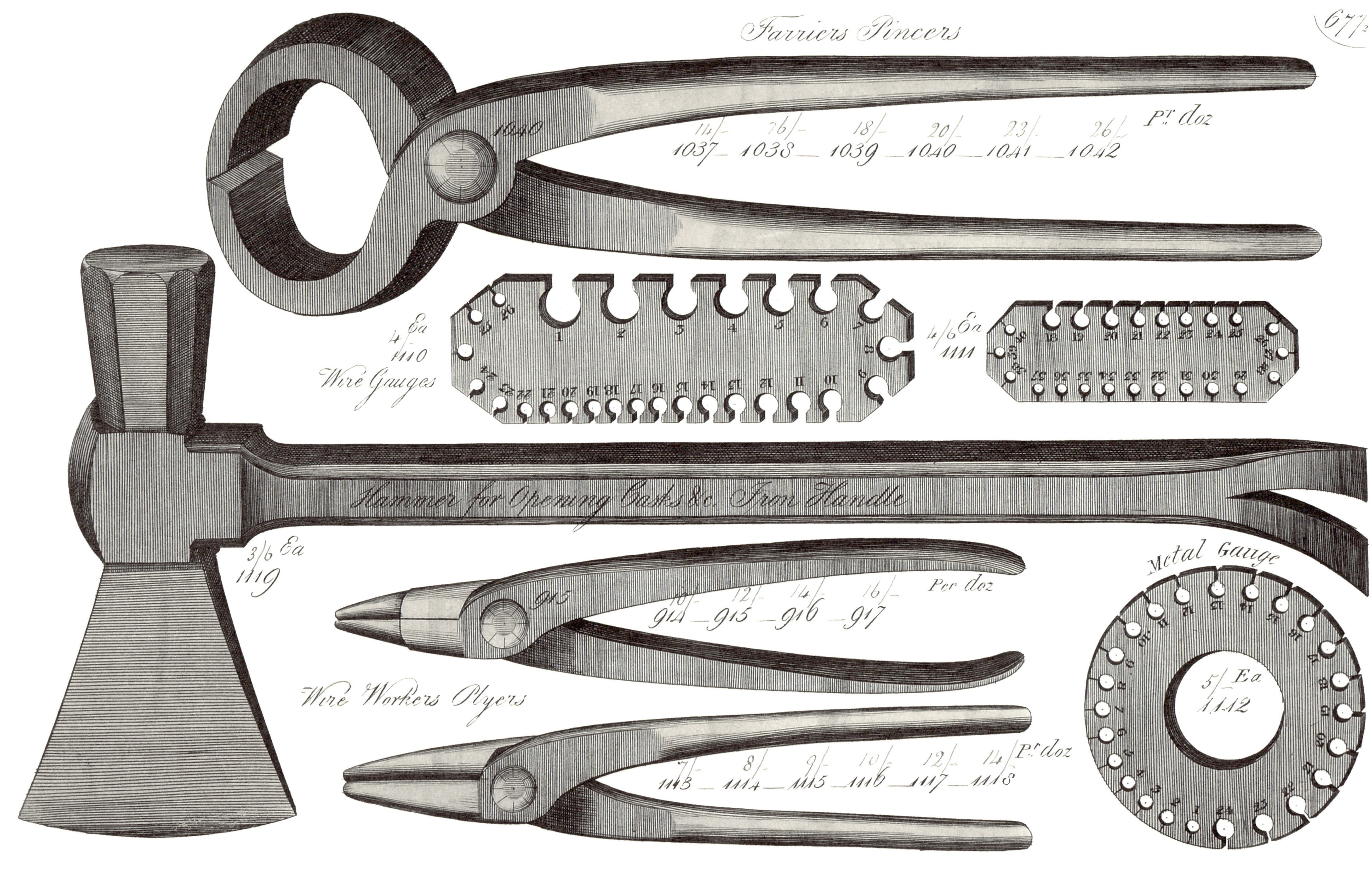
Farriers Pincers
Pr doz
14/- 16/- 18/- 20/- 23/- 26/-
1037 — 1038 — 1039 — 1040 — 1041 — 1042
1040
Wire Gauges
4/ Ea 1110
4/6 Ea 1111
Hammer for Opening Casks &c. Iron Handle
3/6 Ea 1119
Wire Workers Plyers
915
Per doz
10/- 12/- 14/- 16/-
914 — 915 — 916 — 917
Pr doz
7/- 8/- 9/- 10/- 12/- 14/-
1113 — 1114 — 1115 — 1116 — 1117 — 1118
Metal Gauge
5/ Ea 1112

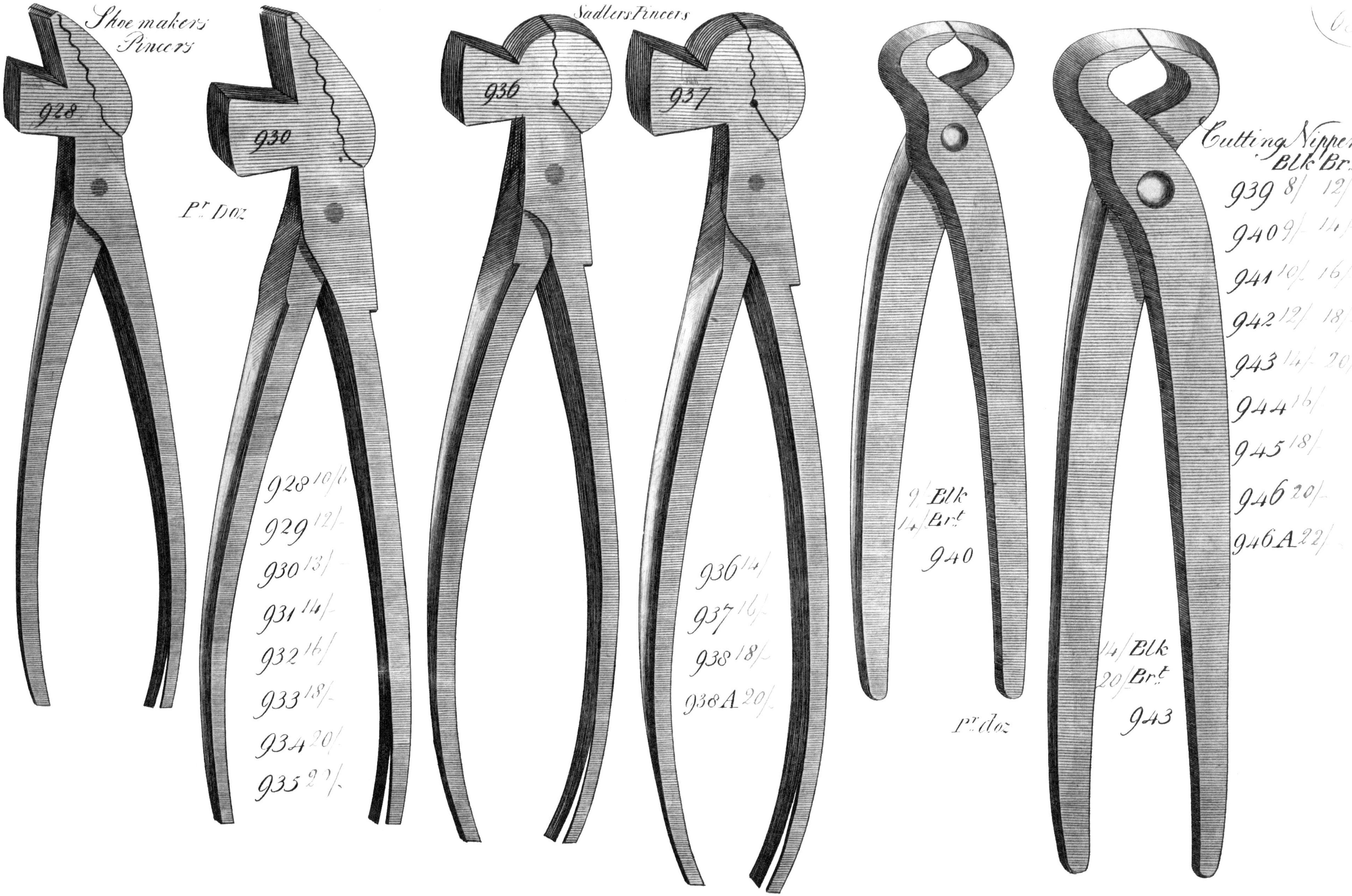
Shoe makers Pincers
928
930
Pr. Doz
928 10/6
929 12/-
930 13/-
931 14/-
932 16/-
933 18/-
934 20/-
935 22/-
Sadlers Pincers
936
937
936 14/-
937 16/-
938 18/-
938 A 20/-
9/- Blk
14/- Brt.
940
Pr. doz
Cutting Nippers
Blk Brt.
939 8/- 12/-
940 9/- 14/-
941 10/- 16/-
942 12/- 18/-
943 14/- 20/-
944 16/-
945 18/-
946 20/-
946 A 22/-
14/- Blk
20/- Brt.
943

London Pattern Shoe Pincers

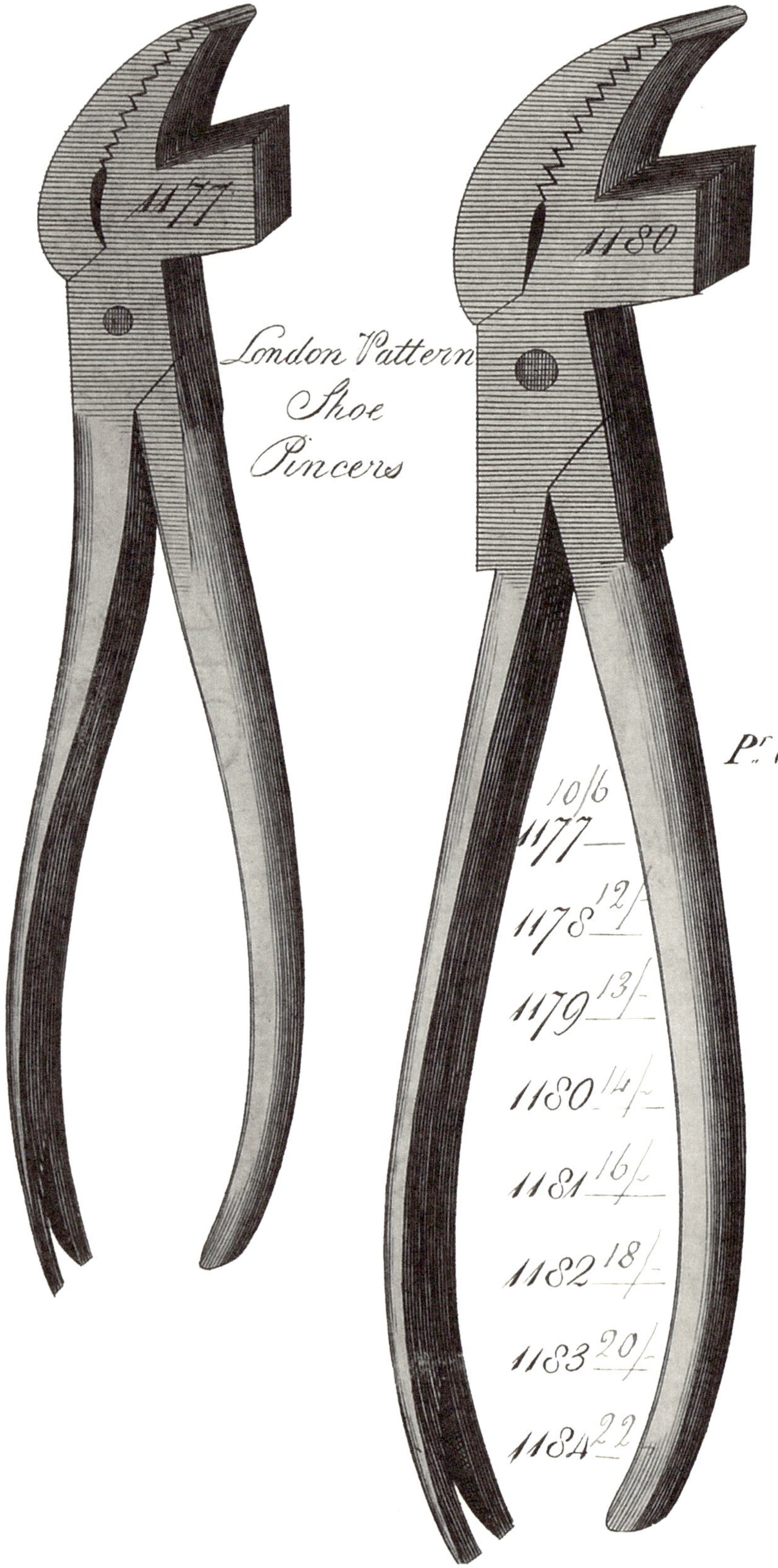

	Pr doz
1177	10/6
1178	12/-
1179	13/-
1180	14/-
1181	16/-
1182	18/-
1183	20/-
1184	22/-

Tower or Carpenters Best Pincers of Superior Quality

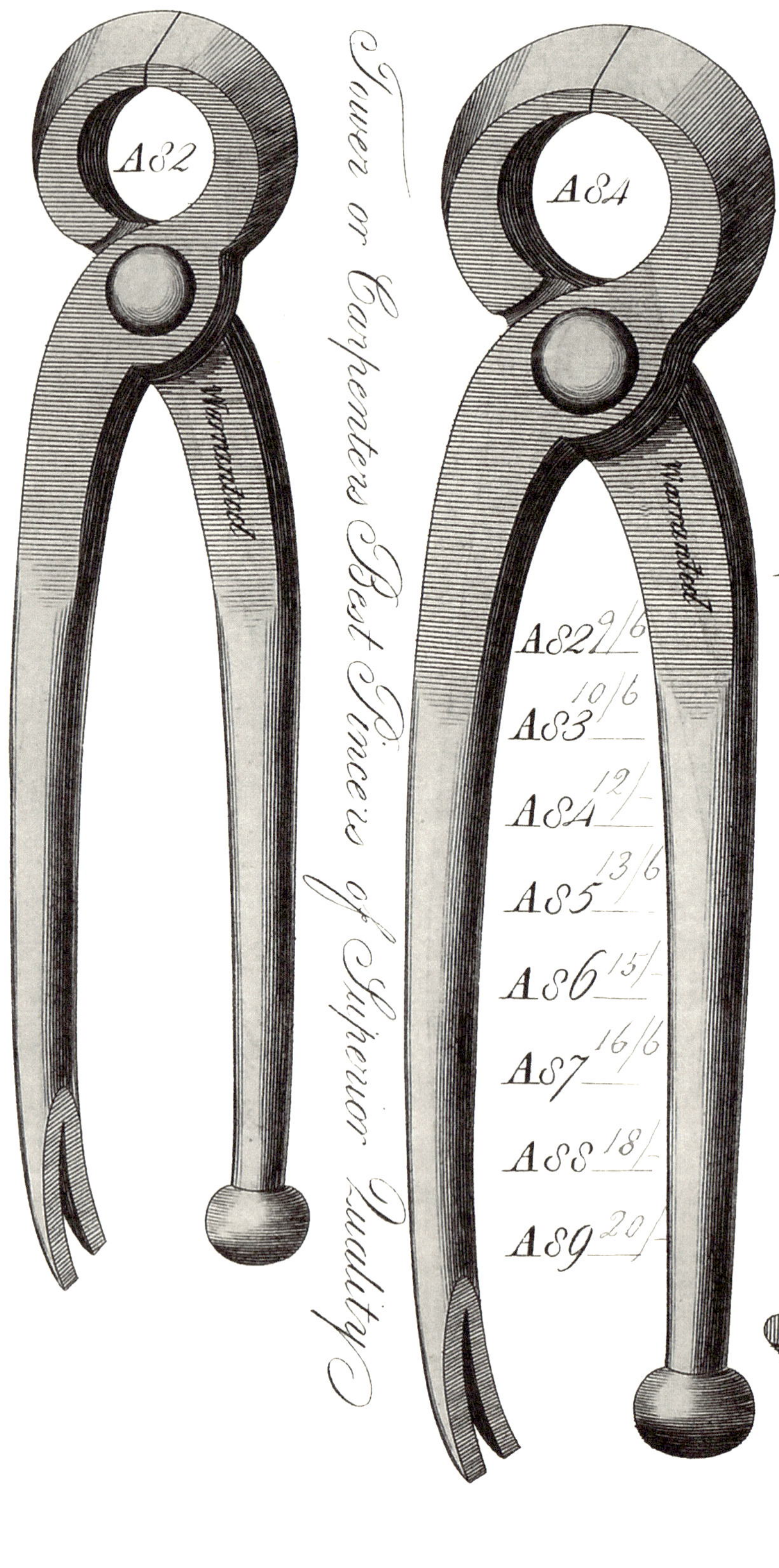

	Pr doz
A82	9/6
A83	10/6
A84	12/-
A85	13/6
A86	15/-
A87	16/6
A88	18/-
A89	20/-

Best Lancashire Hammers

Pr doz

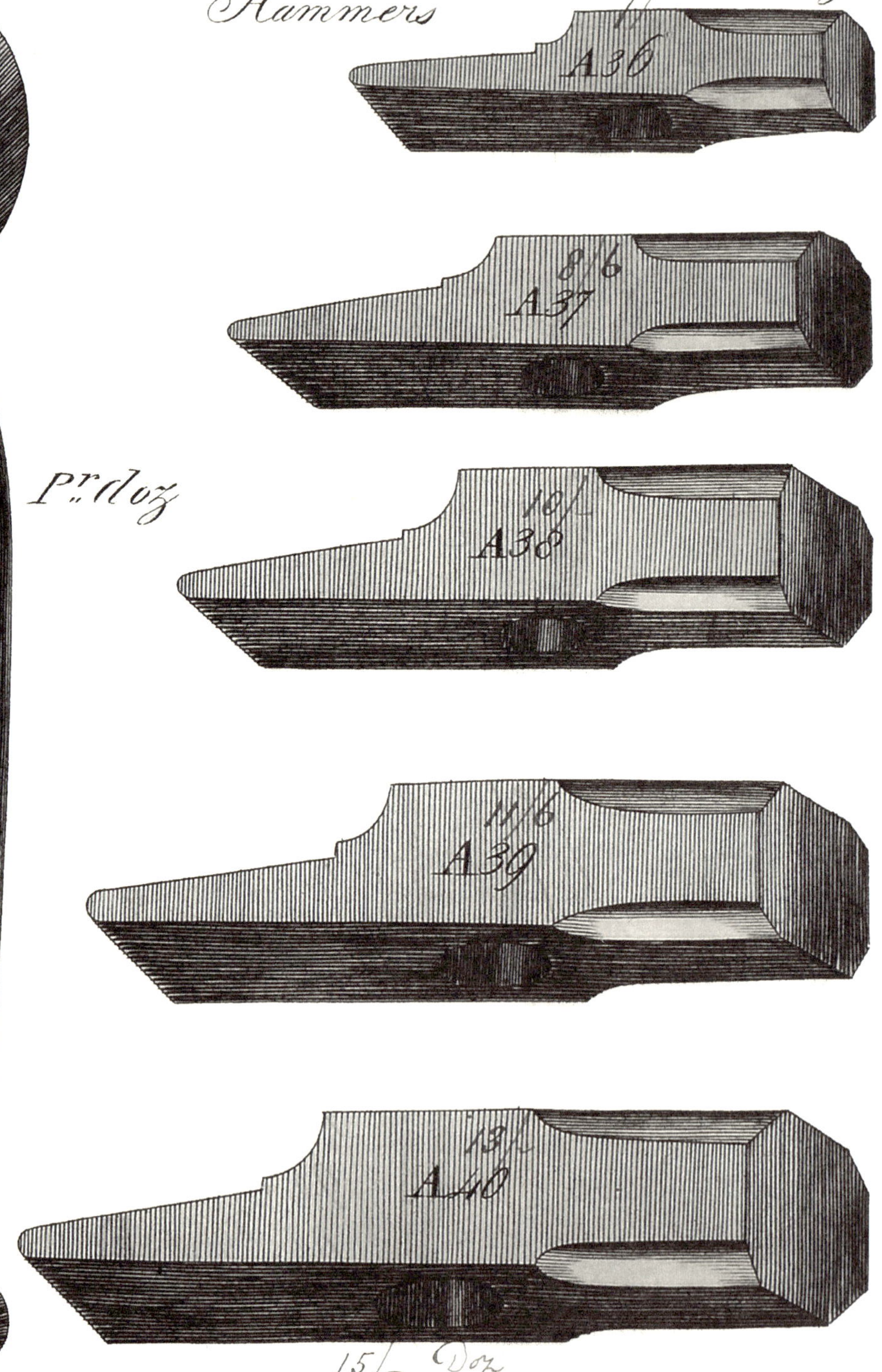

15/- Doz

A41. a Size Larger

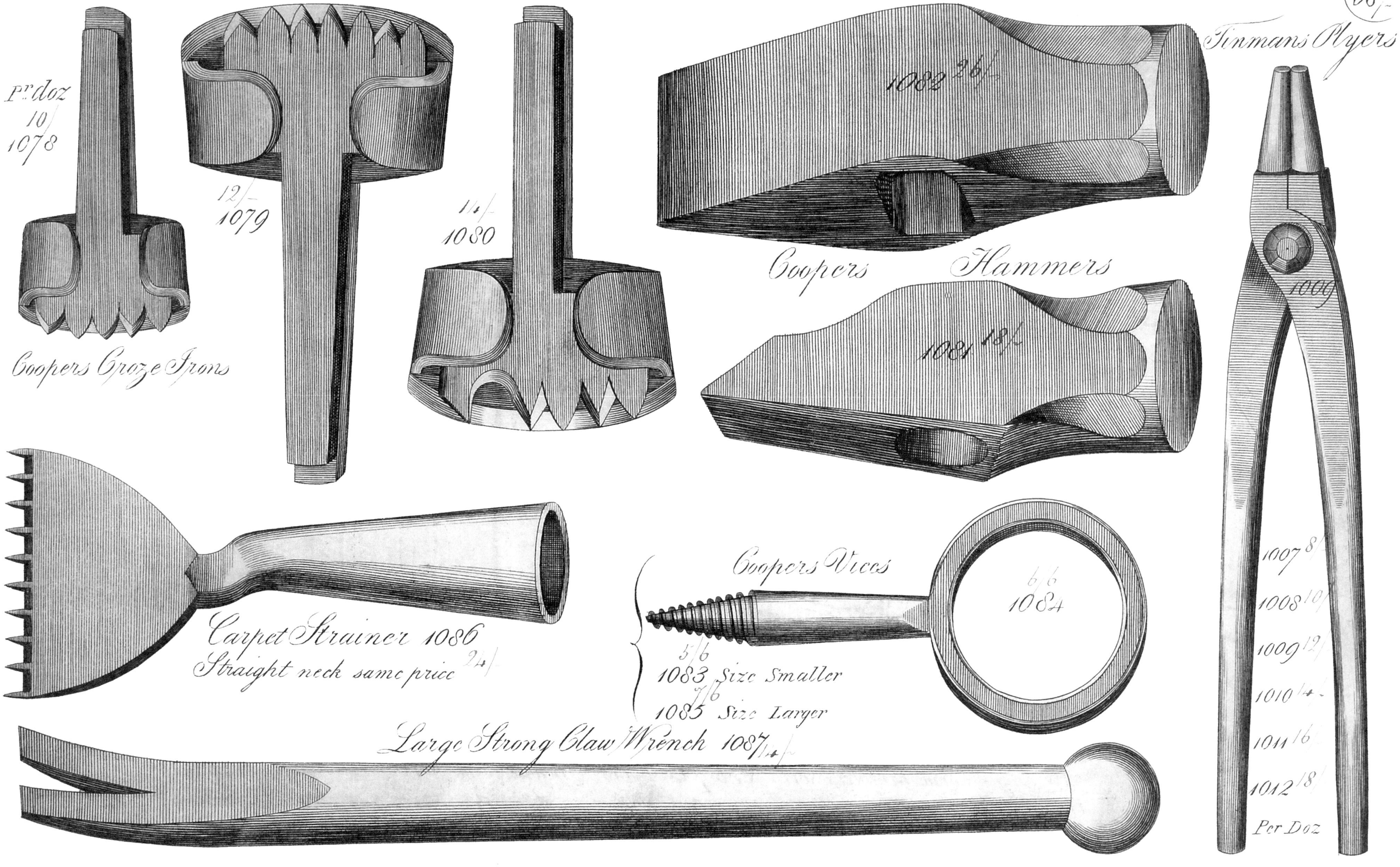
Pr doz
10/
1078
12/
1079
14/
1080
Coopers Croze Irons
1082 26/
Coopers Hammers
1081 18/
Tinmans Plyers
1006
1007 8/
1008 10/
1009 12/
1010 14/
1011 16/
1012 18/
Per Doz
Carpet Strainer 1086
Straight neck same price 24/
Coopers Vices
6/6
1084
5/6
1083 Size Smaller
7/6
1085 Size Larger
Large Strong Claw Wrench 1087 14/

Bright Gimblets with Best Heads

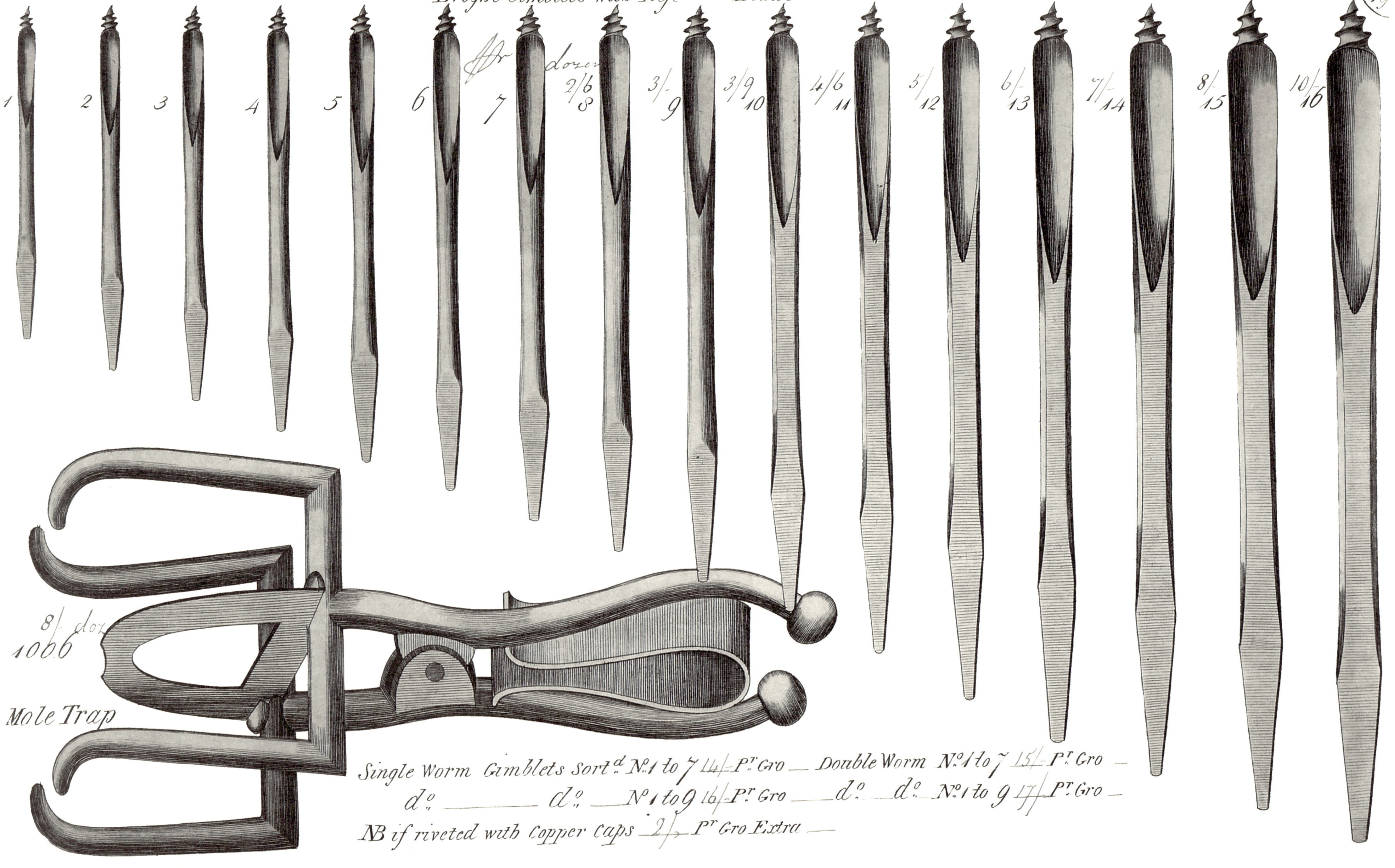

Single Worm Gimblets Sortd. No. 1 to 7 14/- Pr. Gro — Double Worm No. 1 to 7 15/- Pr. Gro —

do. ——— do. — No. 1 to 9 16/- Pr. Gro — do. — do. No. 1 to 9 17/- Pr. Gro —

NB if riveted with Copper Caps 2/- Pr Gro Extra —

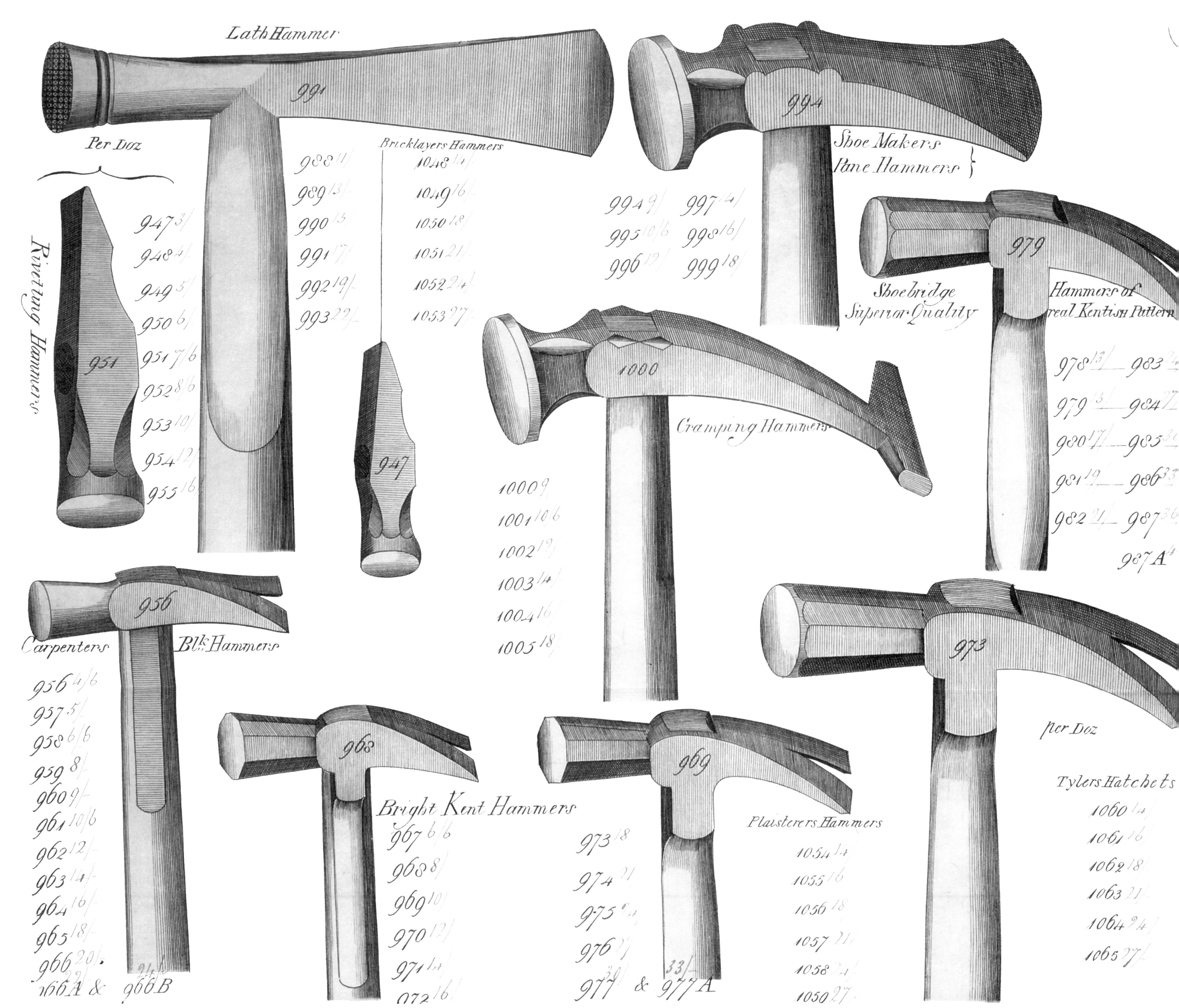
Lath Hammer
991
Per Doz
Riveting Hammers
951
947 3/
948 4/
949 5/
950 6/
951 7/6
952 8/6
953 10/
954 12/
955 16/
988 11/
989 13/
990 15/
991 17/
992 19/
993 22/
Bricklayers Hammers
1048 14/
1049 16/
1050 18/
1051 21/
1052 24/
1053 27/
947
994
Shoe Makers
Pane Hammers
994 9/
995 10/6
996 12/
997 14/
998 16/
999 18/
979
Shoebridge
Superior Quality
Hammers of
real Kentish Pattern
978 13/ — 983 24
979 15/ — 984 27
980 17/ — 985 30
981 19/ — 986 33
982 21/ — 987 36
987A
1000
Cramping Hammers
1000 9/
1001 10/6
1002 12/
1003 14/
1004 16/
1005 18/
956
Carpenters
Blk. Hammers
956 4/6
957 5/
958 6/6
959 8/
960 9/
961 10/6
962 12/
963 14/
964 16/
965 18/
966 20/
22/ 24/
966A & 966B
968
Bright Kent Hammers
967 6/6
968 8/
969 10/
970 12/
971 14/
972 16/
969
973 18
974 21
975 24
976 27
977 30 & 977A 33/
Plaisterers Hammers
1054 14
1055 16
1056 18
1057 21
1058 24
1059 27
973
per Doz
Tylers Hatchets
1060 14/
1061 16
1062 18
1063 21
1064 24
1065 27/